FIFTH EDITION

P9-DFM-270

GRAMMAR *in* CONTEXT

Teacher's Edition

The cover photo shows the
Ann W. Richards Congress
Avenue Bridge over Lady Bird
Lake in Austin, Texas.

HEINLE
CENGAGE Learning™

Australia • Brazil • Japan • Korea • Mexico • Singapore • Spain • United Kingdom • United States

Grammar in Context Basic, Fifth Edition
Teacher's Edition

Publisher: Sherrise Roehr

Acquisitions Editor: Tom Jefferies

Development Editor: Sarah Sandoski

Director of Global Marketing: Ian Martin

Director of U.S. Marketing: Jim McDonough

Product Marketing Manager: Katie Kelley

Marketing Manager: Caitlin Driscoll

Content Project Manager: Andrea Bobotas

Senior Print Buyer: Susan Spencer

Contributing Writers: Sarah J. Brown and
Hilary Grant

Project Manager: Chrystie Hopkins

Production Services: Nesbitt Graphics, Inc.

Interior Design: Nesbitt Graphics, Inc.

Cover Design: Muse Group, Inc.

© 2010 Heinle, Cengage Learning

Library of Congress Control Number: 2010923821

ISBN 13: 978-1-4240-8096-0

ISBN 10: 1-4240-8096-7

Heinle

20 Channel Center Street

Boston, Massachusetts 02210

USA

Cengage Learning is a leading provider of customized learning solutions with office locations around the globe, including Singapore, the United Kingdom, Australia, Mexico, Brazil, and Japan. Locate our local office at **international.cengage.com/region**

Cengage Learning products are represented in Canada by Nelson Education, Ltd.

Visit Heinle online at **elt.heinle.com**

Visit our corporate Web site at **www.cengage.com**

Printed in the United States of America.
1 2 3 4 5 6 7 8 9 10 — 14 13 12 11 10

Contents

Grammar in Context Basic, Fifth Edition

Welcome to
Grammar in Context
TEACHER'S EDITION!

Grammar in Context, Fifth Edition, contains a rich variety of material, making it easy to customize to any program's needs. The new *Teacher's Edition* includes extra resources to make planning your syllabus and preparing lessons easier than ever before.

NEW! Pacing guides for every activity provide a timing framework useful for lesson planning.

NEW! Ten easy solutions for customizing *Grammar in Context, Fifth Edition*, to meet your needs and your students' needs (see page v).

NEW! Presentation Ideas suggest alternative ways of presenting select grammar charts.

NEW! Practice Ideas include ways to adapt grammar exercises to target specific skills: reading, writing, listening, and speaking.

NEW! Online Lesson Planner saves you time by planning lessons online. This new tool provides instructors with complete, customizable lesson plans using the pacing guide from the *Teacher's Edition*. Go to elt.heinle.com/technology.

NEW! "Fast Track" option (indicated by this icon: ⎯★) identifies essential readings, charts, and exercises for courses that don't have the time to present and practice the full range of readings, grammar charts, and exercises available in *Grammar in Context, Fifth Edition*. Teaching these essential items gives students a basic understanding and practice of the most important grammar in each unit. Additional material can be used in the following ways:

- Struggling students can understand core grammar by doing extra practice exercises.

- Stronger students can be challenged by studying additional grammar charts and Expansion activities.

- Additional exercises may be used for students who have completed the in-class assignments ahead of other students.

Ten Tips for
Customizing *Grammar in Context,*
Fifth Edition, to fit your program:

1. Work within your curriculum.

Let your curriculum guide you on what to cover from this rich, comprehensive series. For example, if your program doesn't expect students to learn about nonessential adjective clauses at this level, you could skip the chart about nonessential adjective clauses. Also, it may be enough to teach unreal conditions in the present without getting into unreal conditions in the past. The Online Lesson Planner allows you to move, edit, and add to lessons to meet your program's needs. These lesson plans can be created by individual teachers or shared across the program.

**2. Administer a test or quiz using the Assessment CD-ROM with Exam*View*®
test banks at the start of each lesson.**

One way to find out how much practice your students need is to give them a test or quiz using the Assessment CD-ROM with Exam*View*® test banks at the beginning of the lesson. If you find that most of your students do well with relatively few errors, then you could skip the lesson altogether or focus only on the sticking points.

3. Assign the readings as homework.

All the readings are important in introducing the grammar in context and should not be skipped. To save class time, however, students can read the readings at home. The reading level is low enough that classroom instruction on how to read should not be necessary. The reading is not meant to challenge or improve the students' reading skills; it is meant to illustrate the grammar topic in a stimulating context. In class, you can ask questions about the reading or the vocabulary to ensure that students read and understood the assignment. You can lead a short discussion on the Before You Read questions, too, if time permits.

4. Set a time limit for each fill-in-the blank exercise.

Set a maximum time limit for each exercise. Suggested times are provided in the *Teacher's Edition*. Once the time limit has been reached, ask students to put down their pens and move on to the next exercise. Students can complete the rest of the exercise at home.

5. Assign audio-based exercises for lab time.

Many exercises contain audio tracks (indicated by the listening icon ◀))). These exercises can take time to set up, so you may wish to assign these exercises for lab credits or homework. You may also decide to do only one of these exercises per class to add variety.

6. Use one of the "About You" exercises in each class.

If you find your students' attention waning, you can insert one of these fun activities in each lesson. If your students attend another class for speech and/or conversation, you can skip these exercises.

7. Use Expansion activities if there is time.

If you have extra time at the end of the lesson, choose one of the fun Expansion activities which your class will enjoy. Students are likely to remember the lesson better if there is a fun element.

8. Assign exercises for extra credit.

Students can go beyond the basic curriculum and work on exercises at home for extra credit.

9. Let students check answers at home.

Print the answer key for each unit from the Heinle Web site (elt.heinle.com/ grammarincontext). Give students the answer key at the start of each unit so they can check their answers at home. Set aside ten minutes every week for troubleshooting particular grammar points.

10. Use the *Teacher's Edition*.

Each level of *Grammar in Context* has an accompanying *Teacher's Edition* which offers comprehensive teaching suggestions on how to present and teach each grammar point and the corresponding exercises. The *Teacher's Edition* also identifies fast-track material to help you quickly identify essential material when you're pressed for time and have to prioritize grammar topics.

Unit Overview

1. Point out and say the unit title. (*Welcome to the U.S.*) Activate students' prior knowledge. Say: *In this unit, we will talk about a new life in the United States. How is your life different in the U.S.? Are stores different? Are prices different? What else is different?* Have students share their personal experiences. Write students' answers on the board.

2. Direct students' attention to the photos. Say: *This is a supermarket. That's a laundromat. What are the people doing?* (buying food, washing clothes) Ask: *Do you like American supermarkets? American laundromats?* Encourage students to share their knowledge and personal experiences.

Presentation Ideas

The topic for this unit can be enhanced with the following items:

1. A large map or atlas to locate students' countries

2. An American passport and, if possible, passports from other countries

3. Pictures of urban, small town, and rural scenes in the U.S.

Lesson 1 Overview

GRAMMAR

1. Point out the objectives on page 2 of the book. Write on the board: *Subject Pronouns* and *Be*. Have a male student and a female student stand in front of the class. Introduce them using *he* and *she* (e.g., *He is Paulo. She is Ma Li.*). Write the sentences on the board. Underline the pronouns. Say: *He* and she *are subject pronouns.* Point to the male student and say: *he.* Point to the female student and say: *she.*

2. List subject pronouns and forms of *be* on the board (*I am; you are; he/she/it is; we are; you are; they are*). Have students repeat the items after you.

CONTEXT

1. Say: *We will read about two people who help. I am a teacher. I help you learn English. John is my friend. He helps me with the computer. Who helps you?* Elicit responses from students. Prompt students to name people and use pronoun references in sentences. (*Mi San. She helps me.*)

2. Direct students' attention to the picture. Say: *This is Dorota and Simon. They help people. Who do they help?* (immigrants in the U.S.) *Are they helping now?* (yes)

We Are Here to Help

READING

1. Have students look at the picture. Point to the people sitting down. Ask: *Are these people new in the U.S.?* (yes) *Who helps them?* (Dorota and Simon)

2. Have students look at the title of the reading. Ask: *What is the reading about? Is it about Simon and Dorota?* Have students use the title and picture to make predictions about the reading.

BEFORE YOU READ

5-10 mins

1. Go over each statement as a class. Have a volunteer read the statements or read them to the class yourself. Ask students to circle *yes* or *no*.

2. Ask a few volunteers to share their answers with the class.

Context Note

Many immigrants in the U.S. come from ten countries: Mexico, India, the Philippines, China, El Salvador, the Dominican Republic, Vietnam, Colombia, Guatemala, and Russia.

CD 1
TR 01

10-15 mins

Reading ≡★

1. Have students read the dialogue silently. Tell them to pay special attention to the verb *be*. Then play the audio and have students read along silently.

2. Check students' basic comprehension. Ask questions such as: *Is Simon from the U.S.?* (no) *Where is Dorota from?* (Poland) *Where is Simon from?* (Mexico) *Is life different here?* (yes) *What is different?* (supermarket, laundromat, bank, doctor's office)

Practice Idea: Listening

To practice listening skills, have students listen to the audio before opening their books. Ask a few comprehension questions: *Who is talking?* (Dorota and Simon) *Who are they talking to?* (new immigrants) Repeat the audio if necessary. Then have students open their books and read along as they listen to the audio.

Practice Idea: Speaking

Have students practice the conversation in pairs. Ask volunteers to role-play the conversation in front of the class.

VOCABULARY IN CONTEXT

5-10 mins

1. Model the pronunciation of each new vocabulary item and have students repeat.

2. Make sure students understand the meaning of each vocabulary item. Review the examples in the book and create additional example sentences. For example, say: *citizen. Dorota is a citizen of the U.S.* Then say: *I am a citizen of the U.S.* Show an American passport. *Is Simon a citizen of the U.S.?* (yes) To elicit a negative response, ask a student who is not a U.S. citizen if he or she is a U.S. citizen. Go over each vocabulary item similarly, using visuals and realia when appropriate. For example, for *different* display two items, one a variation of the other (e.g., a jar of peanut butter and a jar of jelly); for *confused* bring in a strange-looking gadget and mime confusion. When possible, point to pictures in the book that illustrate the new vocabulary items, such as *laundromat* and *supermarket* on page 1.

3. Have students underline an example of each vocabulary item in the reading. Point out that

the word *helpful* is not in the reading, but that it is a useful word to describe Dorota and Simon.

Practice Idea: Speaking

To check comprehension, have volunteers in pairs or groups act out selected vocabulary, such as *both, laundromat, supermarket, bank, helpful,* and *confused.*

Did You Know?

Point out the information to students. Ask: *Do you ever go to the supermarket/laundromat late at night?*

 LISTENING ACTIVITY

CD 1 TR 02

Answers: 1. False; **2.** False; **3.** False; **4.** True; **5.** True; **6.** False

10-15 mins

1. Make sure students understand the meaning of *true* and *false*. Demonstrate with students in the class. Say: *True or false?* [Name of student] *is from* [student's native country]. *True or false?* [Name of student] *is from New York.*

2. Say: *Listen to the sentences about Dorota and Simon. Circle* true *or* false. Play the listening selection one time without pausing. Then play it through again, pausing and replaying as necessary.

3. Have students compare their answers in pairs, then play the audio again and check the answers as a class.

Practice Idea: Listening

Create true or false statements about the class: [Name of student] *is a U.S. citizen.* Say the sentences out loud and have students write *true* or *false* on a piece of paper. Go over the answers as a class.

1.1 Subject Pronouns

5-10 mins

Have students look at the pictures in grammar chart **1.1** on page 4. Give students time to read the dialogue bubbles in the chart. Ask: *Who does he mean?* (Simon) Have them turn to the reading on page 3 if they have trouble remembering Simon's name. Repeat with *I, you,* and *we*. Use the photos of the supermarket and laundromat on page 1 to demonstrate *it*. If students have difficulty with *I*, have them find *I* in the reading and match it to the speaker's name in the text.

> ### Practice Idea: Writing
>
> Have students work in pairs to create similar dialogues using students from the class. Have students write new sentences (e.g., *I am Juliana.*).

EXERCISE 1

ANSWERS: 1. She; **2.** I; **3.** He; **4.** We; **5.** It; **6.** They; **7.** You

 5-10 mins

1. Have students read the direction line. Ask: *What words do we use here?* (I, you, he, she, it, we, they) Go over the example in the book. Then do #1 with the class.

2. Have students complete the rest of Exercise 1 individually. Remind students to review grammar chart **1.1** on page 4 if necessary. Check the answers as a class.

1.2 *Be*—Affirmative Statements

10-15 mins

1. Have students look at grammar chart **1.2** on page 5. Say: *There are three forms of* be: am, is, *and* are. *For* I, *use* am. *For a subject that is one person or thing, use* is. *For* you *and subjects that are more than one person or thing, use* are. Ask volunteers to read the examples.

2. Have students close their books. List some subjects on the board, such as *Dorota, I, it, the bank, Simon, you, Halina and Dorota, we,* and *My name.* Activate students' prior knowledge. Point to each subject and ask: *Is [subject] one subject or more than one? What form of* be *goes with [subject]?* Say each subject and pause for students to call out the verb form.

3. Have students refer to grammar chart **1.1** on page 4. Ask students to underline the verb *be* in the dialogues and match each form to its subject.

4. Go over the Language Note. Help students create examples for each category. Write on the board: *Boston _____ in _____.*

It _____ a city. Elicit additional examples from students.

EXERCISE 2

ANSWERS: 1. am; **2.** are; **3.** are; **4.** are; **5.** is; **6.** are; **7.** is

5-10 mins

1. Have students read the direction line. Go over the example in the book. Have a volunteer do #1.

2. Have students complete the rest of Exercise 2 individually. Then have students check their answers in pairs. Remind them to review grammar chart **1.2** on page 5 if necessary. Check the answers as a class.

> ### Practice Idea: Writing
>
> Have students work in pairs to create four sentences telling the national origin of students in the class. Tell students to use different forms of the verb *be*.

EXERCISE 3

CD 1 TR 03

ANSWERS: 1. are; **2.** am; **3.** am; **4.** are; **5.** am; **6.** is; **7.** is; **8.** are; **9.** is; **10.** are

5-10 mins

1. Have students read the direction line. Ask: *What are the forms of* be? (*am, is, are*) Have a volunteer complete #1.

2. Have students complete the rest of Exercise 3 individually. Remind them to review grammar chart **1.2** on page 5 if necessary. Have students compare their answers with a partner. Play the audio and check the answers as a class.

> ### Practice Idea: Speaking
>
> Have students practice the dialogue in pairs. Monitor and help students with pronunciation.

EXERCISE 4
Answers will vary.

5-10 mins

1. Say: *This exercise is about you.* Have students read the direction line. Go over the examples in the book. Have volunteers model the first three items.

2. Have students complete Exercise 4 individually. Remind them to review grammar chart **1.2** on page 5 if necessary. Then have students compare their answers with a partner. Say: *Read the sentences you checked to your partner.* Monitor pair work. Give help as needed.

Practice Idea: Speaking

Have students compare their answers with a different partner. Say: *Now read the sentences you checked to your new partner.* Monitor pair work. Give help as needed.

EXERCISE 5 =★
Answers will vary.

10-15 mins

1. Say: *This exercise is about you.* Have students read the direction line. Say: *Fill in the blanks with information that is true about you.* Go over the example in the book. Model the example and then have a volunteer model the example.

2. Have students complete Exercise 5 individually. Remind them to review grammar chart **1.2** on page 5 if necessary. Then have students share their answers with a partner. Monitor pair work. Give help as needed.

Practice Idea: Speaking

Have students share their answers to #4, #5, and #6 with the class. Ask: *What are you confused about? Who is helpful in your life? What is different for you?* Write students' ideas on the board.

Lesson 2 Overview

GRAMMAR

Ask: *What did we study in Lesson 1?* (subject pronouns and *be*) *What will we study in Lesson 2?* Point to each objective in the book, read it out loud, and give an example, such as: *I am = I'm* (contractions); *one bank, two banks* (singular and plural). For *this, that, these,* and *those,* point to objects in the room and make phrases such as: *This is a book. That is a clock. These are pens.* Ask volunteers for more examples and write them on the board.

CONTEXT

1. Say: *We're going to talk about the laundromat. Laundromats are helpful. Washing machines are helpful. You don't have to wash clothes by hand. Do you have laundromats like this in your country?* Have volunteers share their answers and personal experiences with the class.

2. Direct students' attention to the picture. Ask volunteers to read the labeled items.

Presentation Ideas

The topic for this lesson can be enhanced with the following items:

1. Items found at a laundromat (e.g., packets of laundry detergent and softeners)

2. Different types of clothing labels with washing instructions and symbols

Help at the Laundromat
READING

1. Have students look at the picture of the laundromat on page 8. Say: *Dorota and Shafia are at the laundromat now.*

2. Have students look at the title of the reading. Ask: *Who needs help—Dorota or Shafia?* (Shafia) *What does Shafia want to do?* (wash her clothes) Have students use the title and picture to make predictions about the reading.

BEFORE YOU READ

5-10 mins

1. Go over each statement as a class. Have a volunteer read the statements or read them to the class yourself. Ask students to circle *yes* or *no.*

2. Ask a few volunteers to share their answers with the class.

Context Note

In some parts of the U.S., laundromats are called *washettes* or *washaterias.*

Reading

CD 1
TR 04

10-15 mins

1. First, have students read the dialogue silently. Then play the audio and have students read along.

2. Check students' basic comprehension. Ask true or false questions, such as: *Dorota is confused. True or false?* (false) *Shafia helps Dorota. True or false?* (false)

Practice Idea: Listening

To practice listening skills, have students listen to the audio before opening their books. Ask a few comprehension questions such as: *Where are Dorota and Shafia?* (at the laundromat) Repeat the audio if necessary. Then have students open their books and read along as they listen to the audio.

Practice Idea: Speaking

Have students practice the conversation in pairs. Monitor to help students with pronunciation. Ask volunteers to role-play the conversation in front of the class.

VOCABULARY IN CONTEXT

5-10 mins

1. Model the pronunciation of each new vocabulary item and have students repeat.

2. Make sure students understand the meaning of each vocabulary item. Review the examples in the book and create additional example sentences. For example, say: *Don't worry. Teacher, I don't speak English. Don't worry. I'm here to help you.* Go over each new vocabulary item similarly, using visuals and realia when appropriate. For example, for *together* ask a volunteer to stand next to you at the front of the classroom. Stand close to the student and then far away from the student. For *right* hold up two objects, such as pens, then ask: *How many [pens] do I have?* (two) Then say: *You're right!* Repeat with another quantity. For *empty* display a container with pencils and pens in it and another that is empty. When possible, point to pictures that illustrate the new vocabulary items, such as *clothes* on page 8.

---

3. Have students underline an example of each vocabulary item in the reading. Point out that the word *clean* is not in the reading, but that it is useful to describe clothes.

Practice Idea: Speaking

To check vocabulary comprehension, have volunteers in pairs or groups act out selected vocabulary, such as *don't worry, together,* and *(you're) right.*

Did You Know?

Point out the information to students. Say: *Labels on clothes can tell you how to wash them.* Bring in some of your own articles of clothing and show students their washing labels. Point out the written instructions and symbols. Draw a rectangle with a circle in it. Say: *This means you can put the clothing in the dryer.* Draw many dots in the circle. Say: *Dots in the circle tell how hot the dryer can be. Many dots mean that it is safe to put the clothing in a very hot dryer.*

LISTENING ACTIVITY

CD 1
TR 05

ANSWERS: 1. True; **2.** False; **3.** True; **4.** True; **5.** False

10-15 mins

1. Say: *Listen to the sentences about the conversation. Circle* true *or* false. Play the audio one time without pausing. Then play it through again, pausing and replaying as necessary.

2. Have students compare their answers, then play the audio again and check the answers as a class.

1.3 Contractions (Short Forms)

10-15 mins

1. Have students look at grammar chart **1.3** on page 10. If possible, use an overhead projector to review the chart with the class. Discuss the rule for each contraction Say: *For* I'm, *take out the* a *and add an apostrophe.*

2. Have students close their books. Say: *Here are a subject and verb:* Life/is. *What is the contraction?* (Life's) Continue with more examples, such as *Everything/is, Simon/is, They/are.* Then reverse the procedure. Give students a contraction and ask for the separate subject and verb. If this task is difficult for students, allow them to keep their books open.

3. Go over the Language Notes. Write these sentences on the board: *The towels're big. The blankets are dirty.* Ask: *Which is right? Why?*

Practice Idea: Writing

Have students work in pairs to create a similar grammar chart using people and things in the class. Students write new sentences with contractions for the chart (e.g., *I'm new. You're a student.*).

EXERCISE 1

ANSWERS: **1.** Simon's; **2.** He's; **3.** Dorota's; **4.** She's; **5.** They're; **6.** The laundromat's; **7.** It's; **8.** You're; **9.** I'm; **10.** We're

 1. Have students read the direction line. Go over the example in the book.
5-10 mins
2. Have students complete Exercise 1 individually. Remind them to review grammar chart **1.3** on page 10 if necessary. Go over the answers as a class.

EXERCISE 2

CD 1
TR 06

ANSWERS: **1.** 'm; **2.** 's; **3.** 'm; **4.** 'm; **5.** 're; **6.** 's; **7.** are; **8.** 's; **9.** 's; **10.** 's; **11.** 's; **12.** 's; **13.** 's; **14.** 're; **15.** 're

10-15 mins
1. Have students read the direction line. Say: *You are going to complete the conversation. Use contractions where possible.* Go over the example.
2. Have students complete the rest of Exercise 2 individually. Remind them to review grammar chart **1.3** on page 10 if necessary. Then have students compare their answers with a partner. Monitor pair work. Give help as needed. Then play the audio and check the answers as a class.

Practice Ideas: Speaking

1. Have students practice the dialogue in pairs. Monitor and help students with pronunciation.
2. Create a short conversation, based on Exercise 2, with a volunteer. Substitute your information for the book's information, such as: *I'm from the U.S. You're from the U.S. too, right?* Then have students work in pairs to create their own conversation with information that is true for them. Monitor pair work.

1.4 Singular and Plural

5-10 mins
1. Have students close their books. Write the nouns from grammar chart **1.4** on the board. Write some as singular nouns and others as plural, such as *machines, coin, towel,* and *blankets.*
2. Ask students if the nouns are singular or plural. Then have students look at grammar chart **1.4** on page 12. Say: *Check your work.* Ask: *What do we add to make a noun plural?* (-s)

EXERCISE 3

ANSWERS: **1.** quarters; **2.** dimes; **3.** dryers; **4.** nickels; **5.** machines; **6.** towels; **7.** items; **8.** blankets; **9.** coins; **10.** dollars

5-10 mins
1. Have students read the direction line. Go over the example in the book.
2. Have students complete Exercise 3 individually. Remind them to review grammar chart **1.4** on page 12 if necessary. Check the answers as a class.

1.5 *This, That, These, Those*

5-10 mins
1. Have students close their books. Use simple objects such as books to demonstrate *this, that, these,* and *those.* For example, hold a book in your hand and say: *This book.* Place a second book on a student's desk, step away and point to it. Say: *That book.* Repeat the procedure for *these* and *those.*
2. Have students look at grammar chart **1.5** on page 12. Say: *This and these are for objects that are close to you. That and those are for objects that are not close to you. This and that are singular. These and those are plural.*
3. Go over the Language Note. Review the rule and the example sentence. Go over the Pronunciation Note and pronounce the sentences in the chart. Then say: *Listen to these words. Raise your hand when you hear the word* this: *this machine/these machines; this sister/ these sisters; these seats/this seat; these sheets/ this sheet.*

Practice Idea: Speaking

Have students practice the sentences in grammar chart **1.5** in groups. Have groups make a circle. Ask students to take objects out of their bags and to place some objects close to them and some far away. Have students take turns making sentences with the objects and the demonstrative pronouns (e.g., *This is a cell phone. Those are pencils.*). Monitor and help students as needed.

EXERCISE 4 ⬛ ⭐

ANSWERS: 1. This is; **2.** These are; **3.** Those are OR These are; **4.** These are; **5.** This is; **6.** Those are

5-10 mins

1. Have students read the direction line. Remind students that only *that is* can be contracted (*that's*). Go over the example in the book.

2. Have students complete Exercise 4 individually. Remind them to review grammar chart **1.5** on page 12 if necessary. Check the answers as a class.

EXERCISE 5 ⬛

ANSWERS: 1. are; **2.** These; **3.** They're; **4.** Quarters; **5.** Those

5-10 mins

1. Have students read the direction line. Go over the example in the book.

2. Have students complete Exercise 5 in pairs. Remind them to review grammar chart **1.5** on page 12 if necessary. Then check the answers as a class.

Lesson 3 Overview

GRAMMAR

1. Ask: *What did we study in Lesson 2?* (contractions, singular and plural, *this/that/these/those*). *What will we study in this lesson?* Read the objectives out loud (negative statements with the verb *be*, adjectives, expressions with *It*, and singular and plural spelling rules).

2. Activate students' prior knowledge. Write *blanket* on the board. Ask: *What is the plural of* blanket? (blankets) *What is the singular of* blankets? (blanket) Give examples of adjectives and expressions with

It that students have learned, such as *It's hot.* Ask volunteers for additional examples and write them on the board.

CONTEXT

1. Say: *We're going to learn about buying food in the U.S. We buy food at supermarkets. Most American supermarkets are big. They sell many things: food, kitchen things, medicine, and toys. Are American supermarkets different from supermarkets in your country?* Have students share their knowledge and personal experiences.

2. Direct students' attention to the picture. Ask: *Where are they?* (supermarket)

Presentation Ideas

The topic for this unit can be enhanced with the following items:

1. Circulars from nearby supermarkets

2. U.S. coins and bills, a checkbook, a debit card, and a credit card

3. Supermarket coupons

Help at the Supermarket
READING

1. Have students look at the picture of the supermarket on page 14. Say: *Dorota and Halina are at the supermarket now.*

2. Have students look at the title of the reading. Ask: *What is the reading about?* (learning to shop in a supermarket) *Who needs help—Dorota or Halina?* (Halina) *Why does she need help?* (She's new. This is her first time in an American supermarket.) Have students use the title and photo to make predictions about the reading.

BEFORE YOU READ

5-10 mins

1. Go over each statement as a class. Have a volunteer read the statements or read them to the class yourself. Ask students to circle *yes* or *no*.

2. Ask a few volunteers to share their answers with the class.

Context Note

Supermarkets are big stores that sell groceries, meat, and produce. Many have a deli and a bakery. Generally, supermarkets carry thousands of different items.

 ### Reading

**CD 1
TR 07**

**10-15
mins**

1. Have students read the dialogue silently. Then play the audio and have students read along.

2. Check students' basic comprehension. Ask true or false questions such as: *The parking lot's not crowded. True or false?* (true) *Halina is confused. True or false?* (true) *Prices change. True or false?* (true)

Practice Idea: Listening

To practice listening skills, have students listen to the audio before opening their books. Ask a few comprehension questions: *Where are they?* (at the supermarket) *What's on sale?* (bananas) Repeat the audio if necessary. Then have students open their books and read along as they listen to the audio.

Practice Idea: Speaking

Have students practice the conversation in pairs. Ask volunteers to role-play the conversation in front of the class.

VOCABULARY IN CONTEXT

**5-10
mins**

1. Model the pronunciation of each new vocabulary item and have students repeat.

2. Make sure students understand the meaning of each vocabulary item. Review the examples in the book and create additional example sentences. For example, point to objects in the room and identify them: *This is a clock.* Then say: *I know. I'm sure* [this is a clock]. Go over each new vocabulary item similarly, using visuals and realia when appropriate. For example, for *free* hold up two books and say: *This book cost $30.* Write $30 on the board. Say: *This book was free.* Write on the board: *free = $0.* For *the same* hold up two identical

books, then hold up a different book and say: *This book is not the same.* Point to items in the picture on page 15 that illustrate some of the vocabulary items, such as *shelves* and *product*.

3. Have students underline an example of each vocabulary item in the reading.

Practice Idea: Speaking

To check comprehension, have volunteers in pairs or groups act out selected vocabulary, such as *sure* and *cashier*.

Did You Know?

Point out the information to students. Make sure they understand *their own bags.* Ask: *Do you bring your own bags to the supermarket?'*

 ### LISTENING ACTIVITY

**CD 1
TR 08**

ANSWERS: 1. True; **2.** False; **3.** False; **4.** True; **5.** False; **6.** True

**5-10
mins**

1. Say: *Listen to the sentences about the supermarket. Circle true or false.* Play the listening selection one time without pausing. Then play it through again, pausing and replaying as necessary.

2. Have students compare their answers, then play the audio again and check the answers as a class.

1.6 *Be*—Negative Statements

**5-10
mins**

1. Have students look at grammar chart **1.6** on page 17. Demonstrate the rule for making negative contractions with *be.* Write on the board: *You are not serious.* Cross out *a* and write *You're not.* Rewrite the sentence. Cross out *o* and write *You aren't.* Stress the use of the apostrophe. Write on the board:
I am not. = I'm not. Say: *There is only one way to do the negative contraction for* I am not. Review each example in the chart.

2. Go over the Language Notes. Point out the columns in the chart where the language notes are exemplified.

3. Have students look at the comparison chart. Review the examples in the chart.

pairs. Remind them to review grammar chart **1.6** on page 17 if necessary. Check the answers as a class.

Practice Idea: Listening

Create false affirmative statements about the class, such as: [Maria] *is a U.S. citizen.* Say the sentences out loud and have volunteers give you the true negative statement ([Maria] *isn't a U.S. citizen.*).

Practice Idea: Writing

Have students create negative statements from the affirmative statements in the comparison chart (e.g., *We aren't in the supermarket.*).

EXERCISE **1** ≡★

ANSWERS: 1. isn't OR 's not; **2.** aren't OR 're not; **3.** aren't OR 're not; **4.** 'm not; **5.** isn't OR 's not; **6.** aren't OR 're not; **7.** aren't OR 're not; **8.** aren't; **9.** isn't OR 's not

1. Have students read the direction line. Ask: *What do you fill in the blanks with?* (the negative of the underlined verb) Go over the example in the book. Do #1 with the class.

2. Have students complete the rest of Exercise 1 individually. Remind them to review grammar chart **1.6** on page 17 if necessary. Check the answers as a class.

Practice Idea: Writing

Have students negate each beginning statement with a contraction (e.g., *The supermarket isn't big.*). Remind students that *I am not* can be contracted only one way—*I'm not.* Also, reiterate that there is only one negative short form for a plural noun + *are.*

EXERCISE **2**
Answers will vary.

1. Have students read the direction line. Go over the examples in the book.

2. Have students complete Exercise 2 individually. Then have students compare their answers in

1.7 Adjectives ≡★

1. Say: *Adjectives describe nouns. For example, they tell if a thing or person is big or small, hot or cold.* Write on the board: *The parking lot is empty.* Write this sentence on the board: *Bags are free.* Ask: *Which word is the noun?* (Bags) *Which word describes the noun?* (free) *Free is an adjective. It describes the bags.*

2. Have students look at grammar chart **1.7** on page 18. Go over the examples. Point out that adjectives come after the verb *be* and that they can also come before a noun. Ask: *What are the adjectives in these sentences?* (empty, crowded, free, big) *Are the adjectives before or after the verb* be? (after)

3. Point out the Language Note. Review the rule and the examples. Write these sentences on the board:

1. *Those are <u>bigs</u> washing machines.*

2. *Those are <u>big</u> washing machines.*

Ask: *Which sentence is correct?* (Sentence 2 is correct.) *Why?* (You can't make adjectives plural.) Stress to students that adjectives in English do not show number (plural or singular) or gender (feminine, masculine, neutral).

🔊 EXERCISE **3** ≡★

CD 1 TR 09

ANSWERS: Conversation A: **1.** different OR new; **2.** helpful; **3.** easy; **4.** crowded; **5.** early; **6.** big Conversation B: **1.** hot; **2.** open; **3.** small OR big; **4.** big OR small; **5.** different

1. Tell students they are going to read two conversations about supermarkets and laundromats. Have students read the direction line. Go over the example in the book.

2. Have students complete Exercise 3 individually. Then have students compare their answers in pairs. Remind them to review grammar chart **1.7** on page 18 if necessary. Play the audio and check the answers as a class.

1.8 Expressions with *It*

🕐 5-10 mins

1. Have students look at grammar chart **1.8** on page 20. Go over the examples and explanations in the chart. Demonstrate the meaning of *temperature*. Draw a thermometer on the board. Draw an arrow going up, say *hot,* and mime sweating. Draw an arrow going down, shiver, and say *cold.*

2. Stress that a *to-* phrase often follows an impersonal expression with *it*. Define *easy* and *hard* and give more examples: *It's hard to learn English. It's easy to speak* [student's language]. Say: Easy *means* no problem. Hard *means* not easy. *Ask: What is easy? It's easy to _____.* Write students' ideas on the board. Repeat for *hard.*

EXERCISE 4
Answers will vary.

🕐 5-10 mins

1. Have students read the direction line. Check that students know the meanings of the adjectives in the box. Elicit things that are *necessary* or *important;* look at your watch and ask if the time is *early* or *late.* Go over the example.

2. Have students complete Exercise 4 individually. Remind them to review grammar chart **1.7** on page 18 and grammar chart **1.8** on page 20 if necessary. Then check the answers as a class.

EXERCISE 5
Answers will vary.

🕐 5-10 mins

1. Have students read the direction line. Tell students this exercise is about them. Go over the example. Model #1 yourself; write your sentence on the board. Have a volunteer do #1; write the answer on the board.

2. Have students complete Exercise 5 individually. Remind them to review grammar chart **1.8** on page 20 if necessary. Then have students share their sentences with a partner. Have volunteers share their sentences with the class.

1.9 Singular and Plural— Spelling Rules

🕐 5-10 mins

1. Have students look at grammar chart **1.9** on page 21.

2. Go over the examples and explanations. Pronounce the singular and plural forms. Remind students that the *-es* on nouns that end in *-sh, -ss, -x,* and *-ch* is pronounced as an extra syllable.

3. Write additional examples on the board: *glass, desk, way,* and *knife.* Ask volunteers to form the plural (*glasses, desks, ways, knives*).

4. Go over the Pronunciation Note. Say: *With some noun endings, we need to pronounce an extra syllable when we add -s. Nouns that end in /s/ and /z/ sounds have an extra syllable in the plural.* Pronounce the example words. Write these additional pairs of singular/plural nouns on the board: *rose > roses, hose > hoses, ace > aces, race > races.* Pronounce the pairs and have students repeat.

EXERCISE 6

ANSWERS: **1.** prices, shelves; **2.** matches; **3.** families; **4.** dishes; **5.** bananas; **6.** babies

🕐 5-10 mins

1. Have students read the direction line. Go over the example.

2. Have students complete Exercise 6 individually. Remind them to review grammar chart **1.9** on page 21 if necessary. Then go over the answers with the class.

Editing Advice

5-10 mins

Have students close their books. Write the sentences without editing marks or corrections on the board. For example:

> **1.** *You is at the laundromat.*
> **2.** *Is 10:15 A.M.*

Ask students to correct each sentence and provide a rule or explanation for each correction, e.g.: 1. You are at the laundromat. (Use the correct form of *be*.) 2. It is 10:15 A.M. (Every sentence has a subject.). This activity can be done individually, in pairs, or as a class. After students have corrected each sentence, tell them to turn to page 22. Say: *Now compare your work with the Editing Advice in the book.*

Editing Quiz

ANSWERS: 1. it's OR it is; **2.** You're; **3.** isn't; **4.** These; **5.** They're; **6.** are; **7.** big; **8.** these; **9.** C; **10.** Ø; **11.** You're; **12.** I'm; **13.** he's OR he is; **14.** He's

5-10 mins

1. Tell students they are going to put the Editing Advice into practice. Have students read the direction line. Ask: *Do all the shaded words have mistakes?* (No) Go over the examples with the class. Then do #1 together.

2. Have students complete the quiz individually. Then have them compare their answers with a partner before checking answers as a class. Elicit the relevant grammar point for each correction. For example, for #1 (Answer: But it's hot in here.), ask: *Why do we use* it's? (Use *it* with impersonal expressions.)

3. For the items students had difficulties with, have them go back and find the relevant grammar chart and review it. Monitor and give help as necessary.

Expansion

These expansion activities provide opportunities for students to interact with one another and further develop their speaking and writing skills. Encourage students to use grammar from this unit whenever possible.

LEARNER'S LOG

5-10 mins

1. Have students close their books. Ask: *What did you learn about American laundromats and supermarkets in this unit? What else do you want to know about them?* Prompt students with questions, such as: *How much does it cost to wash clothes? Do vegetables go on sale?* Write ideas on the board. Discuss ways in which students can find out more about laundromats and supermarkets.

2. Have students complete the Learner's Log.

3. Have students compare logs in pairs.

WRITING ACTIVITY

5-10 mins

1. Point out the picture of the display of apples in a supermarket. Say: *The paragraph in this activity is about different kinds of apples.* Have students read the direction line. Go over the example. Then write the second sentence on the board and rewrite it as a class.

2. Have students complete the activity individually. Then collect for assessment.

Practice Idea: Writing

Have students exchange papers with a partner. Ask students to help their partners edit their paragraph. Refer students to the Editing Advice on page 22.

OUTSIDE ACTIVITIES

1. Have students go to a supermarket in their neighborhood. Tell them to find an item on sale. In class, ask them to tell the usual price and the sale price.

2. Have students go to a laundromat in their neighborhood. Ask them to tell the class the name and location, as well as the price to wash and dry clothes.

INTERNET ACTIVITY

Have students search the words *online grocery store* or *online supermarket* in an online search engine. Ask them to choose an item, then find the price in two different online stores. Have them tell the class about the item and the prices.

Unit 2

Unit Overview

1. Point out and say the unit title. (*Time and Money*) Say: *This unit is about time and money.* Point to your wrist. *I [do/don't] wear a watch. I [always/never] know what time it is. What about you? Is time important?*

2. Direct students' attention to the photos. Ask: *Who has a watch?* (a man) *What's he doing?* (checking the time) *What's this man doing?* (showing/holding money) *What do you get at a bank?* (money) *What are some American banks?* Write names of popular banks on the board. Circle the one you use. Say: *This is my bank.*

Presentation Ideas

The topic for this unit can be enhanced with the following items:

1. A watch, a digital clock, and a clock whose hands can be moved easily
2. A large calendar with holidays circled
3. A list of popular banks in the area
4. A list of services banks provide

Lesson 1 Overview

GRAMMAR

1. Write on the board: *Possessive Nouns.* Touch a student's chair and say: *[Juan]'s chair.* Write the words on the board. Underline the possessive noun. Say: *This is a possessive noun.*

2. Go around the room touching different students' chairs and using the possessive noun.

3. Touch your chair and say: *my chair.* Write the words on the board. Underline the possessive adjective. Say: *This is a possessive adjective.*

CONTEXT

1. Direct students' attention to the picture. Say: *There is a clock in the car, and Victor has a watch.*

2. Point to your watch or to a clock in the classroom. Say: *It's [time].* Ask: *Who has a watch?* Walk around looking at the students' watches and say the time followed by: *Your watch is slow/fast.* Emphasize the time difference between the clock on the wall and each student's watch.

My Clock Is Fast READING

Have students look at the picture and the title of the reading. Ask: *Where is Victor?* (in a car) *Who is he with?* (Dorota) *What is the reading about?* (time in the U.S.) Have students use the title and picture to make predictions about the reading.

BEFORE YOU READ

5-10 mins

1. Go over each statement as a class. Have a volunteer read the statements or read them to the class yourself. Ask students to circle *yes* or *no.*

2. Ask a few volunteers to share their answers with the class.

Context Note

Daylight Saving Time is the expression used for the practice in the United States of turning the clock back in the fall or forward in the spring to "save daylight."

 Reading ═★

CD 1
TR 10

10-15 mins

1. Have students read the text silently. Then play the audio and have students read along.

2. Check students' basic comprehension. Ask questions such as: *Is Simon helping Victor today?* (No, Dorota is.) *Is the bank open?* (no)

Practice Idea: Listening

To practice listening skills, have students listen to the audio before opening their books. Ask a few comprehension questions: *Where is Simon?* (with his kids) *Where is Marta?* (at the hospital) Repeat the audio if necessary. Then have students open their books and read along as they listen to the audio.

Practice Idea: Speaking

Have students practice the conversation in pairs. Ask volunteers to role-play the conversation in front of the class.

VOCABULARY IN CONTEXT

5-10 mins

1. Model the pronunciation of each new vocabulary item and have students repeat.

2. Make sure students understand the meaning of each vocabulary item. Review the examples in the book and create additional example sentences. For example, say: *kids. These are my kids.* (Show a picture if possible.) Then ask: *Do you have kids?* Have volunteers share information. Go over each new vocabulary item similarly, using visuals and realia when appropriate. For example, for *turn* ask students one at a time to do a task, such as go to the board and write his/her name. Point to another student and say: *OK, your turn. Please write your name.* For *broken* bring in a broken clock or use a pen without a spring or ink cartridge. Mime trying to use the object, but failing, several times. When possible, point to pictures in the book that illustrate new vocabulary items, such as *daughter* and *watch* on page 27.

3. Have students underline an example of each vocabulary item in the reading. Let them know that *son* and *daughter* are not in the reading.

Practice Idea: Speaking

To check comprehension, have volunteers use vocabulary in sentences (e.g., *Sports cars are fast.*). Write students' examples on the board.

Did You Know?

Point out the information to students. Tell students about some customs of popular holidays, such as these:

Independence Day: barbecues and picnics, fireworks

Thanksgiving: family gatherings with turkey and pumpkin pie

 LISTENING ACTIVITY

CD 1
TR 11

ANSWERS: 1. False; **2.** False; **3.** False; **4.** True; **5.** False; **6.** True

5-10 mins

1. Say: *Listen to the sentences about Dorota and Victor at the bank. Circle* true *or* false. Play the listening selection one time without pausing. Then play it through again, pausing and replaying as necessary.

2. Have students compare their answers, then play the audio again and check the answers as a class.

Practice Idea: Listening

Create statements about the class: *[Ahmed] is usually late.* Say the sentences out loud and have students write *true* or *false* on a piece of paper. Go over the answers as a class.

2.1 Possessive Nouns ≡★

5-10 mins

Have students look at grammar chart **2.1** on page 28. Review the examples and explanations. Stress that an apostrophe + *s* means ownership. Say: *Whose wife?* (Simon's) *Whose father?* (Marta's) Go around the room and point to students' objects. Say: *[Maria's] desk. Whose desk?* (Maria's) Write the examples on the board.

EXERCISE **1** ≡★

ANSWERS: 1. Simon's; **2.** Marta's; **3.** Simon's; **4.** Dorota's; **5.** Simon's

1. Have students read the direction line. Go over the example in the book. Direct students to the picture of the clock in Dorota's car on page 26.

2. Have students complete Exercise 1 individually. Remind them to review grammar chart **2.1** on page 28 if necessary. Check the answers as a class.

EXERCISE 2

ANSWERS: 1. Victor's daughter; **2.** Simon's children; **3.** Marta's father; **4.** Dorota's car

5-10 mins

1. Have students read the direction line. Go over the example in the book.

2. Have students complete Exercise 2 individually. Then have them compare their answers in pairs. Remind them to review grammar chart **2.1** on page 28 if necessary. Check the answers as a class.

Practice Idea: Writing

Have students work in pairs to create sentences about the class using possessive nouns (e.g., *Jean-Pierre's children are at home.*).

2.2 Possessive Adjectives

1. Have students close their books. Elicit subject pronouns. Begin by saying *I, you.* Write the pronouns on the board. Then write *my* next to *I.* Point to your chair and say: *My chair.* Touch a student's chair and say: *Your chair.* Write *your* on the board next to *you.*

2. Have students look at grammar chart **2.2** on page 29. Say: *Now let's study possessive adjectives.* Review the examples and explanations. Elicit and write on the board the remaining possessive adjectives next to the appropriate subject pronouns.

EXERCISE 3

ANSWERS: 1. her; **2.** their; **3.** my; **4.** his; **5.** our

1. Have students read the direction line. Go over the example in the book. Have a volunteer do #1.

2. Have students complete the rest of Exercise 3 individually. Remind them to review grammar chart **2.2** on page 29 if necessary. Check the answers as a class.

EXERCISE 4

Answers will vary.

1. Say: *This exercise is about you.* Have students read the direction line. Have a volunteer do #1.

2. Have students complete the rest of Exercise 4 individually. Remind them to review grammar chart **2.2** on page 29 if necessary. Then have students share their answers with a partner. Monitor pair work. Give help as needed.

Practice Idea: Speaking

Do a class survey. How did students respond to each question? Write the results on the board.

EXERCISE 5

CD 1 TR 12

ANSWERS: 1. Our OR My; **2.** Their; **3.** my; **4.** Your

1. Have students read the direction line. Direct students to the picture on page 29. Say: *Simon and Dorota are talking on the phone.*

2. Have students complete Exercise 5 individually. Remind them to review grammar chart **2.2** on page 29 if necessary. Have students compare their answers in pairs. Then play the audio and check the answers as a class.

Practice Ideas: Speaking

1. Have students practice the conversation in pairs. Ask volunteers to role-play the conversation in front of the class.

2. Have students work in pairs to create a similar conversation. Ask volunteers to role-play their new conversations in front of the class.

Lesson 2 Overview

GRAMMAR

1. Elicit a *yes/no* response by asking a student: *Are you [name]?* Say: *That's a yes/no question.* Go around the room asking the same question.

2. Say: *In this lesson we're going to learn about yes/no questions and short answers with be. We're also going to learn irregular plural forms of nouns.*

CONTEXT

1. Say: *In this lesson we're going to talk about time. Americans say, "Time is money." What does this mean?* (Time is important; being late makes people lose money.)

2. Say: *Sometimes students are late for class. Is it OK to be late for appointments? Is it important to be on time in your country?* Have students share their ideas and experiences. If students say it is OK to be late, encourage them to say by how long (e.g., *Twenty minutes is OK. One hour is not OK.*)

3. Direct students' attention to the picture. Ask: *Who can you see?* (Simon and Victor) *What can you see?* (a clock, the temperature) *Where is Victor?* (outside the bank)

Time Is Money READING

Say: *Do you remember the conversation in Lesson 1? Dorota and Victor went to the bank. Was the bank open?* (no) *Why?* (It was Columbus Day, a holiday.) *What's happening now? Is the bank open?* (yes) Have students look at the title of the reading. Have students use the title and picture to make predictions about the reading. Ask: *What is the reading about? What do you think Simon says to Victor? What does Victor say?*

BEFORE YOU READ

5-10 mins

1. Go over each statement as a class. Have a volunteer read the statements or read them to the class yourself. Ask students to circle *yes* or *no*.

2. Ask a few volunteers to share their answers with the class.

Context Note

Being on time is very important in the U.S. If you are late for business and social occasions, it's considered rude and disrespectful. If you know you're going to be late by more than a few minutes, you should call and let the person know.

 Reading

CD 1
TR 13

10-15 mins

1. First, have students read the dialogue silently. Then play the audio and have students read along.

2. Check students' basic comprehension. Ask true or false questions, such as: *Simon is late. True or false?* (true) *People in the U.S. are always late. True or false?* (false)

Practice Ideas: Listening

1. To practice listening skills, have students listen to the audio before opening their books. Ask a few comprehension questions: *Is Simon late?* (yes) *Are doctors ever on time?* (no) Repeat the audio if necessary. Then have students open their books and read along as they listen to the audio.

2. Alternatively, have students begin by listening to the audio as they read along.

Practice Idea: Speaking

Have students practice the conversation in pairs. Ask volunteers to role-play the conversation in front of the class.

VOCABULARY IN CONTEXT

5-10 mins

1. Model the pronunciation of each new vocabulary item and have students repeat.

2. Make sure students understand the meaning of each vocabulary item. Review the examples in the book and create additional example sentences. For example, say: *on my mind. I think about my students every day. You're always on my mind.* On the board, draw a teacher with a thought bubble. In the thought bubble, draw students. Go over each new vocabulary item similarly, using visuals and realia when appropriate. For example, for *appointment* draw a page from a desk calendar that includes specific times on the board. Write in: "Appointment with Dr. Garcia" in one of the time slots. Say: *Use appointment*

for business and medical meetings. When possible, point to pictures in the book that illustrate the new vocabulary items, such as *outside* and *temperature* on page 30.

3. Have students underline an example of each vocabulary item in the reading. Let them know that *inside* is not in the reading.

Practice Idea: Speaking

To check comprehension, have volunteers in pairs or groups act out selected vocabulary, such as *serious*, *polite*, and *on my mind*.

Did You Know?

Point out the information to students. Explain to students why the U.S. continues to use Fahrenheit to measure temperature. Say: *Fahrenheit was invented in 1714. Celsius was invented in 1742 and many countries began to use Celsius. Today, English-speaking countries say it is too expensive to change. Also, the U.S. and Great Britain like the old Fahrenheit system and do not want to change it.*

 LISTENING ACTIVITY

CD 1
TR 14 **ANSWERS: 1.** No, he isn't. **2.** Yes, they are. **3.** No, they aren't. **4.** No, it isn't. **5.** No, they aren't.

1. Say: *Listen to the questions about Simon and Victor's conversation. Circle the correct short answer.* Play the listening selection one time without pausing. Then play it through again, pausing and replaying as necessary.

2. Have students compare their answers with a partner, then play the audio again and check the answers as a class.

2.3 *Be—Yes/No Questions*

1. Have students look at grammar chart **2.3** on page 33. Review the questions and answers in the chart. Explain that in a question, the verb comes before the subject. Point out that only the subject and the verb are included in a short answer.

2. Direct students to the Language Note. Point out the explanations of contraction use there. Ask the questions with different subject pronouns,

e.g., *Is he late? Are they on time?* Have students respond with negative and positive answers, using contractions appropriately.

3. Compare statements and questions with *be*. Ask volunteers to point out the differences between the statements and the questions (the position of subjects and verbs is reversed).

4. Point out the first Pronunciation Note. Explain that *yes/no* questions have rising intonation. Demonstrate with the example sentences in both charts.

5. Point out the second Punctuation Note. Ask: *What punctuation goes at the end of a question?* (question mark)

Practice Idea: Writing

Have students turn to Vocabulary in Context on page 3. Say: *Make the statements into questions* (e.g., *Is Dorota a citizen of the United States?*). Then ask students to write short answers for the questions. (*Yes, she is.*)

Practice Idea: Speaking

Review how to tell time with students. Use a clock with movable hands or draw a clock on the board. Elicit times from students. Write the times out on the board (e.g., *It's three o'clock. It's 1:45. It's 12:30. It's twenty minutes 'til two.*). Then ask *yes/no* questions about the times (e.g., *Is it six o'clock? Is it 1:40?*).

EXERCISE 1

ANSWERS: 1. Is the bank; **2.** Am I; **3.** Is it; **4.** Are Simon and Victor; **5.** Are we; **6.** Is Simon

1. Have students read the direction line. Ask: *What do we write on the blanks?* (the correct form of the verb *be* and a noun or a pronoun) Go over the examples in the book.

2. Have students complete Exercise 1 individually. Remind them to review grammar chart **2.3** on page 33 if necessary. Check the answers as a class.

EXERCISE 2

1. Tell students that this exercise is based on the reading on page 31. Have students read the direction line. Direct students to the picture of the bank on page 30. Ask: *Is the bank open or closed?* (open) Go over the example in the book.

2. Have students complete Exercise 2 individually. Remind them to review grammar chart **2.3** on page 33 if necessary. Then have students compare their answers with a partner. Say: *Take turns asking and answering questions.* Monitor pair work. Give help as needed.

EXERCISE 3 ═★
Answers will vary.

1. Say: *This exercise is about you.* Have students read the direction line. Go over the example in the book. Model the example with a volunteer. Then have a pair of volunteers model the example again.

2. Have students complete Exercise 3 orally in pairs. Remind them to review grammar chart **2.3** on page 33 if necessary. Say: *Take turns asking and answering questions.* Monitor pair work. Give help as needed.

Practice Idea: Speaking

Take a class survey. How did students answer the questions? Write the results of the survey on the board.

 EXERCISE 4

CD 1
TR 15
ANSWERS: Conversation A: 1. are; **2.** Are we; **3.** are; **4.** Is it (OR the bank); **5.** isn't OR 's not. **Conversation B: 1.** Are you; **2.** 'm not; **3.** Is it (OR the supermarket); **4.** is; **5.** Are you; **6.** Are they (OR bananas); **7.** are; **8.** Is it (OR bread); **9.** isn't OR 's not

1. Tell students this exercise has two conversations: Conversation A and Conversation B. Explain that they will complete questions and answers. Go over the example. Say: *Victor is asking a question. How do you know?* (question mark punctuation) Then do #1 as a class. Point out the questions in the rest of the conversation. Tell students to use short *yes/no* answers to questions. Have students complete the rest of Conversation A individually.

2. Ask: *Are Simon and Marta together, in the same place?* (no) Have students complete Conversation B individually. Remind them to review grammar chart **2.3** on page 33 if necessary. Then have students compare their answers in pairs. Play the audio and check the answers as a class.

Practice Idea: Speaking

Have students practice the conversations in pairs. Have volunteers role-play the conversations in front of the class.

2.4 Irregular Plural Forms ═★

1. Write the following examples on the board:
   1. *person/people*
   2. *man/men*

   Say: *Some plural forms are different words.* Point to #1. Say: *Some plural forms only have a vowel change.* Circle *a* in *man* in #2 and draw an arrow to *e* in *men.* Write *vowel* on the board.

2. Have students look at grammar chart **2.4** on page 35. Go over the singular and plural forms and the explanations.

3. Go over the Pronunciation Note. Model the pronunciation of *woman* and *women.* Then say: *I am going to say some words. For singular, hold up one hand. For plural, hold up two hands.* Say: *people/person, child/children, book/books, woman/women.*

EXERCISE 5

ANSWERS: 1. person, people; **2.** woman, children;
3. child; **4.** man; **5.** women; **6.** men

5-10 mins

1. Have students read the direction line. Go over the example in the book. Point out the picture of the figures in line.

2. Have students complete Exercise 5 individually. Remind them to review grammar chart **2.4** on page 35 if necessary. Check the answers as a class.

EXERCISE 6

ANSWERS: 1. is; **2.** are; **3.** is; **4.** is; **5.** are; **6.** is

5-10 mins

1. Have students read the direction line. Go over the example in the book.

2. Have students complete Exercise 6 individually. Then have students compare their answers with a partner. Remind them to review grammar chart **2.4** on page 35 and **1.2** on page 5 if necessary. Check the answers as a class.

Lesson 3 Overview

GRAMMAR

1. Say: *Listen to these questions: "Are you at the bank?" "Why are you at the bank?" Can you answer yes or no to both questions?* (no) *Which question wants information, not just yes or no?* (the second) Activate prior knowledge. Ask: *What are some information question words?* (who, what, when, where, why, how) *What are some information questions?* Have volunteers work together to make questions. Write the questions on the board.

2. Say: *We're also going to study the articles* a *and* an. Say: *This is a book. This is an envelope.* Ask: *Can you hear the difference between* a *and* an?

CONTEXT

1. Say: *We're going to talk about banks and money again. In the U.S., people often get money from an ATM. What is an ATM?* (a machine that gives money when you put in a special card) *Do people in your country*

use ATMs? How often? Have volunteers share their knowledge and experiences with the class.

2. Direct students' attention to the picture. Ask: *What is happening in the picture? Where are they? Is it early or late? Why do people use ATMs?*

Presentation Items

The topic for this lesson can be enhanced with the following items:

1. An ATM card

2. Maps of the location of bank branches and/or ATM machines in the area

At the ATM READING

Have students look at the title of the reading. Ask: *Where are Dorota and Victor? What is the reading about?* Have students look at the picture on page 37. Ask: *What is Dorota doing?* (getting cash from an ATM) *Who is inside the bank?* (security guard) Have students use the title and picture to make predictions about the reading.

BEFORE YOU READ

5-10 mins

1. Go over each statement as a class. Have a volunteer read the statements or read them to the class yourself. Ask students to circle *yes* or *no*.

2. Ask for a few volunteers to share their answers with the class.

Reading

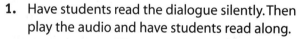

CD 1 TR 16

10-15 mins

1. Have students read the dialogue silently. Then play the audio and have students read along.

2. Check students' basic comprehension. Ask true or false questions such as: *The bank is closed. True or false?* (true) *Victor needs cash. True or false?* (false) *A PIN is not necessary. True or false?* (false)

Practice Idea: Listening

To practice listening skills, have students listen to the audio before opening their books. Ask a few comprehension questions: *Why does Dorota need cash?* (She needs to go to the supermarket.) Repeat the audio if necessary. Then have students open their books and read along as they listen to the audio.

Practice Idea: Speaking

Have students practice the conversation in pairs. Ask volunteers to role-play the conversation in front of the class.

VOCABULARY IN CONTEXT

5-10 mins

1. Model the pronunciation of each new vocabulary item and have students repeat.

2. Make sure students understand the meaning of each vocabulary item. Review the examples in the book and create additional example sentences. For example, to illustrate the word *cash*, take out both a credit card and cash from your wallet. Hold up the cash and say: *I have only [amount] in cash.* For *secret* whisper something simple into a student's ear, such as *I like apples.* Then say out loud: *It's a secret. Don't tell!* For *account* write the name of a bank on the board. Say: *I put my money in this bank. I put it in my account. Do you have a bank account? Where do you put your money?* Elicit answers to check comprehension. Go over each new vocabulary item similarly, using visuals and realia when appropriate. When possible, point to pictures in the book that illustrate the new vocabulary items, such as *security guard* and *ATM* on page 37.

3. Have students underline an example of each vocabulary item in the reading.

Practice Idea: Speaking

Have volunteers act out selected vocabulary, such as *security guard* and *cash.*

Did You Know?

Point out the information to students. Explain to students that online banking is also called *PC banking, home banking, electronic banking,* and *Internet banking.*

 LISTENING ACTIVITY

CD 1
TR 17

ANSWERS: 1. It's 7:30. **2.** Monday through Saturday; **3.** 24 hours a day; **4.** It's a machine for cash. **5.** to get cash; **6.** It's a secret.

1. Say: *Listen to the questions about the conversation we just read between Dorota and Victor. Circle the correct answer.* Play the listening selection one time without pausing. Then play it through again, pausing and replaying as necessary.

2. Go over the answers as a class. Ask a few volunteers to share their answers with the class.

2.5 *Be*—Information Questions =★

10-15 mins

1. Have students look at grammar chart **2.5** on page 40. Stress that information questions begin with a question word. Go over the list of question words (*where, what, what time, why, when, who, whose money, how old*). Review the word order of questions. Go over the examples and answers.

2. Have students cover their charts. Write on the board: *Where is the ATM? It's outside.* Ask students to identify the word order in each sentence.

3. Review the meanings of question words. Read each question in the chart. Ask: *What kind of information is wanted?* (e.g., *Where = place. We want to know the place*). Explain that question words can be contracted with *is.* Go over the examples.

4. Direct students to the Language Note. Ask a few volunteers to make and say contractions from the question words and forms of *be* in the chart.

5. Have students compare statements and information questions in the second part of the chart on page 40. Ask students to identify the subject and the verb in both the statements and questions. Have students underline the subject once and the verb twice (e.g., <u>The bank</u> <u>is</u> open.).

6. Direct students to the Pronunciation Note. Explain that information questions have a falling intonation. Have students close their books. Pronounce the statements and questions in the chart in random order. Have students raise their hands when they hear a question.

Context Note

Today most banks offer online banking and regular banking. Some small banks do not offer online services. Other banks are only online. These banks are called "virtual" banks.

Practice Idea: Speaking

Have students work in pairs. One partner makes a statement with *be*. The other turns it into a question using a question word from grammar chart **2.5** on page 40, e.g., *The school is open. When is the school open?* Tell partners to take turns making statements and questions.

Practice Idea: Speaking

Have students work in pairs to practice the falling intonation of information questions found in **2.5** on page 40. Monitor pair work.

 EXERCISE 1

CD 1
TR 18
ANSWERS: 1. Where; **2.** What; **3.** Why; **4.** Who; **5.** When; **6.** What time

---

5-10 mins

1. Have students read the direction line. Ask: *What do we write on the blanks?* (question words) Go over the example in the book.

2. Have students complete Exercise 1 individually. Remind them to review grammar chart **2.5** on page 40 if necessary. Then have them compare their answers in pairs. Play the audio and check the answers as a class.

Practice Idea: Speaking

Have students practice the conversation in pairs. Ask volunteers to perform the conversation in front of the class.

EXERCISE 2

ANSWERS: 1. are we late; **2.** is it (OR the ATM); **3.** is she (OR that woman); **4.** money is; **5.** old is

---

5-10 mins

1. Have students read the direction line. Say: *In this exercise, you will be completing questions.* Go over the example in the book.

2. Have students complete Exercise 2 individually. Then have students compare their answers in pairs. Check the answers as a class.

EXERCISE 3

Answers will vary.

5-10 mins

1. Say: *This exercise is about you.* Have students read the direction line. Say: *The answers to the questions should be true for you.* Have a volunteer model #1.

2. Have students complete Exercise 3 individually. Remind them to review grammar chart **2.5** on page 40 if necessary. Then have students take turns asking and answering questions in pairs. Monitor pair work. Give help as needed.

Practice Idea: Speaking

Write five information questions on the board. Then create two rings of students. Have half of the students stand in an outer ring around the classroom. Have the other half stand in an inner ring, facing the outer ring. Instruct students to ask and answer the questions on the board. Call out *turn* every minute or so. Students in the inner ring should move one space clockwise. Students now ask and answer the questions with their new partner. Have students ask questions in random order. Make sure students look at each other when they're speaking.

2.6 Articles *A* and *An* ≡★

5-10 mins

1. Have students close their books. Ask: *How do we use the articles* a *and* an? *It depends on sounds and singular and plural nouns.*

2. Write this matching exercise on the board to do with the class:

   1. *It's a bank.*
   2. *It's an ATM.*
   3. *They're ATMs.*
   4. *The bank is big./It's a big bank.*

   a. *Do not use* a *or* an *before a plural noun.*
   b. *Use* an *before a vowel sound.*
   c. *Use* a *before a consonant sound.*
   d. *Use* a *or* an *before an adjective only if a noun follows the adjective.*

3. Say: *Let's match the examples with the rules.* Read each rule and ask students to name the example. Ask students to explain their choices.

4. Have students look at grammar chart **2.6** on page 42. Go over the examples and explanations together as a class.

EXERCISE 4 ≡★

ANSWERS: 1. an; **2.** a; **3.** a; **4.** an; **5.** a; **6.** an; **7.** an; **8.** a

5-10 mins

1. Have students read the direction line. Go over the examples in the book. Elicit from students the rules for using *a* and *an* in the examples (*a* before a consonant: *bank*; *an* before a vowel: *envelope*)

2. Have students complete Exercise 4 individually. Remind them to review grammar chart **2.6** on page 42 if necessary. Then check the answers as a class.

EXERCISE 5 ≡★

CD 1 TR 19

ANSWERS: 1. 's a; **2.** are; **3.** 's a; **4.** is a; **5.** 's a; **6.** are; **7.** are; **8.** are; **9.** 're; **10.** 's an

10-15 mins

1. Have students read the direction line. Remind students that *a* and *an* are not used with plural nouns. Go over the example in the book.

2. Have students complete Exercise 5 individually. Remind them to review grammar chart **2.6** on page 42 if necessary. Then have students

compare their answers in pairs. Play the audio and check the answers as a class.

Practice Idea: Speaking

Have students practice the conversation in pairs. Ask volunteers to perform the dialogue in front of the class.

EXERCISE 6

ANSWERS: 1. That's a new ATM. **2.** Columbus Day is an American holiday. **3.** This is an identification number. **4.** This is an easy way to get cash. **5.** That's a big envelope. **6.** That's an old clock.

5-10 mins

1. Have students read the direction line. Ask: *When do we use* a *with an adjective?* (in front of an adjective that begins with a consonant sound) *When do we use* an? (in front of an adjective that begins with a vowel sound) Go over the example in the book.

2. Have students complete Exercise 6 individually. Remind them to review grammar chart **2.6** on page 42 if necessary. Then have students compare their answers in pairs. Check the answers as a class.

Practice Idea: Writing

Have students work in pairs to create new sentences with the adjectives from Exercise 6. Write an example on the board (e.g., *That's a big dryer.*).

Editing Advice

Have students close their books. Write the example sentences without editing marks or corrections on the board. For example:

10-15 mins

1. *The new people is late.*
2. *She is with his father.*

Ask students to correct each sentence and provide a rule or explanation for each correction, e.g., 1. The new people are late. (*People* is a plural word. Use a plural verb.) 2. She is with her father. (Use the correct possessive adjective.) This activity can be done individually, in pairs, or as a class. After students have corrected each sentence, tell them to turn to page 44. Say: *Now compare your work with the Editing Advice in the book.*

Editing Quiz

ANSWERS: 1. are we; **2.** an; **3.** a machine; **4.** C; **5.** isn't she; **6.** Her; **7.** C; **8.** Is her son small; **9.** C; **10.** a; **11.** Dorota's son; **12.** C; **13.** C; **14.** C; **15.** are; **16.** men; **17.** Ø; **18.** You're

10-15 mins

1. Tell students they are going to put the Editing Advice into practice. Have students read the direction line. Ask: *Do all the shaded words have mistakes?* (no) Go over the examples with the class. Then do #1 together.

2. Have students complete the quiz individually. Then have them compare their answers with a partner before checking the answers as a class. Elicit the relevant grammar point for each correction. For example, for #1 (Answer: *Why ~~we are~~ are we here?*), ask: *What's the rule for questions?* (The verb comes before the subject.)

3. For the items students had difficulties with, have them go back and find the relevant grammar chart and review it. Monitor and give help as necessary.

Expansion

These expansion activities provide opportunities for students to interact with one another and further develop their speaking and writing skills. Encourage students to use grammar from this unit whenever possible.

LEARNER'S LOG

5-10 mins

1. Have students close their books. Ask: *What did you learn about time and money in the U.S.? What else do you want to know?* Prompt

students with questions, such as *How do you use an ATM? Are banks open every day? When are they open?* Write ideas on the board. Discuss ways in which students can find out more about time and ATMs in the U.S.

2. Have students open their books to complete the Learner's Log.

3. Have students compare logs in pairs.

WRITING ACTIVITIES

10-15 mins

1. Have students read the direction line. Go over the example. Write a second sentence about Marta and her daughter together on the board. Have students complete the activity individually.

2. Have students read the direction line. Go over the examples. On the same piece of paper that they used for part 1, have students write their five questions. Collect for assessment.

Practice Idea: Writing

Have students exchange papers with a partner. Ask students to help their partners edit their sentences. Refer students to Editing Advice on page 44.

OUTSIDE ACTIVITY

Have students find a bank in their neighborhood. Ask them to tell the class the name and address of the bank. When is the bank open? Where is the ATM machine?

INTERNET ACTIVITY

In an online search engine, have students search the words *exact time* or *official clock*. Ask them to find the time in their country.

Unit 3

Unit Overview

1. Say: *In the United States, we use many forms.* If available, hold up a form that students will recognize (e.g., a school application, a financial aid form). Otherwise, direct students' attention to the form on page 48. Say: *This is a form. What will we talk about in this unit?* (filling out forms)

2. Direct students' attention to the photos. Ask: *What are they doing?* (filling out forms)

3. Ask: *Where do you fill out forms: at the bank? at the supermarket? Is it easy or hard?* Have students share their personal experiences.

Presentation Ideas

The topic for this unit can be enhanced with the following items:

1. Forms for school admissions and financial aid, for bank cards and supermarket cards

2. Enlarged examples of hand-printed information and written information on forms

Lesson 1 Overview

GRAMMAR

Ask: *What's an imperative?* Demonstrate by performing the actions as you say the commands: *Stand! Sit!* Write *Imperatives* and the verbs on the board. Turn to the class, gesture, and say: *Stand! Sit!* After students are seated, say: *Imperatives are commands. Commands say* Do it! *or* Don't do it! *They can be affirmative or negative.*

CONTEXT

1. Say: *This lesson is about applications.* Direct students' attention to the pictures. Ask: *What are these?* (a Social Security card and an application for a Social Security card). Say: *You need this card to work. Who gets it?* (U.S. citizens and other workers in the U.S.) *In this country, workers pay money to Social Security.*

Social Security pays money to you when you are old, sick, or cannot work. Ask: *What information is on the card?* (a number; your name) *How do you get a card?* (fill out a form) Point to the boxes on the form. Ask: *How many boxes of information do you fill out?* (17; many)

2. Ask: *Did you fill out this form? Who helped you? Was it hard? Do you write or print the information?* Write your own name on the board both in script and print to show the difference. Have students share their experiences.

Getting a Social Security Card
READING

Have students look at the title of the reading. Say: *Dorota and Halina are talking. Dorota has something for Halina. What is it? Will Halina know what to do?* Have students use the title to make predictions about the reading.

BEFORE YOU READ

5-10 mins

1. Go over each statement as a class. Have a volunteer read the statements or read them to the class yourself. Ask students to circle *yes* or *no*.

2. Ask a few volunteers to share their answers with the class.

Context Note

The official Web site of the Social Security Administration gives information in 16 different languages.

 ### Reading ≡★
CD 1 TR 20

1. Have students read the dialogue silently. Then play the audio and have students read along silently.

10-15 mins

2. Check students' basic comprehension. Ask true or false questions, such as: You *use a pencil to fill out a Social Security application. True or false?* (false) *Halina's birthday is in June. True or false?* (true) *Halina was born in 1907. True or false?* (false) You *take two identity documents to the Social Security office. True or false?* (true)

Practice Ideas: Listening

1. To practice listening skills, have students listen to the audio before opening their books. Ask a few comprehension questions: *What is the application for?* (a Social Security card) *When is Halina's birthday?* (June 11) Repeat the audio if necessary. Then have students open their books and read along as they listen to the audio.

2. Alternatively, have students begin by listening to the audio as they read along.

Practice Idea: Speaking

Have students practice the conversation in pairs. Ask volunteers to role-play the conversation in front of the class.

VOCABULARY IN CONTEXT

5-10 mins

1. Model the pronunciation of each new vocabulary item and have students repeat.

2. Make sure students understand the meaning of each vocabulary item. Review the examples in the book and create additional example sentences. For example, say: *print.* Then tell a student volunteer: *Print your name on the board.* Go over each new vocabulary item similarly, using visuals and realia when appropriate. For example, for *forget* write a long number on the board (e.g., 670789321). Say: *Everyone look at this number. Memorize it. Don't forget it.* Then erase the number. Ask: *What's the number? Did you forget?* Ask volunteers to try and remember the number. When possible, point to pictures in the book that illustrate the vocabulary items, such as *application* on page 48 and *birth certificate* on page 50.

3. Have students underline an example of each vocabulary item in the reading.

Practice Idea: Speaking

Have volunteers act out selected vocabulary, such as *fill out* and *sign your name.*

Did You Know?

Point out the information to students. Explain to students that the U.S. does not have a national identity card. Say: *Most people use a driver's license as their identity card. States also offer non-drivers an identity card.*

 LISTENING ACTIVITY

CD 1
TR 21

ANSWERS: 1. True; **2.** True; **3.** False; **4.** False; **5.** True; **6.** False

___

1. Say: *This listening activity is based on Dorota and Halina's conversation about Social Security card applications. Listen to the instructions. Circle* true *or* false. Play the listening selection one time without pausing. Then play it through again, pausing and replaying as necessary.

2. Have students compare their answers, then play the audio again and check the answers as a class.

3.1 Imperatives—Affirmative

1. Have students look at grammar chart **3.1** on page 51. Say: *We use imperatives when we explain or suggest what to do. We also use them to get someone's attention.*

2. Go over the examples and explanations in the chart. Say: *Tell me the imperative: To use a pen./Using a pen./Use a pen.* (Use a pen.) *How do you know?* (base form of verb) Stress that the base form is used for the imperative. Stress that adding the word *please* to an imperative makes the command polite.

3. List examples for each use of imperatives. Write on the board and say: *Instructions: Print your name. Suggestions: Use this pen. It's black. Get someone's attention: Look over there.* Have students give examples. Write their examples on the board.

EXERCISE 1

ANSWERS: **1.** Help; **2.** Fill; **3.** Use; **4.** Write; **5.** Go; **6.** Take; **7.** Sign OR Write

 5-10 mins

1. Have students read the direction line. Go over the example in the book. Say: Make a copy *means to make a photocopy on a machine.*

2. Have students complete Exercise 1 individually. Remind them to review grammar chart **3.1** on page 51 if necessary. Check the answers as a class.

3.2 Imperatives— Negative

 5-10 mins

1. Have students look at grammar chart **3.2** on page 51. Ask volunteers to read the examples. Explain that the negative is formed with *do not* or the contraction *don't*.

2. Have volunteers write the long form of *don't worry*, *don't write*, and *don't be* on the board.

EXERCISE 2

ANSWERS: **1.** Don't forget; **2.** Don't go; **3.** Don't use; **4.** Don't be; **5.** Don't put; **6.** Don't print

 5-10 mins

1. Have students read the direction line. Go over the example in the book. Point out the picture of a person's hand signing his name. Say: *Don't forget to sign your name. Did he forget?* (no)

2. Have students complete Exercise 2 individually. Remind them to review grammar chart **3.2** on page 51 if necessary. Check the answers as a class.

EXERCISE 3

ANSWERS: **1.** Don't use; **2.** Don't forget; **3.** Take; **4.** Write OR Use; **5.** Don't put OR Don't write

 5-10 mins

1. Have students read the direction line. Go over the example.

2. Have students complete Exercise 3 individually. Then have students compare their answers with a partner. Remind them to review grammar charts **3.1** and **3.2** on page 51 if necessary. Check the answers as a class.

EXERCISE 4

CD 1 TR 22

ANSWERS: **1.** Don't touch; **2.** don't ask; **3.** Give; **4.** Be; **5.** let; **6.** Make; **7.** Say; **8.** wash; **9.** Say

 10-15 mins

1. Have students read the direction line. Point out the picture on page 53 of Amy and Marta. Ask: *What's Amy doing? What's Marta doing?* Encourage students to make predictions. Go over the example in the book.

2. Have students complete Exercise 4 individually. Then have students compare their answers with a partner. Remind them to review grammar charts **3.1** and **3.2** on page 51 if necessary. Play the audio and check the answers as a class.

Lesson 2 Overview

GRAMMAR

1. Say: *Let's begin Lesson 2. Let's learn about subject and object pronouns. Is this a command?* (no) Say: Let's *is a strong suggestion. Let's take a break. Let's sing a song.* Write a few verbs on the board (e.g., *go, eat, walk*). Ask volunteers to make suggestions with the verbs using *Let's.*

2. Say: *Let's look at subject and object pronouns.* Write on the board:

    John: I gave the book to Mary. I gave it to her.

    Mary: John gave me the book. He gave it to me.

    Underline the pronouns. Ask students to identify the subject and object pronouns in the sentences and name the referents.

CONTEXT

1. Say: *Let's talk about applications for financial aid. You can fill out many applications online. How do you do it? Is it fast? Do you use a password?* Have students share their knowledge and experiences.

2. Direct students' attention to the picture. Say: *What are they doing?* (filling out a financial aid application) *Where are they?* (at home) *Are they working online?* (maybe)

Presentation Ideas

The topic for this lesson can be enhanced with the following items:

1. A financial aid application
2. A copy of instructions for completing an online application

Financial Aid Application
READING

Have students look at the picture of Halina and Shafia on page 54. Ask a volunteer to read the title of the reading. Ask: *Where are Halina and Shafia?* (at a computer; at home) *What are they doing?* (filling out an application) *What will the conversation be about?* (filling out applications online) Have students use the title and picture to make predictions about the reading.

BEFORE YOU READ

5-10 mins

1. Go over each statement as a class. Have a volunteer read the statements or read them to the class yourself. Ask students to circle *yes* or *no.*

2. Ask a few volunteers to share their answers with the class.

Context Note

The word *college* is often used for both college and university in the U.S. When someone says, "I go to college" or "How many college credits do you have?" he or she can mean *college* or *university.*

  Reading
CD 1 TR 23

10-15 mins

1. First, have students read the dialogue silently. Then play the audio and have students read along.

2. Check students' basic comprehension. Ask *yes/no* and information questions, such as: *Where do Halina and Shafia go to* fill out *an application?* (Internet) *Is it difficult to fill out the application online?* (No, it's easy.) *Is it before 10 P.M.?* (no) *Do they call Dorota?* (no)

Practice Ideas: Listening

1. To practice listening skills, have students listen to the audio before opening their books. Ask a few comprehension questions, such as: *Is college in the U.S. expensive?* (yes) *Does Halina use dashes?* (no) Repeat the audio if necessary. Then have students open their books and read along as they listen to the audio.

2. Alternatively, have students begin by listening to the audio as they read along.

Practice Idea: Speaking

Have students practice the conversation in pairs. Ask volunteers to role-play the conversation in front of the class.

VOCABULARY IN CONTEXT

5-10 mins

1. Model the pronunciation of each new vocabulary item and have students repeat.

2. Make sure students understand the meaning of each vocabulary item. Review the examples in the book and create additional example sentences. For example, say: *password. Let's create passwords.* Go around the room and ask volunteers to make up a password. Go over each new vocabulary item similarly, using visuals and realia when appropriate. For example, for *look up* have students look up a few words in the dictionary, such as *look up* and *password.* For *what about* ask a student in the class his or her name. Then turn to another student and say: *What about you? What's your name?* When possible, point to pictures in the book that illustrate the vocabulary items, such as *dash* on page 55.

3. Have students underline an example of each vocabulary item in the reading.

> ### Practice Idea: Speaking
>
> To check comprehension, have volunteers in pairs or groups act out selected vocabulary, such as *expensive, dashes, create a password, middle initial,* and *bother.*

Did You Know?

Point out the information to students. Say: *Most Americans have middle names, but they don't always use them.* Explain that the middle initial is often used when filling out forms.

 LISTENING ACTIVITY

CD 1 TR 24 **ANSWERS: 1.** True; **2.** False; **3.** True; **4.** False; **5.** False; **6.** True

5-10 mins

1. Say: *Listen to the sentences about Halina and Shafia's conversation. Circle true or false.* Play the listening selection one time without pausing. Then play it through again, pausing and replaying as necessary.

2. Have students compare their answers, then play the audio again and check the answers as a class.

3.3 Let's—Affirmative and Negative

5-10 mins

1. Have students look at grammar chart **3.3** on page 56. Read the examples and explanations in the chart.

2. Point out that the contraction is almost always used because *Let us* is very formal.

> ### Practice Idea: Writing
>
> Have students work in pairs to create a schedule for the next week. Say: *Think about things you need and want to do. For each day, write down a suggestion.* Write the following example on the board: *On Monday, let's go to the laundromat.* Monitor pair work. Give help as needed.

EXERCISE 1

ANSWERS: 1. Let's walk; **2.** Let's not walk, Let's drive; **3.** Let's get; **4.** Let's fill it out; **5.** Let's call; **6.** Let's not call

5-10 mins

1. Have students read the direction line. Say: *You have to write* let's *or* let's not *AND a verb from the box.* Go over the example in the book.

2. Have students complete Exercise 1 individually. Remind them to review grammar chart **3.3** on page 56 if necessary. Check the answers as a class.

3.4 Subject and Object Pronouns

5-10 mins

1. Have students close their books. Elicit a list of subject pronouns and a list of object pronouns. Write the lists on the board.

2. Write the following sentences from the chart on the board:

   I am confused. Help me.

   We are busy. Don't bother us.

   Ask a volunteer to underline the subject pronouns and circle the object pronouns. Ask students: *Does the subject pronoun come before or after the verb?* (before) *What about the object pronoun?* (after)

3. Have students look at grammar chart **3.4** on page 57. Go over the examples and the explanations. Point out that object pronouns come after prepositions. Ask volunteers to demonstrate the meaning of *with*, *on*, and *in*.

EXERCISE 2

ANSWERS: 1. her; **2.** me; **3.** us; **4.** me; **5.** him; **6.** him; **7.** them; **8.** it; **9.** it; **10.** you

5-10 mins

1. Have students read the direction line. Go over the example in the book.

2. Have students complete Exercise 2 individually. Remind them to review grammar chart **3.4** on page 57 if necessary. Check the answers as a class.

EXERCISE 3

ANSWERS: 1. You, me; **2.** He, her; **3.** We, them; **4.** I, you; **5.** They, her

5-10 mins

1. Have students read the direction line. Go over the example in the book. Point out to students that the second sentence of each item repeats what the first sentence says, but in reverse order.

2. Have students complete Exercise 3 individually. Have students compare their answers in pairs. Remind them to review grammar chart **3.4** on page 57 if necessary. Check the answers as a class.

🔊 EXERCISE 4
CD 1
TR 25

ANSWERS: 1. us; **2.** them; **3.** us; **4.** it; **5.** It; **6.** she; **7.** her; **8.** He; **9.** him; **10.** them; **11.** we; **12.** it

10-15 mins

1. Have students read the direction line. Go over the example in the book. Ask students what *it* refers to. (*that*) Go over #1. (It's very expensive for *us*.) Ask students what *us* refers to. (*immigrants*)

2. Have students complete Exercise 4 individually. Then have students compare their answers with a partner. Remind them to review grammar chart **3.4** on page 57 if necessary. Play the audio and check the answers as a class.

Editing Advice

5-10 mins

Have students close their books. Write the example sentences without editing marks or corrections on the board. For example:

> **1.** *Let's don't be late.*
> **2.** *Don't to write on this line.*

Ask students to correct each sentence and provide a rule or explanation for each correction, e.g.: 1. Let's not be late. (Use *not* after *let's* to make the negative.) 2. Don't write on this line. (Don't use *to* after *don't*.). This activity can be done individually, in pairs, or as a class. After students have corrected each sentence, tell them to turn to page 59. Say: *Now compare your work with the Editing Advice in the book.*

Editing Quiz

ANSWERS: 1. C; **2.** him; **3.** not; **4.** C; **5.** C; **6.** Don't; **7.** Ø; **8.** them; **9.** Let's; **10.** it; **11.** C; **12.** C; **13.** me

10-15 mins

1. Tell students they are going to put the Editing Advice into practice. Have students read the direction line. Ask: *Do all the shaded words have mistakes?* (no) Go over the examples with the class. Then do #1 together.

2. Have students complete the quiz individually. Then have them compare their answers with a partner before checking answers as a class. Elicit the relevant grammar point for each correction.

3. For the items students had difficulties with, have them go back and find the relevant grammar chart and review it. Monitor and give help as necessary.

Expansion

These expansion activities provide opportunities for students to interact with one another and further develop their speaking and writing skills. Encourage students to use grammar from this unit whenever possible.

LEARNER'S LOG

10-15 mins

1. Have students close their books. Ask: *What did you learn about Social Security cards and financial aid applications? What else do you want to know about them?* Discuss ways in which students can find out more about applications for Social Security cards and financial aid.

2. Have students open their books to complete the Learner's Log.

3. Have students compare logs in pairs.

WRITING ACTIVITIES

10-15 mins

1. Say: *These are the steps you take to get a Social Security card, but the steps are out of order.* Have students read the direction line. Note that some steps can be done at different times (e.g., copying your birth certificate). Decide as a class which is the first step and write it on the board. Have students complete the activity individually. Collect for assessment.

2. Have students read the direction line. Do the first line in the paragraph with the class on the board. Have students complete the activity individually. Collect for assessment.

Practice Idea: Writing

Have students exchange papers with a partner. Ask students to help their partners edit their paragraph. Refer students to the Editing Advice on page 59.

OUTSIDE ACTIVITY

Have students go to the school's financial aid office to pick up a financial aid application. Ask them to practice filling it out.

INTERNET ACTIVITY

Tell students to go to the Social Security Administration Web site (www.ssa.gov) and use their zip code to find the address of a Social Security Administration office near them. Ask them to bring it to class. In class, have students read the addresses to each other in pairs or small groups. Help with pronunciation.

Unit 4

Unit Overview

1. Say: *Americans like to work and have fun. They go to the movies. They like to eat. They often eat popcorn at the movies. Pizza is a favorite food.* Relate the topic to students' experience. Ask: *What's your lifestyle?*

2. Direct students' attention to the photos. Ask: *What is this man bringing to the door?* (pizza) *What are these people doing?* (watching a movie) *What are they eating?* (popcorn) *What are these people doing?* (riding bikes)

3. Ask students about the lifestyles of their countries: *What's the [Venezuelan] lifestyle like?* Prompt with questions about picnics, travel, exercise, movies, dancing, and favorite foods. Have students share ideas and experiences.

Presentation Ideas

The topic for this unit can be enhanced with the following items:

1. Pictures of family barbecues/picnics which show typical picnic foods, such as fried chicken, hamburgers, chips, and pies
2. A flyer from a local pizzeria that delivers
3. A flyer from a local gym
4. Invitations to children's parties or other events

Lesson 1 Overview

GRAMMAR

1. Write *Simple Present Tense* on the board. Say: *In Lesson 1 we will study the simple present tense.* Say and write on the board: *I go to the movies.* Underline *go*.

2. Say: *We will also study frequency words.* Write *always* and *usually* on the board. Say: *I always go to movies.*

I usually go with a friend. Elicit similar sentences from students about their free-time activities. Write verb and frequency phrases on the board (e.g., *always go shopping, usually watch T.V.*).

CONTEXT

1. Ask: *What are we going to talk about in this lesson?* (free-time activities) Say: *Americans have fun. They like music. They often go to concerts. They like art and exercise.*

2. Direct students' attention to the pictures. Ask: *What is this couple doing?* (watching a movie) *Are they at the movies?* (No, they're at home.) *What about these people? Are they at home?* (No, they're at an art museum.)

Having Fun READING

Have students look at the title of the reading and the first sentence. Ask: *Who is the reading about?* (Americans) *What are we going to read about—work or free time?* (free time) Have students use the title and the pictures on pages 64–65 to make predictions about the reading.

BEFORE YOU READ

5-10 mins

1. Go over each question as a class. Have students discuss the questions in groups. Say: *Say what you like to do in your free time.* Write on the board: *I like to _____ in my free time.* If possible, put students in groups with people from different countries. Monitor group work.

2. Ask a few volunteers to share their answers with the class. Find out what favorite activities or hobbies students have in common.

Context Note

Surveys say that Americans spend much of their free time watching TV.

Reading ≡★

CD 1
TR 26

1. Have students read the text silently. Then play the audio and have students read along silently.

10–15 mins

2. Check students' comprehension. Ask *true* or *false* questions, such as: *Americans don't work very hard. True or false?* (false) *Visitors usually don't need an invitation. True or false?* (false) *Friends watch sports on TV together. True or false?* (true)

Practice Ideas: Listening

1. To practice listening skills, have students listen to the audio before opening their books. Ask a few comprehension questions, such as: *When is the Super Bowl?* (in January or February) *What do theaters sell?* (popcorn) Repeat the audio if necessary. Then have students open their books and read along as they listen to the audio.

2. Alternatively, have students begin by listening to the audio as they read along.

VOCABULARY IN CONTEXT

5–10 mins

1. Model the pronunciation of each new vocabulary item and have students repeat it.

2. Make sure students understand the meaning of each vocabulary item. Review the examples in the book and create additional example sentences. For example, say: *have fun. I have fun in this class. I like to be with you.* Go over each new vocabulary item similarly, using visuals and realia when appropriate. For example, for *invite/invitation* display an example of a child's birthday party invitation. Say: *Children invite their friends to a birthday party.* For *best* show a picture of a famous soccer player or singer and ask: *What is the #1 soccer team in the world? Who is the best singer?* When possible, point to pictures in the book that illustrate new vocabulary items, such as *activity* and *enjoy* on pages 63–64, and *grill* on page 65.

3. Have students underline an example of each vocabulary item in the reading.

Practice Idea: Speaking

Bring in objects to illustrate some of the new vocabulary items, such as posters of different sports teams. Have volunteers act out selected vocabulary items, such as *have fun, activity, team,* and *invite.*

Did You Know?

Point out the information to students. Say: *Movie times before 6 p.m. are often called* matinees.

LISTENING ACTIVITY

CD 1
TR 27

ANSWERS: 1. False; **2.** True; **3.** True; **4.** True; **5.** False; **6.** False; **7.** True

5–10 mins

1. Say: *Listen to the sentences about the journal entry on page 65. Circle* true *or* false. Play the listening selection one time without pausing. Then play it through again, pausing and replaying as necessary.

2. Have students compare their answers in pairs, then play the audio again and check the answers as a class.

4.1 The Simple Present Tense—Affirmative Statements ≡★

5–10 mins

1. Have students cover up grammar chart **4.1** on page 66. Write the following sentences on the board:

   > I <u>like</u> concerts.
   > You <u>like</u> sports.
   > He <u>likes</u> football.
   > She <u>likes</u> tennis.
   > We <u>like</u> English class.
   > They <u>like</u> popcorn.

   Say: *Read these sentences. Look at the verb* like. Point to the verb in each sentence. Say: *Is* like *the same?* (no) *How is it different?* (There is an *-s* on the end when *he* or *she* is the subject.)

2. Explain that in the simple present tense, the base form of the verb is used for all subjects except for *he/she/it* and singular nouns.

3. Have students look at the grammar chart. Go over the sentences. Point out the Language Notes. Say: *Some verbs have irregular forms.* Go over the irregular verbs. Explain that *family* and *team* are singular nouns. Direct students' attention to the examples in the chart and give more examples, such as: *My family is big. My family is fun. Their team always wins.*

Practice Idea: Writing

Have students work in pairs to rewrite the examples in the grammar chart by changing the subjects and/or the complements (e.g., My sister likes concerts.).

EXERCISE 1

ANSWERS: **1.** like; **2.** has; **3.** invites; **4.** spend; **5.** call; **6.** visit; **7.** play

5-10 mins

1. Have students read the direction line. Go over the example in the book.

2. Have students complete Exercise 1 individually. Remind students to review grammar chart **4.1** on page 66 if necessary. Check the answers as a class.

4.2 Spelling of the *-s* Form

5-10 mins
1. Have students look at grammar chart **4.2** on page 67. Go over the examples and explanations in the chart.

2. Write two spellings on the board for these verbs:

   carry: carrys/carries

   walk: walks/walkes

   stay: stays/staies

   mix: mixs/mixes

   splash: splashs/splashes

   Ask students which spelling is correct and why. Refer students to the rules in the grammar chart.

3. Pronounce the verbs. Have students repeat.

Practice Idea: Writing

Have students work in pairs to create sentences with the verbs from grammar charts **4.1** and **4.2**. Say: *Write five sentences using the -s form.* Monitor pair work. Give help as needed. Ask volunteers to read some of their sentences.

EXERCISE 2

ANSWERS: **1.** tries; **2.** watches; **3.** enjoys; **4.** goes; **5.** worries; **6.** washes; **7.** spends; **8.** does

5-10 mins
1. Have students read the direction line. Go over the example in the book. Point out the picture of the football player on page 68.

2. Have students complete Exercise 2 individually. Remind students to review grammar chart **4.2** on page 67 if necessary. Check the answers as a class.

4.3 Uses of the Simple Present Tense

5-10 mins
1. Have students look at grammar chart **4.3** on page 68. Go over the examples and explanations.

2. Write more examples on the board and elicit rules from students.

   I have a Social Security card.

   My daughter wants a computer.

   Children get gifts at birthday parties.

Practice Idea: Writing

Have students come up with other examples of facts, repeated actions, and examples for *like*, *need*, and *want*.

EXERCISE 3

ANSWERS: **Answers may vary. Possible answers: 1.** American museums have many learning activities. **2.** A park has a lot of fun activities. **3.** Two teams play in the Super Bowl.

4. People sometimes invite their friends to their homes. **5.** A movie theater sells popcorn. **6.** Americans sometimes cook on a grill in the summer. **7.** On weekends, American families enjoy movies.

1. Have students read the direction line. Then go over the example. Say: *The ideas for the sentences are from the reading on page 65.*

2. Have students complete Exercise 3 individually. Remind them to review grammar chart **4.3** on page 68 if necessary. Then have students compare their answers with a partner. Monitor pair work. Give help as needed. If needed, go over the sentences with the class.

Practice Idea: Writing

Have students work in pairs to create sentences about their own countries and cultures (e.g., Korean families like to eat barbecue). Monitor to help students with vocabulary. Have volunteers share their sentences with the class.

4.4 Frequency Words

1. Have students cover up grammar chart **4.4** on page 69. Draw a similar scale on the board. Write the frequency words on the scale in a jumbled order. Say: *Try to put the frequency words in the correct order.* Have students call out suggestions as you reorder the list from top to bottom on the board.

2. Have students look at grammar chart **4.4** on page 69. Go over the frequency words and the examples.

3. Point out the Language Notes. Say: *Some frequency words go before the verb, and some words can go at the beginning or the end of a sentence.* Say: *Frequency words go after the verb* be. Go over the example sentences.

EXERCISE 4
Answers will vary.

1. Say: *This exercise is about you.* Have students read the direction line. Go over the example in the book. Say: *Remember to write sentences about yourself.*

---

2. Have students complete Exercise 4 individually. Remind them to review grammar chart **4.4** on page 69 if necessary. Then have students compare their answers with a partner. Monitor pair work. Give help as needed. Have a few students share their answers with the class.

Practice Idea: Speaking

Have students get into groups to discuss their statements. Then have groups report to the class. Write example sentences about students on the board, e.g.: *[Students name or names] hardly ever cook(s) dinner at home.*

EXERCISE 5

ANSWERS: 1. Usually an American invites OR An American usually invites; **2.** A dinner guest always comes; **3.** Usually guests bring OR Guests usually bring; **4.** Sometimes they bring OR They sometimes bring; **5.** guests often say; **6.** Sometimes guests ask OR Guests sometimes ask

---

1. Say: *Dorota is talking about American customs.* Point out the picture. Say the words and have students repeat. Have students read the direction line. Say: *To complete the sentences, put the words in parentheses in the correct order.* Go over the example in the book. Remind students to capitalize the first word of every sentence.

2. Have students complete Exercise 5 individually. Remind them to review grammar chart **4.4** on page 69 if necessary. Then have students compare their answers with a partner. Check the answers as a class.

Practice Idea: Speaking

Have students talk about their customs in groups. Ask: *When you are invited to dinner in your country, what are the customs? Do you bring flowers? Is it important to be on time?*

EXERCISE 6

CD 1
TR 28

ANSWERS: 1. enjoy; **2.** pays; **3.** plays; **4.** have; **5.** sells;
6. likes; **7.** enjoy; **8.** need; **9.** have

⏱
10-15
mins

1. Have students read the direction line. Point out the picture. Ask: *What are the people doing?* (They're at the park/listening to the band/music/ having a picnic, etc.) Go over the example. Ask a volunteer to complete the next sentence.

2. If you think students will have difficulty with the vocabulary, review or pre-teach words such as *Maya* (Victor and Lisa's daughter), *Lisa* (Victor's wife), *Central Street* (a place), *Logan Park* (a place), *chairs* (things that you sit on).

3. Have students complete Exercise 6 individually Remind them to review grammar charts **4.1** on page 66 and **4.2** on page 67 if necessary. Then have students compare their answers with a partner. Play the audio and check the answers as a class.

Practice Idea: Writing

Have students draw a poster advertising the concert in the conversation. Put an example on board for students to complete.

TONIGHT!

_____ *CONCERT*

At _____ *on Central* _____

Date: _____ *evening*

Time: _____ - _____

Post the posters around the classroom. Invite students to read them and say which concert they want to go to.

Lesson 2 Overview

GRAMMAR

1. Write the following sentences on the board:

   I don't work on [Sundays].

   I work [five] days a week.

   I like to relax on [Sundays].

2. Point to each example and say: *First, we're going to learn how to form the negative. Then, we're going to learn time expressions and infinitives.* Elicit more examples of each objective from volunteers.

CONTEXT

1. Say: *Some Americans do not relax. They work five days a week and on weekends. They work eight hours a day.* Ask: *What will we talk about in this lesson—having fun or working in the United States?* (working in the United States)

2. Direct students' attention to the pictures on page 72. Ask: *What are these places?* Point to each place. (a factory, an office, a classroom, a laboratory)

3. Relate the topic to students' knowledge and experience. Ask: *Do you work? Where do you work? Do you work in any of these places?* Point to the pictures on page 72. Have a few volunteers tell where they work.

Working in the U.S. READING

Have students look at the title of the reading. Ask: *Is the reading about working?* (yes) *Working where?* (in the U.S.) *What do you think it will say about working in the U.S.?* Have students use the title to make predictions about the reading.

BEFORE YOU READ

⏱
5-10
mins

1. Go over each question as a class. Have a volunteer read the questions or read them to the class yourself. Ask students to discuss their answers in pairs.

2. Ask a few volunteers to share their answers with the class.

Reading ≡★

CD 1
TR 29

⏱
10-15
mins

1. First, have students read the text silently. Then play the audio and have students read along silently.

2. Check students' basic comprehension. Ask true or false questions, such as: *American workers talk about salaries. True or false?* (false) *American workers usually work six days a week. True or false?* (false) *All Americans relax on their days off. True or false?* (false)

Unit 4   **37**

Practice Idea: Listening

To practice listening skills, have students listen to the audio before opening their books. Ask a few comprehension questions, e.g.: *Do young people often change jobs?* (yes) *How many days a week do Americans usually work?* (five) Repeat the audio if necessary. Then have students open their books and read along as they listen to the audio.

VOCABULARY IN CONTEXT

🕐 5-10 mins

1. Model the pronunciation of each new vocabulary item and have students repeat.

2. Make sure students understand the meaning of each vocabulary item. Review the examples in the book and create additional example sentences. For example, say: *salary. Doctors in the U.S. have big salaries. They usually make between $90,000 and $600,000 a year.* For *overtime* tell students that the work week in the U.S. is 40 hours. Someone that works over 40 hours is working *overtime.* Review each new vocabulary item similarly, using visuals and realia when appropriate. For example, for *complain* say: *Let's complain about the room.* Point to the problems as you say them (e.g., *The room is too small. We need more desks. There aren't enough windows.*).

3. Have students underline one example of each vocabulary item in the reading.

Practice Idea: Speaking

Have volunteers act out selected vocabulary, such as *relax* and *complain.*

Did You Know?

Point out the information to students. Explain to students that they can find the minimum wage for each state by looking on the U.S. Department of Labor's Web site.

LISTENING ACTIVITY

ANSWERS: 1. False; **2.** True; **3.** False; **4.** False; **5.** False; **6.** True; **7.** False

CD 1
TR 30

🕐 5-10 mins

1. Say: *Listen to the sentences about the journal entry on page 73. Circle* true *or* false. Play the listening selection one time without pausing. Then play it through again, pausing and replaying as necessary.

2. Have students compare their answers, then play the audio again and check the answers as a class.

4.5 The Simple Present Tense— Negative Statements ≡★

🕐 10-15 mins

1. Have students turn to the reading on page 73. Say: *Do you see negatives? What are they?* (*don't* and *doesn't*)

2. Have students look at grammar chart **4.5** on page 74. Read the examples in the chart. Say: *There are two forms for the negative with* do. Point out that *doesn't* is used with *he, she,* and *it,* and singular nouns. *Don't* is used with all other subjects. Explain that the base form is always used with the negative.

3. Direct students to the Language Notes. Explain that irregular verbs, such as *have* and *get,* have regular negative forms. Go over the examples. Stress to students that *hardly ever, never,* and *rarely* are negative. Therefore, we do not use them with a negative verb.

Practice Idea: Writing

Have students work in pairs to create new sentences for the negative verbs listed in the grammar chart (e.g., *She doesn't work on Sundays.*).

EXERCISE **1** ≡★

ANSWERS: 1. don't keep; **2.** doesn't complain; **3.** don't make; **4.** don't have; **5.** doesn't talk; **6.** doesn't mean

🕐 5-10 mins

1. Have students read the direction line. Go over the example in the book.

2. Have students complete Exercise 1 individually. Remind them to review grammar chart **4.5** on page 74 if necessary. Check the answers as a class.

EXERCISE 2

ANSWERS: 1. Simon (OR He) doesn't get paid every week. **2.** *Salary* (OR It) doesn't mean money for an hour of work. **3.** Dorota and Simon don't complain about long work hours. **4.** I don't get weekends off. **5.** Halina (OR She) doesn't work 40 hours a week. **6.** You and I (OR We) don't work overtime.

🕐 10-15 mins

1. Have students read the direction line. Say: *In this exercise, you rewrite each sentence. You make the verb negative, and then change the information based on the words in parentheses.* Go over the examples in the book. Point out that the two examples illustrate two kinds of sentences that students might make. Have a volunteer complete #1.

2. Have students complete the rest of Exercise 2 individually. Remind them to review grammar chart **4.5** on page 74 if necessary. Check the answers as a class.

Practice Idea: Writing

Have students work in pairs to create sentences true for them or their country (e.g., *Workers in my country don't get two days off a week.*). Ask volunteers to share information with the class.

4.6 Time Expressions with the Simple Present Tense

🕐 5-10 mins

1. Have students look at grammar chart **4.6** on page 76. Go over the examples. Point out the subject, verb, complement, and time expression in each example.

2. Draw a large monthly calendar on the board. Use the calendar to help illustrate the time expressions. For example, cross out five days in a week for *five days a week*.

3. Direct students to the Language Note. Explain that time expressions with two or more words usually come at the end of a sentence.

Illustrate with examples. Say: *Listen. Which is correct?*

1. *She on weekends doesn't work.*
2. *She doesn't work on weekends.*

EXERCISE 3
Answers will vary.

🕐 10-15 mins

1. Tell students that this exercise is about them. Have students read the direction line. Go over the example in the book.

2. Have students complete Exercise 3 individually. Remind them to review grammar chart **4.6** on page 76 if necessary. Then have students compare their answers in pairs. Monitor pair work. Give help as needed. Have a few volunteers share their answers with the class.

Practice Idea: Speaking

Have students compare their answers to Exercise 3 in groups. Say: *Ask your group members new questions, such as: How often do you eat? How often do you do the laundry?*

4.7 Infinitives with Simple Present Tense

🕐 5-10 mins

1. Write on the board: *Infinitive Form.* Ask: *What is an infinitive?* Say: *The infinitive is the base form of the verb with "to" in front.* Write an example such as *to relax.*

2. Have students look at grammar chart **4.7** on page 77. Say: *We use the infinitive after specific verbs in the simple present tense, such as:* like, want, expect, try, *and* need. Go over the examples in the chart. Point out the subject, verb, the infinitive form, and the complement in each example. Elicit further examples with *like/want/need*.

3. Explain that the infinitive form never changes. It is always the same.

Unit 4 **39**

EXERCISE 4

ANSWERS: 1. like to complain; **2.** doesn't want to leave; **3.** need to take; **4.** don't expect to work; **5.** doesn't like to work; **6.** tries to; **7.** needs to find

1. Have students read the direction line. Say: *You can complete the sentence with the negative or the affirmative.* Go over the examples in the book. Have a volunteer complete #1.

2. Have students complete the rest of Exercise 4 individually. Then have students compare their answers in pairs. Remind them to review grammar chart **4.7** on page 77 if necessary. Check the answers with the class.

5-10 mins

Practice Idea: Writing

Have students work in pairs to create sentences about work (e.g., *I expect to have a day off every week.*). Brainstorm topics and list them on the board. Topics might include days off/vacation, salary/wage, and insurance. Monitor pair work. Give help as needed.

EXERCISE 5

ANSWERS: 1. Many Americans try to get a second job. **2.** The workers don't expect to work on Sundays. **3.** I don't want to complain about my job. **4.** Simon doesn't need to work overtime.

1. Have students read the direction line. If necessary, clarify that students will change the verb to verb + infinitive. Go over the examples in the book.

5-10 mins

2. Have students complete Exercise 5 individually. Then have students compare their answers with a partner. Remind them to review grammar chart **4.7** on page 77 if necessary. Check the answers with the class.

◀)) EXERCISE 6

CD 1
TR 31

ANSWERS: 1. don't like; **2.** don't work; **3.** doesn't pay; **4.** doesn't like; **5.** don't want; **6.** don't find

1. Have students read the direction line. Go over the example in the book. Remind

10-15 mins

students that they are going to complete the conversation with the negative form only.

2. Have students complete Exercise 6 individually. Remind them to review grammar chart **4.5** on page 74 if necessary. Then have students compare their answers with a partner. Play the audio and check the answers as a class.

Practice Idea: Speaking

Have students practice the conversation in pairs. Ask volunteers to role-play the conversation in front of the class.

EXERCISE 7

ANSWERS: 1. gets OR doesn't get; **2.** spend OR don't spend; **3.** pays OR doesn't pay; **4.** like to work OR don't like to work; **5.** complain OR don't complain; **6.** get OR don't get; **7.** pay OR don't pay; **8.** takes OR doesn't take; **9.** expect to get OR don't expect to get; **10.** go OR don't go; **11.** changes OR doesn't change; **12.** keeps OR doesn't keep; **13.** make OR don't make; **14.** work OR don't work; **15.** work OR don't work

1. Say: *In this exercise, you'll write true sentences about work in your town or country.* Then have students read the direction line. Go over the example in the book. Have a volunteer model the example. Elicit and review difficult vocabulary, such as *overtime.*

10-15 mins

2. Have students complete Exercise 7 individually. Remind them to review grammar charts **4.1** on page 66, **4.2** on page 67, **4.5** on page 74, and **4.7** on page 77 if necessary. Then have students compare their answers with a partner. Monitor pair work. Give help as needed. Have a few volunteers share their answers with the class.

Practice Idea: Speaking

Have students compare their answers in groups. If possible, put students from different countries together. Do a survey. Ask: *Which country do you think is the best to work in?*

Lesson 3 Overview

GRAMMAR

Ask: *What tense did we study in Lesson 2?* (simple present) Write the following sentence on the board: *Do you eat hamburgers?* Repeat the question and elicit *yes* and *no* responses in complete sentences from several students (e.g., Yes, I eat hamburgers; Yes, I do.). Then say: *In Lesson 3, we're going to study yes/no questions in the simple present tense.*

CONTEXT

1. Say: *We're going to talk about eating customs. Many Americans eat lunch at noon. I usually eat dinner at 6:00. I like to get Chinese takeout.* Elicit yes/no responses. Ask: *Do you eat Chinese food? Do you get takeout?*

2. Direct students' attention to the photo. Ask: *What place is this?* (a restaurant) *Who is serving food?* (a woman; a waitress)

Eating Customs READING

Have students look at the title of the reading. Ask: *What is the reading about?* (eating customs) *Is it about Indian food or American food?* (American food) Have students use the title and the pictures on pages 80–81 to make predictions about the reading.

BEFORE YOU READ

5-10 mins

1. Go over each question as a class. Have a volunteer read the questions or read them to the class yourself.

2. Ask volunteers to name foods and restaurants they like.

Context Note

Americans eat out more than the people of any other country. More than 65 percent eat in a restaurant one or more times a week. Getting takeout food is even more popular.

Reading
CD 1
TR 32
10-15 mins

Reading

1. First, have students read the dialogue silently. Then play the audio and have students read along.

2. Check students' comprehension. Ask yes/no questions, such as: *Does lunch hour in the U.S. often begin at 11 a.m.?* (yes) *Do supermarkets have prepared food?* (yes)

Practice Ideas: Listening

1. To practice listening skills, have students listen to the audio before opening their books. Ask a few comprehension questions: *Do Americans often eat in restaurants?* (yes) *Is prepared food popular?* (yes) Repeat the audio if necessary. Then have students open their books and read along as they listen to the audio.

2. Alternatively, have students begin by listening to the audio as they read along.

Practice Idea: Speaking

Have students work in pairs to create a similar conversation using information about their native cultures and food customs.

VOCABULARY IN CONTEXT

5-10 mins

1. Model the pronunciation of each new vocabulary item and have students repeat.

2. Make sure students understand the meaning of each vocabulary item. Review the examples in the book and create additional example sentences. For example, say: *convenient. It's convenient to eat out. I don't have to cook dinner or wash dishes.* Go over each new vocabulary item similarly, using visuals and realia when appropriate. For example, for *vegetarian* say: *I'm a vegetarian. I don't like meat. I eat a lot of pasta and vegetables.* For *order* mimic a waiter by using a small notebook and pencil to take an order. Say: *I am a waiter. Can I take your order? What would you like to eat?* When

possible, point to pictures in the book that illustrate the new vocabulary items, such as *deli* and *prepared food* on page 82.

3. Have students underline an example of each vocabulary item in the reading.

Practice Idea: Speaking

To check comprehension, have volunteers in pairs or groups act out selected vocabulary, such as *order* and *deliver*.

Did You Know?

Point out the information to students. Tell students that there are different kinds of vegetarians. For example, some vegetarians eat dairy and egg products, but don't eat meat. *Vegans* don't eat any animal products, including eggs or honey, and don't wear clothes made from animal skins or fur.

LISTENING ACTIVITY

CD 1
TR 33

ANSWERS: 1. False; **2.** True; **3.** True; **4.** True; **5.** False; **6.** False; **7.** False

5-10
mins

1. Say: *This listening activity is based on the conversation about American eating customs. Listen to the instructions. Circle* true *or* false. Play the listening selection one time without pausing. Then play it through again, pausing and replaying as necessary.

2. Have students compare their answers, then play the audio again and check the answers as a class.

4.8 The Simple Present Tense —*Yes/No* Questions ≡★

5-10
mins

1. Have students look at grammar chart **4.8** on page 82. Say: *Questions in the simple present tense begin with* do *or* does *followed by the subject and the base form of the verb.* Write on the board in two columns: *I, you, we, they, plural nouns,* and *he, she, it, singular nouns.* Ask: *Which subjects take* does *and which take* do? (first column *do*, second column *does*) Hold up the book and run your finger down the column of subjects and then verbs to make sure students can follow the chart.

2. Read through all the questions and short answers in the chart. Ask volunteers questions to check understanding (e.g., *Do you like Chinese food?* [Yes, I do.]).

3. Review word order for questions. Then write scrambled questions on the board, such as: *go/ to a deli for lunch/she/does/?* Ask volunteers to put the words in the correct order.

Practice Idea: Speaking

Have students go back to the reading on page 81. Say: *Find the questions in the reading. Circle* do *or* does *and the subject of each question.* In pairs, have students practice asking and answering the questions they found.

EXERCISE 1 ≡★

ANSWERS: 1. Does/No, it doesn't. **2.** Does/No, she doesn't. **3.** Do/Yes, they do. **4.** Do/No, they don't. **5.** Do/Yes, they do. **6.** Does/Yes, it does. **7.** Do/No, they don't.

10-15
mins

1. Have students read the direction line. Point out that the answers are based on the conversation on page 81. Go over the example in the book. Have a volunteer do #1.

2. Have students complete the rest of Exercise 1 individually. Remind them to review grammar chart **4.8** on page 82 if necessary. Check the answers as a class.

EXERCISE 2

ANSWERS: 1. Do you work Monday through Friday? **2.** Do you use your car? **3.** Does the job pay well? **4.** Does Joe's Pizza have pizza for vegetarians too?

10-15
mins

1. Have students read the direction line. Go over the example in the book. Say: *Use the words in the parentheses to make a question.* Have a volunteer do #1.

2. Have students complete the rest of Exercise 2 individually. Remind them to review grammar chart **4.8** on page 82 if necessary. Check the answers as a class.

Practice Idea: Speaking

Have students practice the short conversations in pairs. Circulate to observe pair work.

EXERCISE 3

ANSWERS: 1. Does Victor (OR he) like salads? **2.** Does Halina (OR she) buy prepared food? **3.** Does that restaurant (OR it) have vegetarian food? **4.** Do you go to lunch at 11:00 A.M.? **5.** Do Halina and Dorota (OR they) want to order sandwiches? **6.** Does this restaurant (OR it) deliver sandwiches? **7.** Do Americans (OR they) eat it in the supermarket?

10-15 mins

1. Have students look at the picture. Ask: *What do you think Victor's job is?* (delivering pizza) Have students read the direction line in the book.

2. Have students complete Exercise 3 individually. Have students compare their answers in pairs. Remind them to review grammar chart **4.8** on page 82 if necessary. Check the answers as a class.

Practice Idea: Speaking

Have students practice the conversation in pairs. Have volunteers role-play the conversation in front of the class.

EXERCISE 4

ANSWERS: Student responses will vary. Correct questions: 1. Do you like pizza? **2.** Do you like to cook? **3.** Do you eat dinner with your family? **4.** Do you sometimes order takeout food? **5.** Do you eat lunch at home? **6.** Does someone cook for you? **7.** Do restaurants in your country deliver? **8.** Do supermarkets in your country have deli sections? **9.** Do most people in your country eat meat?

10-15 mins

1. Say: *This exercise is about you. You're going to ask your partner* yes/no *questions.* Have students read the direction line in the book. Go over the example by modeling it with a student. Then have two volunteers model #1.

2. Have students complete the rest of Exercise 4 in pairs. Remind them to review grammar chart **4.8** on page 82 if necessary. Monitor pair work. Give help as needed. Have volunteers tell the class about their partner.

Practice Idea: Speaking

Create two rings of students. Have half of the students stand in an outer ring around the classroom. Have the other half stand in an inner ring, facing the outer ring. Write four questions from Exercise 4 on the board. Instruct students to ask and answer the questions on the board. Call out *turn* every minute or so. Students in the inner ring should move one space clockwise. Students now ask and answer the questions with their new partner. Have students ask questions in random order. Make sure students look at each other when they're speaking.

 EXERCISE 5
CD 1
TR 34 **ANSWERS: 1.** Do you have; **2.** Does the food taste; **3.** Does it have; **4.** Do they have; **5.** Do you like to cook; **6.** Does the supermarket prepare; **7.** Do you and Peter eat

10-15 mins

1. Have students look at the picture on page 85. Ask: *What are they doing?* (eating) *What do you think they are eating?* Have students read the direction line. Go over the example in the book.

2. Have students complete Exercise 5 individually. Then have students compare their answers in pairs. Remind them to review grammar chart **4.8** on page 82 if necessary. Then play the audio and check the answers as a class.

Practice Idea: Speaking

Have students practice the conversation in groups of four. Ask volunteers to role-play the conversation in front of the class.

Lesson 4 Overview

GRAMMAR

1. Say: *In Lesson 3, we studied yes/no questions in the simple present. In Lessons 1 and 2, we studied time expressions.* Elicit examples, such as: *Do you eat vegetables?* and *three times a week.* Write the examples on the board.

2. Say: *In Lesson 4, we will study information questions. Information questions begin with question words.* Write the two objectives on the board. Say: *Listen to the questions. Tell me the question words: Who are you? Where do you live? Why do Americans exercise?* Write the question words on the board.

CONTEXT

1. Say: *Are you healthy? Do you exercise? I go to the gym three times a week. I run. I swim. In this lesson, we're going to talk about staying healthy.* Ask: *Do you go to a gym? Do you run in the park? What kind of exercise do you do?*

2. Direct students' attention to the picture. Ask questions about the people in the picture: *Why is this woman wearing sneakers?* (e.g., She walks to work for exercise and wears comfortable shoes.) *What is that woman doing?* (exercising at the gym)

Exercise READING

Have students look at the title of the reading. Ask: *What is the reading about? What are Dorota and Halina talking about?* (exercise) *What do you think they will say about exercising in America?* Have students use the title of the reading and the picture on page 86 to make predictions about the reading.

BEFORE YOU READ

5-10 mins

1. Go over each question as a class. Have a volunteer read the questions or read them to the class yourself. Ask students to discuss their answers in pairs.

2. Ask a few volunteers to share their answers with the class. Write students' answers on the board.

Reading

CD 1
TR 35

10-15 mins

1. First, have students read the dialogue silently. Then play the audio and have students read along silently.

2. Check students' basic comprehension. Ask questions such as: *Do some American workers exercise during their lunch hour?* (yes) *Do most Americans exercise?* (no) *Does Dorota try to exercise almost every day?* (yes)

VOCABULARY IN CONTEXT

5-10 mins

1. Model the pronunciation of each new vocabulary item and have students repeat it.

2. Make sure students understand the meaning of each vocabulary item. Review the examples in the book and create additional example sentences. For example, say: *desk job. My husband has a desk job. He works at a desk in an office all day.* Go over each new vocabulary item similarly, using visuals and realia when appropriate. When possible, point to pictures in the book that illustrate new vocabulary

items, such as *sneakers*, *gym*, *next door*, and *ride a bicycle* on page 86.

3. Have students underline one example of each vocabulary item in the reading.

Practice Idea: Speaking

Have volunteers act out selected vocabulary, such as *ride a bicycle* and *exercise*.

Context Note

Many Americans have serious health problems because they overeat and don't exercise enough. As a result, approximately 65 percent of U.S. adults are overweight or obese.

Did You Know?

Point out the information to students. Explain to students that the U.S. government recommends 30 minutes a day of moderate exercise, such as walking, golfing, and water aerobics.

 LISTENING ACTIVITY

CD 1
TR 36

ANSWERS: **1.** True; **2.** True; **3.** False; **4.** True; **5.** True; **6.** False

5-10 mins

1. Say: *Listen to the sentences about Halina and Dorota's conversation. Circle* true *or* false. Play the audio one time without pausing. Then play it through again, pausing and replaying as necessary.

2. Have students compare their answers, then play the audio again and check the answers as a class.

4.9 The Simple Present Tense—Information Questions ≡★

10-15 mins

1. Have students look at grammar chart **4.9** on pages 88–89. Elicit word order for information questions from students. Write on the board:

   Question word + do/does + subject + verb (base form)

Elicit which subjects take *do/does* from students. Write on the board: Do *is used with* I, you, we, they, *and plural nouns.* Does *is used with* he, she, it, *and singular nouns.*

2. Elicit question words from students and their meaning. Write on the board:

   How often → *frequency*

   Why → *reason*

   Where → *place*

   When → *time*

   How → *in what way*

   What kind → *type*

   What → *thing*

   How much/many → *amount*

   Who → *person*

   Say: *Information questions ask for information about people, places, time, and other things.* Activate students' knowledge. Elicit examples of each kind of information.

3. Go over short answers. Have students look at the answers in the first part of the chart. Say: *Some short answers are a phrase. The phrase gives a piece of information.* Direct students' attention to the answers in the second part of the chart. Say: *Some short answers may be given in a short sentence.* Have students read the questions and answers in the chart.

4. Point out the Language Notes. Ask students to identify the examples with *How often* and *Why* in the chart.

Practice Idea: Speaking

Have students go back to the reading on page 87. Have them find the information questions. Ask students to underline the question word, the subject, *do/does*, and the verb. In pairs, have students practice asking and answering the questions they found.

EXERCISE 1 ≡★

ANSWERS: **1.** What; **2.** Why; **3.** How many; **4.** What kind of; **5.** How much; **6.** How; **7.** How often; **8.** When

---

1. Have students read the direction line. Say: *First, look at the underlined words. Then decide what question word you need.* Go over the example in the book. Have a volunteer do #1.

2. Have students complete the rest of Exercise 1 individually. Remind them to review grammar chart **4.9** on pages 88–89 if necessary. Check the answers as a class.

Practice Idea: Speaking

Have students practice the short conversations in pairs. Ask volunteers to role-play the conversations in front of the class.

EXERCISE 2

ANSWERS: 1. What kind of exercise does Dorota do? She walks. **2.** Where does Dorota exercise? She exercises in a park. **3.** When does Louisa exercise? She exercises during her lunch hour. **4.** How often does Dorota exercise? She exercises (OR tries to exercise) five days a week. **5.** Why do people need to exercise? Because they want to stay healthy. OR Because they sit all day. OR Because they have desk jobs. **6.** What does "bike" mean? It (OR "Bike") means "bicycle."

1. Tell students they are going to make questions and answers. Have students read the direction line. Review meanings of question words. Ask: *What does* where *ask about?* (place/location) Go over the example in the book. Have a volunteer complete #1. Point out that the exercise is based on the conversation on page 87.

2. Have students complete the rest of Exercise 2 individually. Then have students compare their answers in pairs. Remind them to review grammar chart **4.9** on pages 88–89 if necessary. Check the answers as a class.

EXERCISE 3

ANSWERS: 1. Why does she wear sneakers? **2.** When does she have a day off (each week)? **3.** What kind of shoes do you have? **4.** How often does she go to the gym in the winter?

5. How many bikes does Halina (OR she) see in the street? **6.** Why do bike messengers (OR they) ride fast?

1. Tell students they are going to make questions. Have students read the direction line. Review the example. Say: *Look at the question word in parentheses.*

2. Point to the picture on page 86. Write (*where*) on the board. Say: *The answer is:* Dorota goes to the park. *What is the question?* (Where does Dorota go?)

3. Have students complete Exercise 3 individually. Remind them to review grammar chart **4.9** on pages 88–89 if necessary. Then have students compare their answers in pairs. Check the answers as a class.

Practice Idea: Speaking

Have students practice the statements and questions in pairs.

4.10 The Simple Present Tense—Subject Questions

1. Have students look at grammar chart **4.10** on page 91. Say: *When the subject is a question word, do not use* do *or* does. Read through the questions in the chart. Point out that the verb is either the base form or the -*s* form. Stress that the base form is used with plural nouns (e.g., *which workers, what kind of people*), and that the -*s* form is used with *who* and singular nouns (e.g., *which company*).

2. Say: *Look at the short answers. They give the subject and* do *or* does. *They do not repeat the verb.* Go over the questions and short answers. Ask: *Do you always answer with a sentence?* (No, you can answer with a phrase.)

3. Point out the Language Notes. Ask students to identify the examples in the chart that relate to the notes.

EXERCISE 4

ANSWERS: 1. Who wants to exercise? **2.** What kinds of jobs pay well? **3.** How many people ride their bicycles to work? **4.** Who works three days a week? **5.** Which workers exercise during their lunch hours? **6.** How many people in your company exercise before work? **7.** Whose company has a gym for the workers? **8.** What happens after lunch?

⏱ **10-15 mins**

1. Have students read the direction line. Go over the example in the book.
2. Have students complete Exercise 4 individually. Remind them to review grammar chart **4.10** on page 91 if necessary. Check the answers as a class.

Practice Idea: Speaking

Have students practice the statements and questions in pairs.

EXERCISE 5

ANSWERS: Answers may vary. Possible answers: 1. Why do people (OR Americans) exercise? **2.** Whose friend exercises during lunch hour? OR Whose friend wears sneakers with a business suit? **3.** When do some office workers exercise? **4.** What does a bike messenger do? **5.** How much does that bike cost? **6.** How often does Louisa exercise? **7.** Who works on a bicycle? **8.** How many bike messengers do Halina and Dorota see?

⏱ **10-15 mins**

1. Have students read the direction line. Go over the example in the book.
2. Review #6. Elicit the difference between *when* (general time), *how often* (frequency), and *what time* (specific/exact time).
3. Have students complete Exercise 5 individually. Then have students compare their answers in pairs. Remind them to review grammar chart **4.10** on page 91 if necessary. Check the answers as a class.

Practice Idea: Speaking

Have students ask and answer questions about exercise in a partner's country. Have them ask questions such as: *How many people in [country] exercise during their lunch hour? What do people in [country] wear to the office? Do many people in [country] ride bicycles to work?* Pair students from different countries if possible.

Editing Advice

⏱ **10-15 mins**

Have students close their books. Write the example sentences without editing marks or corrections on the board. For example:

1. *Dorota work in an office.*
   She have a good job.
2. *She doesn't has a new job.*
   Where does she works?

Ask students to correct each sentence and provide a rule or explanation for each correction, e.g.: 1. Dorota works in an office. She has a good job. (Use the *-s* form in the affirmative with *he, she, it,* and singular subjects.) 2. She doesn't have a new job. Where does she work? (Don't use the *-s* form after *does* or *doesn't*.) This activity can be done individually, in pairs, or as a class. After students have corrected each sentence, tell them to turn to page 93. Say: *Now compare your work with the Editing Advice in the book.*

Editing Quiz

ANSWERS: 1. does a bike messenger deliver; **2.** delivers; **3.** Who works; **4.** C; **5.** happens; **6.** People sometimes open OR Sometimes people open; **7.** C; **8.** C; **9.** C; **10.** they often ride OR often they ride; **11.** means; **12.** C; **13.** C; **14.** They never need

⏱ **10-15 mins**

1. Tell students they are going to put the Editing Advice into practice. Have students read the direction line. Ask: *Do all the shaded words have mistakes?* (no) Go over the examples with the class. Then do #1 together.
2. Have students complete the quiz individually. Then have them compare their answers with a partner before checking the answers as a class.

Elicit the relevant grammar point for each correction.

3. For the items students had difficulties with, have them go back and find the relevant grammar chart and review it. Monitor and give help as necessary.

Expansion

These expansion activities provide opportunities for students to interact with one another and further develop their speaking and writing skills. Encourage students to use grammar from this unit whenever possible.

LEARNER'S LOG

10-15 mins

1. Have students close their books. Ask: *What did you learn about free-time activities and work in the U.S? What about food and exercise in the U.S? What else do you want to know about them?* Discuss ways in which students can find out more about work and free-time activities.

2. Then have students open their books to complete the Learner's Log.

3. Have students compare logs in pairs.

WRITING ACTIVITY

10-15 mins

Have students read the direction line. Do the first line in the paragraph with the class on the board. Have students complete the activity individually. Collect for assessment.

Practice Idea: Writing

Have students exchange papers with a partner. Ask students to help their partners edit their paragraph. Refer students to the Editing Advice on page 93.

OUTSIDE ACTIVITIES

1. Tell students to visit the deli section of a supermarket. In class, have students discuss the foods they found in a deli section with questions such as: *Do you like this _____? How often do you eat/buy it?*

2. Tell students to get a takeout menu from a restaurant they like. Ask them to choose a meal. In class, have students tell what foods are in the meal, and what the price is.

3. Tell students to find out the cost of food and drinks at a nearby movie theater. Then have them report to the class.

INTERNET ACTIVITIES

1. Tell students to use the Internet to find out about places to exercise (e.g., parks, gyms) in their current town or city. Have them report back to the class.

2. Tell students to use the Internet to find out what the minimum wage is in the state they live in. Tell them that the U.S. Department of Labor has information about minimum wage by state on its Web site (www.dol.gov).

Unit 5

Unit Overview

1. Say: *We're going to learn about driving in the United States. We will talk about safety and driver's licenses.* Ask: *Is driving in the U.S. different from driving in your country? Can teenagers drive? Do you have to wear seatbelts?* Have students share their ideas and personal experiences.

2. Direct students' attention to the photo of the teenage driver. Ask: *Is the driver young or old?* (young) *What is the man with her doing?* (teaching her to drive) Direct students' attention to the other photo. Say: *The mother puts her baby in a car seat. Why?* (for safety)

Presentation Ideas

The topic for this unit can be enhanced with the following items:

1. An infant car seat, a booster seat, or a catalog showing these items
2. A driver's license
3. A copy of a practice driving test
4. A poster or printout of common road signs

Lesson 1 Overview

GRAMMAR

Ask: *What will we study in Lesson 1?* (modal verbs *can* and *should*, and *have to*) Say: *I can drive. I should drive. I have to drive.* Write the sentences on the board. Underline the modals and *have to*. Ask: *Is the meaning of all three sentences the same?* (no) *What is the main verb?* (drive) Say: *A modal verb adds to the meaning of the main verb.*

CONTEXT

1. Say: *We're going to learn about driving in the U.S. You have to have a license to drive in the U.S.* Activate students' knowledge. Ask: *How do you get a driver's license?*

2. Direct students' attention to the pictures. Say: *This is a driver's license. Is it the same as your license?* Have a student show his or her license and briefly compare it with the illustration. Point to the other picture of the Department of Motor Vehicles. Ask: *Where is this?* (Department of Motor Vehicles) *What do people do here?* (get a driver's license; take an eye test and written test; get license photos taken)

3. Ask: *Where do you go to take a driver's test? How many tests do you take? Are they easy or hard?* Have students share their experiences.

Getting a Driver's License
READING

Have students look at the title of the reading. Say: *A father and son are talking about driving. The son is 15 years old.* Ask: *What do you think the son and father are saying?* Have students use the title and pictures on page 98 to make predictions about the reading.

BEFORE YOU READ

5-10 mins

1. Go over each statement as a class. Have a volunteer read the statements or read them to the class yourself. Ask students to circle *yes* or *no*.

2. Ask for a few volunteers to share their answers with the class.

Context Note

Each state issues driver's licenses. In most states drivers have to be 16. Many states give a learner's permit to 14- and 15-year-old teens. An adult must always accompany these learners.

 Reading

CD 2
TR 01

10-15 mins

1. Have students read the dialogue silently. Then play the audio and have students read along silently.

2. Check students' basic comprehension. Ask questions such as: *Can Ed get a license at 15?* (No, but he can get a learner's permit.) *What does he have to do before he can practice in a car?* (pass a vision test and a written test)

VOCABULARY IN CONTEXT

5-10 mins

1. Model the pronunciation of each new vocabulary item and have students repeat it.

2. Make sure students understand the meaning of each vocabulary item. Review the examples in the book and create additional example sentences. For example, say: *permit. I have a permit to ride a motorcycle.* Go over each new vocabulary item similarly, using visuals and realia when appropriate. For example, for *in a hurry* start to rush out of the room and say: *I can't stay after class today—I'm in a hurry.* When possible, point to pictures in the book that illustrate the new vocabulary items, such as *vision test* and *written test* on page 98.

3. Have students underline an example of each vocabulary item in the reading. Point out that the word *over* is not in the reading. Provide other example sentences if students are unsure of its meaning.

Did You Know?

Point out the information to students. Ask students if either males or females have more frequent serious car crashes. Tell them that statistics (insurance and police information) say that males have more frequent serious car crashes than females.

 LISTENING ACTIVITY

CD 2
TR 02   **ANSWERS: 1.** True; **2.** False; **3.** True; **4.** True; **5.** False; **6.** True; **7.** True

5-10 mins

1. Say: *Listen to the sentences about Simon and Ed's conversation. Circle* true *or* false. Play the listening selection one time without pausing. Then play it through again, pausing and replaying as necessary.

2. Have students compare their answers, then play the audio again and check the answers as a class.

5.1 Modal: *Can*—Affirmative and Negative ≡★

10-15 mins

1. Have students look at grammar chart **5.1** on page 101. Say: *We use* can *to show ability, permission, or possibility.* Write these three examples on the board:

   > *ability: I can drive a car.*
   >
   > *permission: Can I use your car?*
   >
   > *possibility: We can go to the park tomorrow. It's going to be a nice day.*

2. Go over the examples in the chart. Review word order with modals. Ask: *Where is the modal in a sentence?* (between the subject and the base form of the verb)

3. Say: *The negative of* can *is* cannot. *The contraction, or short form, for* cannot *is* can't. Write on the board: *cannot = can't*

4. Direct students to the Language and Pronunciation Notes. Go over each note and the examples. To stress the use of *can't* to show rules, say: *can't = don't: "You can't park here"* means *"Don't park here."* To stress the difference in pronunciation of *can* and *can't,* say five minimal sentence pairs with *can* and *can't.* (e.g., *I can go./ I can't go. He can drive./ He can't drive. She can speak English./ She can't speak English.*) Ask students to raise their hands if they hear *can* and to keep their hands down if they hear *can't.*

EXERCISE 1

ANSWERS: **1.** can; **2.** can't; **3.** can; **4.** can; **5.** can't; **6.** can; **7.** can't; **8.** can't

5-10 mins

1. Have students look at the learner's permit on page 101. Say: *This is an example of a learner's permit. People who are learning to drive can get a permit before getting their license.* Then have students read the direction line. Go over the example in the book. Tell students to go back to the conversation on page 99 to help find the answers.

2. Have students complete Exercise 1 individually. Remind them to review grammar chart **5.1** on page 101 if necessary. Check the answers as a class.

5.2 Modal: *Should*—Affirmative and Negative

5-10 mins

1. Have students look at grammar chart **5.2** on page 102. Say: *We use* should *to give advice or a suggestion.*

2. Go over the examples in the chart. Review word order with modals. Ask: *Where is the modal in a sentence?* (between the subject and the base form of the verb)

3. Say: *The negative of* should *is* should not. *The contraction, or short form, for* should not *is* shouldn't.

EXERCISE 2

ANSWERS: **1.** You should wash; **2.** He shouldn't be; **3.** He should practice; **4.** You shouldn't drive; **5.** He should learn; **6.** New drivers shouldn't drive; **7.** You should look

5-10 mins

1. Have students read the direction line. Go over the example in the book.

2. Have students complete Exercise 2 individually. Remind them to review grammar chart **5.2** on page 102 if necessary. Check the answers as a class.

5.3 *Have To*—Affirmative and Negative

5-10 mins

1. Have students look at grammar chart **5.3** on page 103. Go over the examples in the chart. Review word order. Ask: *Where is* have to *in the sentence?* (between the subject and the base form of the verb) Point out the use of *do.* Say: *The negative of* have to *is* doesn't have to *or* don't have to.

2. Go over the Language and Pronunciation Notes. Go over the examples for affirmative and negative. Ask volunteers to give additional examples. Review the pronunciation rule. Say: *In relaxed speech,* have to *is pronounced* /hæftə/ *and* has to *is pronounced* /hæstə/. Demonstrate the pronunciation of both words. Read the examples. Have students repeat.

EXERCISE 3

ANSWERS: **1.** doesn't have to get; **2.** have to pass; **3.** has to practice; **4.** don't have to take; **5.** don't have to be; **6.** have to have; **7.** doesn't have to teach

5-10 mins

1. Have students read the direction line. Say: *You have to decide to use an affirmative or a negative verb.* Go over the example. Tell students to go back to the conversation on page 99 to help them with the answers.

2. Have students complete Exercise 3 individually. Remind them to review grammar chart **5.3** on page 103 if necessary. Check the answers as a class.

EXERCISE 4

Answers will vary.

5-10 mins

1. Say: *This exercise is about you.* Have students read the direction line. Go over the examples in the book. Have a volunteer model the examples for the class.

2. Have students complete Exercise 4 individually. Remind them to review grammar chart **5.3** on page 103 if necessary. Then have students compare their answers in pairs. Have volunteers share their answers with the class.

Practice Idea: Writing

Have students write sentences with *have to* and *don't have to* about another class they are currently taking or have taken in the past. Then have students compare their sentences in pairs. Monitor pair work. Give help as needed.

EXERCISE 5

ANSWERS: Answers will vary. Possible answers:
1. Riders can't ride a bicycle here. OR Riders have to walk with their bicycles or use another street.
2. Drivers can't turn right. OR Drivers have to go straight or turn left. **3.** Drivers have to stop. OR All drivers at the intersection have to stop.
4. Drivers should be careful. OR Pedestrians can cross here. OR Drivers shouldn't drive fast. **5.** Drivers can't enter. OR Drivers have to go another way.
6. Drivers can only go one way. OR Drivers have to go in the direction of the arrow. **7.** Drivers can't go this way. OR Drivers shouldn't enter this road.
8. Drivers should be careful in a school zone. OR Drivers shouldn't drive fast in a school zone.

1. Have students read the direction line. Go over the example in the book. Say: *There can be many ways to say the same thing, so not everyone will have the same answer.*

2. Have students complete Exercise 5 in pairs. Remind them to review grammar charts **5.1** on page 101, **5.2** on page 102, and **5.3** on page 103 if necessary. Monitor pair work. Give help as needed.

Practice Idea: Speaking

Have students compare sentences in groups. Have groups choose the best sentences to present to the class. Then have the class vote on the best sentence for each road sign.

EXERCISE 6

Answers will vary.

1. Say: *This exercise is about you.* Tell students that they will be writing sentences that are true for drivers in their country. Have students read the direction line. Go over the examples in the book.

2. Have students complete Exercise 6 in pairs from the same country if possible. Remind them to review grammar charts **5.1** on page 101, **5.2** on page 102, and **5.3** on page 103 if necessary. Monitor pair work. Give help as needed. Have volunteers share their answers with the class.

Practice Idea: Speaking

Ask volunteers to share some of their sentences about drivers in their countries. Write their sentences on the board.

EXERCISE 7

ANSWERS: Answers may vary. Possible answers:
1. can take; **2.** shouldn't leave; **3.** have to study, don't have to do; **4.** should wash, can't wash; **5.** have to be;
6. has to take, doesn't have to pay, can take;
7. shouldn't wait, can't learn; **8.** should watch

1. Have students read the direction line. Say: *You decide whether to use* can, should, *or* have to. Go over the example in the book.

2. Have students complete Exercise 7 in pairs. Remind them to review grammar charts **5.1** on page 101, **5.2** on page 102, and **5.3** on page 103 if necessary. Check the answers as a class.

EXERCISE 8

CD 2
TR 03

ANSWERS: Conversation A: **1.** can drive; **2.** has to get; **3.** doesn't have to get; **4.** should study; **5.** has to take. Conversation B: **1.** can't see; **2.** shouldn't worry; **3.** have to wear.

1. Have students read the direction line and the description of Conversation A. Ask: *What*

country is Ed's friend from? (Mexico) Have students complete the dialogue individually. Then have students read the description of Conversation B. Ask: *Who is Mr. Brown?* (the driving teacher) Have students complete the dialogue individually.

2. Have students compare their answers to both conversations in pairs. Remind them to review grammar charts **5.1** on page 101, **5.2** on page 102, and **5.3** on page 103 if necessary. Play the audio and check the answers as a class.

Practice Idea: Speaking

Have students practice Conversations A and B in pairs. Have students change roles. Ask volunteers to role-play the conversations in front of the class.

Lesson 2 Overview

GRAMMAR

1. Activate prior knowledge. Write these sentences on the board:

   He drives.

   He goes to work every day.

   Dan drives to work every day.

   Have students make questions: *yes/no* questions (e.g., *Does he drive?*), information questions (e.g., *Where does he go every day?*), and information questions with *who* and other question words as the subject (e.g., *Who drives to work every day?*).

2. Write on the board: *Can, Should,* and *Have To:* Yes/No Questions, Information Questions, and *Subject Questions.* Say: *In this lesson, we're going to learn to write these types of questions with* can, should, *and* have to.

CONTEXT

Say: *In this lesson, we're going to learn about using cars. The U.S. has many laws about car safety. People have to wear seat belts. Children can't sit in the front seat. Babies have to be in car seats.* Ask: *Should there be laws for children?* Have students share their ideas.

Presentation Ideas

The topic for this lesson can be enhanced with the following items:

1. An infant carrier, a car seat, a booster seat
2. Catalogs of child car seats
3. A brochure or large newspaper ad for an outlet mall

Car Safety for Children
READING

Have students look at the title of the reading. Say: *Halina needs to get a car seat for her daughter. What kinds of questions will she ask Dorota?* (e.g., Where can I get a car seat?) Have students use the title and illustrations on page 108 to make predictions about the reading.

BEFORE YOU READ

5-10 mins
1. Go over each question as a class. Have a volunteer read the questions or read them to the class yourself.
2. Discuss the questions as a class.

Context Note

Consumer Reports magazine gives ratings for many products including child and infant car seats.

 Reading =★
CD 2
TR 04

10-15 mins
1. Have students read the dialogue silently. Then play the audio and have students read along silently.
2. Check students' basic comprehension. Ask questions, such as: *What does Halina want to buy?* (a car seat) *How long do children have to be in car seats?* (until age eight or 57 inches tall) *What do they have to do first at the gas station?* (pay) *What does Halina do at the gas station?* (wash the windows)

Practice Idea: Listening

To practice listening skills, have students listen to the audio before opening their books. Ask a few comprehension questions, e.g.: *Should Anna be in the front seat?* (no) *Are things expensive at an outlet mall?* (no) Repeat the audio if necessary. Then have students open their books and read along as they listen to the audio.

Practice Idea: Speaking

Have students practice the conversation in pairs. Ask volunteers to role-play the conversation in front of the class.

VOCABULARY IN CONTEXT

5-10 mins

1. Model the pronunciation of each new vocabulary item and have students repeat.

2. Make sure students understand the meaning of each vocabulary item. Review the examples in the book and create additional example sentences. For example, say: *trip. Every year I go to New York. Every year I take a trip to New York.* Go over each new vocabulary item similarly, using visuals and realia when appropriate. For example, for *on the way* draw a simple map on the board with a house and a store, and a road between them. Draw a line from the store to the house. As you draw, say: *I'm on the way home.* For *outlet mall* try to locate a brochure or large newspaper ad that shows an outlet mall. For *air bag* show a picture of air bags in a car manual. When possible, point to pictures in the book that illustrate words, such as *seat belt* and *pump* on page 108.

3. Have students underline an example of each vocabulary item in the reading.

Practice Idea: Speaking

To check comprehension, have volunteers in pairs or groups act out selected vocabulary, such as *seat belt*, *passenger*, *hurt*, and *pump*.

Did You Know?

Point out the information to students. Say: *You must put car seats in the right way. The National Highway Traffic Safety Administration says that most car seats are not put in the car correctly.*

 LISTENING ACTIVITY

CD 2 TR 05 **ANSWERS: 1.** True; **2.** False; **3.** True; **4.** True; **5.** False; **6.** False; **7.** False

5-10 mins

1. Say: *Listen to each statement about Halina and Dorota's conversation. Circle* true *or* false. Play the listening selection one time without pausing. Then play it through again, pausing and replaying as necessary.

2. Have students compare their answers, then play the audio again and check the answers as a class.

5.4 *Can, Should,* and *Have To*— *Yes/No* Questions ═★

5-10 mins

1. Have students look at grammar chart **5.4** on pages 110–111. Go over the examples with *can* and *should*. Review word order with modals. Stress that short answers for *can* and *should* contain only the subject and the modal, and not the verb. Test comprehension. Write various subjects on the board (e.g., *Mr. and Mrs. Li, the children, the family, the teacher and I*) and ask volunteers to make questions with *can* and *should*.

2. Review questions with *have to*. Ask: *Are questions with* have to *made the same way?* (no) Elicit differences. (*Do/does* comes first; put *have to* after the subject.) Point out that short answers with *have to* contain only the subject and *do* or *does*, and not *have to* or the verb. Go over the examples.

Practice Idea: Speaking

Have students ask and answer questions using *have to* about work or school. Say: *Ask your partner about his or her job. What does he or she have to do?*

EXERCISE 1

ANSWERS: **1.** No, she shouldn't. **2.** Yes, they can. **3.** No, she doesn't. **4.** Yes, they can. **5.** No, they don't. **6.** Yes, they should. **7.** No, she can't.

5-10 mins

1. Have students read the direction line. Say: *Make sure that the answer you give is short. Remember: Short answers for* can *and* should *have the subject plus* can *or* should. Go over the examples in the book. Tell students to go back to the conversation on page 109 to find the answers. Point out the photo to show the meaning of *lap* in #7.

2. Have students complete Exercise 1 individually. Remind them to review grammar chart **5.4** on pages 110–111 if necessary. Check the answers as a class.

EXERCISE 2

ANSWERS: **1.** Should we pay; **2.** Can we go; **3.** Can I put; **4.** Does Anna have to sit; **5.** Should I wash; **6.** Does everyone have to use

5-10 mins

1. Have students read the direction line. Go over the example.

2. Have students complete Exercise 2 individually. Remind them to review grammar chart **5.4** on pages 110–111 if necessary. Then have students compare their answers with a partner. Check the answers as a class.

Practice Idea: Speaking

Have students practice the questions and create answers in pairs. Monitor and give help as needed.

EXERCISE 3

ANSWERS: **1.** Do we have to get; **2.** Should we try; **3.** Can I wash; **4.** Does he have to sit

5-10 mins

1. Have students read the direction line. Go over the example in the book.

2. Have students complete Exercise 3 individually. Remind them to review grammar chart **5.4** on pages 110–111 if necessary. Then have students compare their answers in pairs. Check the answers as a class.

Practice Idea: Speaking

Have students practice the statements and questions in pairs.

EXERCISE 4

ANSWERS: **Student responses will vary. Correct questions: 1.** Do people have to pump; **2.** Does a young child have to sit; **3.** Can a child sit; **4.** Can children sit; **5.** Can people pay

5-10 mins

1. Say: *This exercise is about you.* Tell students that they will be asking a partner about customs in his or her country. Have students read the direction line. Go over the example.

2. Have students complete Exercise 4 in pairs, asking and answering the questions. Remind them to review grammar chart **5.4** on pages 110–111 if necessary. Then have volunteers share their answers with the class.

Practice Idea: Speaking

Write the names of countries represented in your class across the top of the board horizontally. Then write the numbers of the questions vertically down the side. Survey the class: What are the customs in the different countries? Write a check mark when a country has a particular custom. Write an *x* when it doesn't.

5.5 *Can, Should,* and *Have To*—Information Questions

5-10 mins

1. Have students look at grammar chart **5.5** on page 113. Go over the word order and meaning of information questions on the board:

   question word + can *or* should + *subject* + *verb* + *complement*

   Remind students that the verb is in the base form. Go over each example with *can* and *should.* Then review the short answers.

2. Go over the word order of information questions with *have* to on the board:

> *question word + do/does + subject + have to + verb + complement*

Say: *Use* do *or* does *with* have to *in all questions.* Remind students that the verb is in the base form. Review each example with *have to.* Then go over the short answers.

EXERCISE 5

ANSWERS: **1.** A child can sit in the front passenger seat when he or she is 12. **2.** A small child has to sit in the back seat because air bags can hurt children. **3.** They can pay for gas right at the pump. **4.** She has to get a new car seat because Anna is too big for her old infant seat. **5.** Halina (OR She) can buy water in the store. **6.** Halina (OR She) should buy a car seat for older babies. **7.** Dorota (OR She) has to stop at a gas station because she needs gas.

10-15 mins
1. Have students look at the picture on page 113. Ask: *What is this person doing?* (paying for gas with a credit card) Have students read the direction line. Go over the example. Note the phrase *sit in the back seat* in #2 and elicit or explain the meaning to students. Remind students that questions with *why* are answered with *because.*

2. Have students complete Exercise 5 individually. Remind them to review grammar chart **5.5** on page 113 if necessary. Check the answers with the class.

EXERCISE 6

ANSWERS: **1.** do they have to stop for gas? **2.** should Dorota (OR she) drive slowly? **3.** can an air bag (OR it) hurt small children (OR them)? **4.** does Halina (OR she) have to buy for Anna (OR her)? **5.** can Anna (OR she) sit in the front seat? **6.** should I get a new car seat for my daughter?

10-15 mins
1. Have students read the direction line. Go over the example in the book. Tell students not to answer the questions they write.

2. Have students complete Exercise 6 individually. Remind them to review grammar chart **5.5** on page 113 if necessary. Then have students compare their answers in pairs. Check the answers as a class.

Practice Idea: Speaking

Have students practice the questions in pairs. Have students give answers to the questions. Tell students that the answers are not in the reading. Say: *Create your own answers.*

EXERCISE 7

ANSWERS: **1.** Which Web site should I check? **2.** Where can she buy a good one? **3.** What kind of car seat does Halina have to buy for her? **4.** How much should she spend? **5.** Why do they have to sit in car seats?

10-15 mins
1. Have students look at the picture of Halina on page 114. Ask: *What is Halina doing?* (looking at a Web site on child safety) Read the direction line. Go over the example.

2. Have students complete Exercise 7 individually. Remind them to review grammar chart **5.5** on page 113 if necessary. Then have students compare their answers in pairs. Check answers as a class.

Practice Idea: Speaking

Have students practice the short conversations in pairs. Ask volunteers to role-play the conversations in front of the class.

5.6 *Can, Should,* and *Have To—* Subject Questions

10-15 mins
1. Have students look at grammar chart **5.6** on page 115. Direct their attention to the first two questions with *should* and *can.* Write on the board:

> *question word + can or should + verb + complement*

Demonstrate how to form a question with the question word as subject with the modals *can* and *should.* Remind students that the verb is in the base form. Go over the second example. Review the answers. Ask volunteers to choose a question word and make a new question. Have another volunteer answer.

2. Direct students' attention to the questions with *have to*. Say: *Do not use* do *or* does *with* have to *when the subject is a question word.* Read through the questions with *have to* in the chart. Go over the answers with *have to*.

Practice Idea: Speaking

Have students work in pairs to complete the following questions:

1. *Who should pay _____?*

2. *What can happen _____?*

Tell students that the questions don't have to be about driving. They can be on any topic. Then have pairs share their questions with the class. Volunteers can answer the questions.

EXERCISE 8

ANSWERS: 1. Which gas station can give us the best price for gas? **2.** Who should sit in the back seat? **3.** How many people have to take a trip today? **4.** What can hurt children in a car? **5.** Which drivers have to drive with an adult at night? **6.** Who should buy some water?

10-15 mins

1. Have students read the direction line. Go over the example in the book. Then point out several of the underlined words and phrases in the exercise. Ask students what kind of question word they require.

2. Have students complete Exercise 8 in pairs. Remind them to review grammar chart **5.6** on page 115 if necessary. Check the answers as a class.

Practice Idea: Writing

Have students change the long answers to short answers.

EXERCISE 9

CD 2 TR 06

ANSWERS: 1. Can you put; **2.** I have to take; **3.** We can stop; **4.** Ed should learn; **5.** When does he have to take; **6.** He should practice

---

5-10 mins

1. Have students read the direction line. Go over the example. Ask a volunteer to do #1.

2. Have students complete the rest of Exercise 9 individually. Remind them to review grammar charts **5.5** on page 113 and **5.6** on page 115. Then have students compare their answers with a partner. Play the audio and check the answers as a class.

Practice Idea: Speaking

Have students practice the conversation in pairs. Ask volunteers to role-play the conversation in front of the class.

Editing Advice

10-15 mins Have students close their books. Write the example sentences without editing marks or corrections on the board. For example:

1. *She can drives the car.*

2. *The child can't to sit in the front seat.*

Ask students to correct each sentence and provide a rule or explanation for each correction, e.g.: 1. She can drive the car. (Always use the base form after *can, should,* and *have to*.) 2. The child can't sit in the front seat. (Don't use *to* after *can* and *should*.). This activity can be done individually, in pairs, or as a class. After students have corrected each sentence, tell them to turn to page 116. Say: *Now compare your work with the Editing Advice in the book.*

Editing Quiz

ANSWERS: 1. can I drive; **2.** can have; **3.** has to sit; **4.** do we have to practice; **5.** you should practice; **6.** can we do; **7.** C; **8.** has to go; **9.** Does the adult have to be; **10.** C; **11.** has to wear

---

10-15 mins

1. Tell students they are going to put the Editing Advice into practice. Have students read the direction line. Ask: *Do all the shaded words have mistakes?* (no) Go over the examples with the class. Then do #1 together.

2. Have students complete the rest of the quiz individually. Then have them compare their answers with a partner before checking the answers as a class. Elicit the relevant grammar point for each correction.

3. For the items students had difficulties with, have them go back and find the relevant grammar chart and review it. Monitor and give help as necessary.

Expansion

These expansion activities provide opportunities for students to interact with one another and further develop their speaking and writing skills. Encourage students to use grammar from this unit whenever possible.

LEARNER'S LOG

10-15 mins

1. Have students close their books. Ask: *What did you learn about driver's licenses, gas stations, and children's car seats in this unit? What else do you want to know about them?* Prompt students with questions, such as: *How many tests do you take to get a driver's license?* Write students' ideas on the board. Discuss ways in which students can find out more about driving in the U.S.

2. Have students open their books to complete the Learner's Log. Remind students to write three questions about driving in the U.S.

3. Have students compare logs in pairs.

WRITING ACTIVITY

10-15 mins

Have students read the direction line. Say: *You are going to write an affirmative and a negative sentence about each of these pictures.* Go over the example. Elicit ideas for picture A. Then have students complete the activity individually. Collect for assessment.

Practice Idea: Writing

Have students exchange papers with a partner. Ask students to help their partners edit their sentences. Refer students to the Editing Advice on page 116.

OUTSIDE ACTIVITY

Tell students to go to a local department store and find a child's car seat and an infant seat. Have them report to the class how much they cost.

Practice Idea: Speaking

Have students discuss the best prices they found for child and infant car seats. Write the stores and prices on the board. Did anyone compare prices online?

INTERNET ACTIVITY

Tell students to do a search with the words *graduated licenses* and the name of their state. Tell them to find the rules for their state about limited licenses for teenagers. Have them answer the following questions and report back to the class:

• What is the age for a full license?

• How many young people can be in a car with a young driver?

• When does a young driver have to be with an adult driver?

• What hours can he/she drive?

Unit 6

Unit Overview

1. Say: *In Unit 6, we're going to talk about school in the United States.* Relate the topic to students. *Do you have children who go to school? What do you know about schools in the U.S.?* Have students share their knowledge and experiences.

2. Direct students' attention to the first photo. Ask: *Where are these children?* (in a classroom) *Who is the woman?* (their teacher) Direct students' attention to the second photo. Ask: *Where are they?* (in the school cafeteria) *What food are they serving?* (pasta, salad)

Presentation Ideas

The topic for this lesson can be enhanced with the following items:

1. A menu from local elementary school cafeteria
2. A poster of food pyramid
3. Illustrations of foods in each group
4. A chart showing a typical family food budget in dollars

Lesson 1 Overview

GRAMMAR

Say: *Some families must pay the full price for a school lunch. Some have to pay a little. Some don't have to pay.* Write the sentences on the board. Say: *We're going to learn about the modal* must *and more about* have to. Underline *must, have to,* and *don't have to.* Elicit example sentences from students. Prompt with questions, such as: *What's something you must pay full price for? What's something you don't have to pay for?*

CONTEXT

1. Say: *American kids get milk, meat, vegetables, fruit, and grains in a school lunch program.* Relate the topic to students' experience. Ask: *What did you eat for lunch at school? Did you eat a lot of vegetables?*

2. Direct students' attention to the picture of the cafeteria on page 120. Ask: *Where are these children?* (in a school cafeteria/lunchroom) *What are they eating?* (lunch) Activate student's prior knowledge. Have them name specific foods.

School Lunch Programs
READING

Have students look at the title of the reading and read the first sentence. Then have them look at the picture of the sandwich. Ask: *What kind of sandwich is this?* (peanut butter and jelly) *Is this good nutrition? What's the reading about? What will it say about school lunch programs?* Have students use the title and photos on page 121 to make predictions about the reading.

BEFORE YOU READ

1. Go over each question as a class. Have a volunteer read the questions or read them to the class yourself. Have students discuss the questions in pairs. If possible, put students from different countries together.

2. Ask a few volunteers to share their answers with the class.

Context Note

Approximately 30 million students a day buy lunch or receive a free lunch in school cafeterias as part of the National School Lunch Program.

Reading ≡★

10-15
mins

1. Have students read the text silently. Then play the audio and have students read along silently.

2. Check students' basic comprehension. Ask questions, such as: *What kinds of food do schools have to give children?* (meat, vegetables/fruits, grains/bread, and milk) *Does everyone have to pay for lunch?* (No. Some very low-income families don't have to pay; some families pay a little; some have to pay full price.) *Do all children have to buy lunch?* (No. They can bring it from home.)

Practice Ideas: Listening

1. To practice listening skills, have students listen to the audio before opening their books. Ask a few comprehension questions, such as: *Can schools give children a lot of fat, sugar, or salt?* (no) *Do children have to eat the school lunch?* (no) Repeat the audio if necessary. Then have students open their books and read along as they listen to the audio.

2. Alternatively, have students begin by listening to the audio as they read along.

VOCABULARY IN CONTEXT

5-10
mins

1. Model the pronunciation of each new vocabulary item and have students repeat.

2. Make sure students understand the meaning of each vocabulary item. Review the examples in the book and create additional example sentences. For example, say: *nutrition. Good nutrition is very important to me. I don't eat a lot of candy, cake, or cookies.* Review each new vocabulary item similarly, using visuals and realia when appropriate. For example, for *income* say: *A job pays money. This money is income.* Write on the board: *$8,000, $35,000, $190,000.* Pronounce the amounts. Say: *Some people have low incomes. Others have high incomes; they make a lot of money.* For *serve* place glasses on top of a tray, or something you could use as a tray, and say: *I'm a waiter. I serve you drinks.* When possible, point

to pictures in the book that illustrate the new vocabulary items, such as *grains* on page 121.

3. Have students underline an example of each vocabulary item in the reading.

Practice Idea: Speaking

To check comprehension, have volunteers in pairs or groups act out selected vocabulary, such as *serve* and *tell the truth.*

Did You Know?

Point out the information to students. Ask: *Are school lunch programs important? Why or why not?*

LISTENING ACTIVITY

ANSWERS: 1. False; **2.** True; **3.** False; **4.** False; **5.** True; **6.** False; **7.** True

5-10
mins

1. Say: *Listen to the sentences about the reading on school lunch programs. Circle* true *or* false. Play the listening selection one time without pausing. Then play it through again, pausing and replaying as necessary.

2. Have students compare their answers, then play the audio again and check the answers as a class.

6.1 *Must*—Affirmative and Negative Statements ≡★

5-10
mins

1. Have students look at grammar chart **6.1** on page 122. Explain the affirmative use of *must.* Say: *We use* must *to show rules or laws.* Go over the examples.

2. Explain the negative use of *must.* Say: *If the law says not to do something, we say* must not. Go over the examples. Give additional examples, such as: *You must use your seatbelt. It's the law. You must not drink and drive. In some states, you must not use a cell phone while driving.*

3. Review word order in affirmative and negative sentences with *must.* Ask: *Where does the subject go?* (before the modal at the beginning of the sentence) *Where does the modal* (must) *go?* (after the subject and before the verb or *not*)

EXERCISE

ANSWERS: 1. serve; **2.** fill out; **3.** sign; **4.** tell; **5.** be; **6.** serve

⏱ 5-10 mins

1. Have students read the direction line. Go over the example in the book.

2. Have students complete Exercise 1 individually. Remind them to review grammar chart **6.1** on page 122 if necessary. Check the answers as a class.

Practice Idea: Speaking

Ask: *What rules do we have in our class?* Brainstorm a list of rules for the class on the board using *must*.

EXERCISE

ANSWERS: 1. must fill out the application. **2.** must sign your name. **3.** must not write in the last box. **4.** must write your family income. **5.** must use a pen. **6.** must not use a pencil. **7.** must not give false information.

⏱ 10-15 mins

1. Have students look at the application for free and reduced meals at the top of page 123. Give students time to read through the application. Go through each part with students. Ask: *What do we put in Part 1?* (information about your children) *What goes in Part 2?* (names of people who live in your house and their income) *What do we put in Part 3?* (your signature, address, phone number, and Social Security number) You might need to explain new vocabulary, such as *grade* (Part 1) and *household* (Part 2). You also can tell students it is not necessary to fill in their Social Security numbers in the book if they would rather not.

2. Have students read the direction line for Exercise 2. Go over the examples. Ask: *Which statement is imperative?*

3. Have students complete Exercise 2 individually. Remind them to review grammar chart **6.1** on page 122 if necessary. Check the answers as a class.

Practice Idea: Writing

Find or create a relatively simple application to give students (e.g., for a tutoring program or a free-book program). Have students create a list of instructions for filling it out using *must* and *mustn't*.

6.2 *Must* and *Have To*

⏱ 10-15 mins

1. Have students look at grammar chart **6.2** on page 124. To clarify and stress very formal uses of *must*, say: *We often use* must *with people who tell us or advise us what to do.* Relate the explanation to students' personal experience. Ask: *Who tells you what to do? Who gives rules and laws?* (government, parents and grandparents, doctors, schools and teachers) Say: Have to *is often used to express personal necessity. This means things only you must do.* Go over the examples.

2. Write additional examples on the board. Have students decide whether to use *must* or *have to*. Explain that while both are possible, one might be more appropriate than the other.

    1. *I _____ call my grandmother this week. It's her birthday.*

    2. U.S. Citizens _____ pay their income taxes by April 15.

3. Point out the Language Note. Say: *We don't usually use* must *in questions.* Go over the examples.

Practice Idea: Writing

Ask a volunteer to tell the class something they have to do, using a complete sentence. Have students create three statements with *have to* that are true for them (e.g., At home I have to cook dinner every night.). Next, have them create three statements with *must* that are true for their native countries (e.g., In Colombia we must drive with our headlights on.).

ANSWERS: Answers will vary. Possible answers:
1. must follow OR must obey; **2.** must sign;
3. must fill in OR must tell the truth about;
4. must have; **5.** must give OR must serve

5-10 mins

1. Tell students they are going to complete some rules. List key words on the board, such as *obey* and *serve*.

2. Have students read the direction line. Go over the example.

3. Have students complete Exercise 3 in pairs. Remind them to review grammar chart **6.2** on page 124 if necessary. Check the answers as a class.

EXERCISE **4**

Answers will vary.

5-10 mins

1. Have students read the direction line. Go over the example. Have a volunteer model the example.

2. Have students complete Exercise 4 individually. Remind them to review grammar chart **6.2** on page 124 if necessary. Then have students compare their answers in pairs. Have volunteers share their answers with the class.

6.3 *Must Not* and *Don't Have To*

5-10 mins

Have students look at grammar chart **6.3** on page 125. Stress the very different meanings of the negatives. Say: Must not *means something is against the rules or law*. Don't have to *means that something is not necessary*. Go over the examples. Elicit more examples from students (e.g., *You mustn't be rude to a police officer; I don't have to go to class on Sunday*.). Write the examples on the board.

EXERCISE **5**

Answers will vary.

5-10 mins

1. Say: *In this exercise, you tell what is true for you.* Have students read the direction line. Go over the example.

2. Have students complete Exercise 5 in pairs. Remind students to review grammar chart **6.3** on page 125 if necessary. Monitor pair work. Give help as needed. Have volunteers share their answers with the class.

Practice Idea: Speaking

Take a class survey. Find out what students don't have to do.

EXERCISE **6**

Answers will vary.

5-10 mins

1. Say: *This exercise is also about you.* Have students read the direction line. Go over the example.

2. Have students complete Exercise 6 in pairs. Remind students to review grammar chart **6.3** on page 125 if necessary. Monitor pair work. Give help as needed. Have volunteers share their answers with the class. Make a list on the board of what students must not do.

EXERCISE **7**

ANSWERS: 1. don't have to; **2.** doesn't have to;
3. must not; **4.** don't have to; **5.** doesn't have to;
6. must not; **7.** must not

5-10 mins

1. Have students read the direction line. Go over the example.

2. Have students complete Exercise 7 individually. Remind students to review grammar chart **6.3** on page 125 if necessary. Then have students compare their answers in pairs. Check the answers as a class.

Lesson 2 Overview

GRAMMAR

1. Ask: *What did we study in Lesson 1?* (must/must not, have to/don't have to). Say: *In this lesson, we are going to study count and noncount nouns. We're going to talk about quantity.* Say and write on the board: *Quantity Expressions*. Elicit examples and write them on the board (e.g., *much, a lot of, a little, some, any*).

2. Activate students' knowledge. Elicit foods and list them on the board (e.g., *pizza, cheese, potato chips,*

fruit, milk, juice, and *fish*). Ask volunteers to match a quantity expression with a food and make a sentence.

CONTEXT

1. Say: *This lesson is about lunch food.* Relate the topic to students' experience. Ask: *What do you like to eat for lunch?*

2. Direct students' attention to the picture of Victor and Maya on page 126. Say: *What foods do you see?* (pizza, grilled cheese sandwich, macaroni and cheese, a taco) Write the names of the foods on the board.

Maya's School Lunch READING

Have students look at the title of the reading and the picture on page 126. Ask: *What do you think Victor and Maya are talking about? Are they talking about food Maya likes? What is Victor saying?* Have students use the title and picture to make predictions about the reading.

BEFORE YOU READ

5-10 mins

1. Go over each question as a class. Have a volunteer read the questions or read them to the class yourself. Have students discuss the questions in pairs. Ask: *Should children eat candy? Why or why not?*

2. Ask for a few volunteers to share their answers with the class.

CD 2
TR 09

Reading =★

10-15 mins

1. Have students read the dialogue silently. Then play the audio and have students read along silently.

2. Check students' basic comprehension. Ask questions, such as: *Does Maya like all the food at school?* (no) *Do the students like the fruit at school?* (No, sometimes they throw it away.) *What does Victor say about that?* (It's terrible that they throw fruit away.) *Does Victor drink soda?* (yes)

Practice Ideas: Listening

1. To practice listening skills, have students listen to the audio before opening their books. Ask a few comprehension questions, such as: *Does juice have a lot of sugar?* (yes) Repeat the audio if necessary. Then have students open their books and read along as they listen to the audio.

2. Alternatively, have students begin by listening to the audio as they read along.

Practice Idea: Speaking

Have students practice the conversation in pairs. Ask volunteers to role-play all or part of the conversation in front of the class.

VOCABULARY IN CONTEXT

5-10 mins

1. Model the pronunciation of each new vocabulary item and have students repeat.

2. Make sure students understand the meaning of each vocabulary item. Review the examples in the book and create additional example sentences. For example, say: *favorite. My favorite singer is Shakira.* Go over each new vocabulary item similarly, using visuals and realia when appropriate. When possible, point to pictures in the book that illustrate new vocabulary items, such as *bunch of (grapes), lunch box,* and *throw away* on page 127.

3. Have students underline an example of each vocabulary item in the reading.

Practice Idea: Speaking

To check comprehension, have volunteers in pairs or groups act out selected vocabulary, such as *terrible* and *throw away*.

Point out the information to students. Ask: *What is the difference between free lunches and low-cost lunches?*

  LISTENING ACTIVITY

CD 2
TR 10
ANSWERS: 1. False; **2.** False; **3.** True; **4.** False; **5.** False; **6.** False

⏱ 5-10 mins

1. Say: *Listen to the sentences about Victor and Maya's conversation. Circle* true *or* false. Play the listening selection one time without pausing. Then play it through again, pausing and replaying as necessary.

2. Have students compare their answers, then play the audio again and check the answers as a class.

6.4 Count and Noncount Nouns

⏱ 5-10 mins

1. Have students cover up grammar chart **6.4** on page 128. Write some nouns on the board:

   > *bread*
   >
   > *sandwich*
   >
   > *child*
   >
   > *milk*

   Ask: *Which two nouns can you count?* (*sandwich* and *child*)

2. Have students look at grammar chart **6.4**. Say: *Count nouns have a singular form and a plural form. Noncount nouns do not have a plural form.* Go over the examples and the explanations. Review all of the noncount nouns. Point out the pictures of the food items as you go through the list.

3. Explain to students that there are exceptions. When ordering food, for example, some noncount nouns are used as count nouns (e.g., *I'd like three pizzas. I'd like two sugars in my coffee.*).

Practice Idea: Writing

Have students work with a partner to create a list of five count nouns related to a single topic, such as a favorite place or game. Make a list on the board of students' nouns.

⏱ 5-10 mins

1. Say: *In this exercise, you tell what's true for you.* Direct students' attention to the list of food items. Ask: *Are these count or noncount nouns?* (noncount) Have students read the direction line. Go over the examples in the book.

2. Have students complete Exercise 1 in pairs. Remind them to review grammar chart **6.4** on page 128 if necessary. Monitor pair work. Give help as needed. Have volunteers share their answers with the class.

EXERCISE 2
Answers will vary.

⏱ 5-10 mins

1. Say: *In this exercise, you also tell what's true for you.* Direct students' attention to the list of foods. Ask: *Are these count or noncount nouns?* (count nouns) Have students read the direction line. Go over the examples in the book.

2. Have students complete Exercise 2 in pairs. Remind them to review grammar chart **6.4** on page 128 if necessary. Monitor pair work. Give help as needed. Have volunteers share their answers with the class.

Practice Idea: Speaking

Have pairs ask and answer questions. Tell partners to begin their questions with, *How often do you …?* Do a class survey. What are the most popular foods?

6.5 Quantity Expressions with Noncount Nouns

⏱ 5-10 mins

1. Have students look at grammar chart **6.5** on page 130. Say: *To talk about quantity with noncount nouns, we use a unit of measure, such as a cup or a teaspoon, that we can count.* Go over the example sentences.

2. Read through the quantity expressions. Point out the pictures as you read through the list.

3. Have students close their books. Write a matching exercise on the board. Elicit from students ten or fifteen noncount foods and drinks and write them on the board. Write a blank in front of each item. Then list in a separate column the following quantity expressions:

> *a carton*
>
> *a glass*
>
> *a bottle*
>
> *a jar*
>
> *a pound*
>
> *a piece*
>
> *a teaspoon*
>
> *a bowl*
>
> *a can*
>
> *a tablespoon*

4. Have students take turns coming to the board. Ask them to match a quantity expression with a food or drink and then make a sentence.

Practice Idea: Writing

Print names of foods on index cards. Hold up a card and ask students to write down the quantity expression that goes with the food. Ask volunteers to share their answers.

 EXERCISE 3

CD 2
TR 11

ANSWERS: 1. fruit; **2.** jar; **3.** can; **4.** milk

5-10 mins

1. Have students read the direction line. Tell students the conversation is between Amy and her mother, Marta, about food. Have students skim the conversation. Explain that clues to answers may be in information found after the blank. Go over the example.

2. Have students complete Exercise 3 individually. Remind them to review grammar chart **6.5** on page 130 if necessary. Then have students compare their answers in pairs. Play the audio and check the answers as a class.

Practice Idea: Speaking

Have students practice the conversation in pairs. Ask volunteers to role-play the conversation in front of the class.

 EXERCISE 4

CD 2
TR 12

ANSWERS: 1. slices OR pieces; **2.** can; **3.** jar; **4.** tablespoons; **5.** can OR glass; **6.** glass; **7.** piece

5-10 mins

1. Have students read the direction line. Go over the example. Have students skim the conversation.

2. Have students complete Exercise 4 individually. Remind them to review grammar chart **6.5** on page 130 if necessary. Then have students compare their answers in pairs.

Play the audio and check the answers as a class.

Practice Idea: Speaking

Have students use Exercise 4 to tell a partner how to make a different sandwich with another food, such as turkey, ham, or egg salad.

EXERCISE 5

Answers will vary.

5-10 mins

1. Say: *In this exercise, you say what is true for you.* Have students read the direction line. Say: *Say exactly how much you eat or drink of an item. Say what you don't eat or drink too.* Elicit which example sentence gives an exact amount (the first: *I eat two slices of bread a day.*).

2. Have students complete Exercise 5 individually. Remind them to review grammar chart **6.5** on page 130 if necessary. Then have students compare their answers in pairs. Have volunteers share their answers with the class.

6.6 *Much/A Lot Of/A Little* with Noncount Nouns

5-10 mins

1. Have students look at grammar chart **6.6** on page 132. Say: *We use* much, a lot, *and* a little *when we don't want or need to say exactly how*

much. Review the examples and explanations. Point out that the negative example *I don't drink a lot of milk* means *I drink a little milk.*

2. Point out the Language Note. Say: *When we talk about condiments, such as salt, sugar, butter, ketchup, and pepper, we say* use, *not* eat.

3. Have students close their books. Write a food on the board (for example, *pizza*) and ask students to make affirmative sentences with *a lot of* or *a little* (e.g., *He eats a lot of pizza.*). Ask volunteers to say the sentence with another pattern from the chart (e.g., *He doesn't eat much pizza.*).

EXERCISE 6
Answers will vary.

5-10 mins

1. Say: *In this exercise, you tell a partner what is true for you.* Have students read the direction line. Go over the examples.

2. Have students complete Exercise 6 in pairs. Remind them to review grammar chart **6.6** on page 132 if necessary. Monitor pair work. Give help as needed. Have volunteers share their answers with the class.

> ### Practice Idea: Speaking
>
> Do a class survey of students' favorite and least favorite foods. Ask: *What do you eat a lot of? What do you eat a little of?* Write the results on the board.

EXERCISE 7

ANSWERS: Answers may vary. Possible answers:
1. a little milk, a little sugar; **2.** a little meat; **3.** a little butter; **4.** a little salt (OR oil)

5-10 mins

1. Have students read the direction line. Go over the example.

2. Have students complete Exercise 7 individually. Remind them to review grammar chart **6.6** on page 132 if necessary. Check the answers as a class. Note that for #1, two

answers are possible: Put *a little milk* and *sugar* in the coffee, or Put *a little milk* and *a little sugar* in the coffee.

6.7 *Some/Any* with Noncount Nouns

5-10 mins

1. Have students look at grammar chart **6.7** on page 133. Review the explanations and examples. Say and write on the board the following sentences:

> *Do you have some popcorn?*
> *I have any popcorn.*
> *No, I don't have some coffee.*

Have students say which sentences are incorrect and why.

2. To elicit examples of usage from the class, list count and noncount foods on the board, such as *potato chips, sandwiches,* and *candy.* Prompt students with the question: *Do you have any [chips] in your bag?* Have a student answer using *any* or *some.* Then have a second student ask him or her an additional question (e.g., *Do you have any candy bars?*).

EXERCISE 8 =★

ANSWERS: 1. any; **2.** any; **3.** some OR any; **4.** some; **5.** some; **6.** any OR some; **7.** any; **8.** any; **9.** some

5-10 mins

1. Have students read the direction line. Go over the example.

2. Have students complete Exercise 8 individually. Remind them to review grammar chart **6.7** on page 133 if necessary. Check the answers as a class.

> ### Practice Idea: Speaking
>
> Have students write down a list of things they have in their refrigerator at home. Then have students ask and answers questions in pairs (e.g., *Do you have any milk? Yes, I have some milk.*).

Lesson 3 Overview

GRAMMAR

Say: *Look in your bags now. How many notebooks do you have? How many pens do you have? How much homework do you have?* Elicit answers to the questions and write the quantity words on the board: *some, any, a lot of, much, many, a few, a little.* Say: *In Lesson 3, we're going to learn to ask questions with* how much *and* how many.

CONTEXT

1. Ask: *What do you need for your classes?* Write a volunteer's answer on the board. Ask the class if they use the same kind and/or number of items. List additional items on the board. Relate the topic to students' experience. Ask: *Do you need the same things in your country? Is school different in the U.S?* Say: *In this lesson, we're going to talk about school in the U.S.*

2. Direct students' attention to the picture. Ask: *What are these things for?* (school, art, writing, drawing) Go over the names of the supplies in the picture: ruler, glue stick, crayons, notebook paper, spiral notebook, eraser, scissors, tissues, and folders.

School Supplies READING

Have students look at the title of the reading. Ask: *What are school supplies?* Elicit ideas from students. Say: *Supplies are what you need to do something.* Ask: *What do you think Victor and Maya are talking about this time?* (school supplies for Maya) *What is Maya saying? What's Victor saying? Do you think Maya will do a lot of homework?* Have students use the title and picture on page 134 to make predictions about the reading.

BEFORE YOU READ

1. Go over each question as a class. Have a volunteer read the questions or read them to the class yourself.

2. Discuss the questions as a class.

Context Note

Many stores have back-to-school sales in July and August. Students usually buy school supplies, electronics, and clothing.

 Reading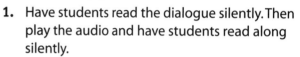

CD 2
TR 13

10-15 mins

1. Have students read the dialogue silently. Then play the audio and have students read along silently.

2. Check students' basic comprehension. Ask questions, such as: *What does Maya have to buy?* (school supplies) *Does Maya have to buy a uniform?* (maybe) *Does Maya have to buy books?* (no) *Do all children in public schools need uniforms?* (no)

Practice Ideas: Listening

1. To practice listening skills, have students listen to the audio before opening their books. Ask a few comprehension questions, such as: *Do American kids get a lot of homework?* (yes) Repeat the audio if necessary. Then have students open their books and read along as they listen to the audio.

2. Alternatively, have students begin by listening to the audio as they read along.

Practice Idea: Speaking

Have students practice the conversation in pairs. Ask volunteers to role-play the conversation in front of the class.

VOCABULARY IN CONTEXT

5-10 mins

1. Model the pronunciation of each new vocabulary item and have students repeat.

2. Make sure students understand the meaning of each vocabulary item. Review the examples in the book and create additional example sentences. For example, say: *uniform. I don't like uniforms. I don't want to wear the same clothing every day.* Review each new vocabulary item similarly, using visuals and realia when appropriate. For example, for *note* write a quick note on a piece of paper and hand it to a student. Say: *I wrote a note to [student's name].* When possible, point to pictures that illustrate new vocabulary items, such as *school supplies* on page 134.

3. Have students underline an example of each vocabulary item in the reading.

Practice Idea: Speaking

To check comprehension, have volunteers in pairs or groups act out selected vocabulary, such as *note* and *advice.*

Did You Know?

Point out the information to students. Ask: *How old are children when they start school in other countries?* Discuss what the best age to start is. Ask: *Is 5 years old too young?*

CD 2
TR 14

LISTENING ACTIVITY

ANSWERS: 1. True; **2.** True; **3.** False; **4.** False; **5.** False; **6.** False

5-10 mins

1. Say: *Listen to the sentences about the conversation about Maya's school supplies. Circle true or false.* Play the listening selection one time without pausing. Then play it through again, pausing and replaying as necessary.

2. Have students compare their answers, then play the audio again and check the answers as a class.

6.8 Count and Noncount Nouns: *Some* vs. *Any*

5-10 mins

1. Have students look at grammar chart **6.8** on page 136. Elicit the rule for *some* and *any* with noncount nouns. Write these examples on the board and have students say if they are correct and why or why not: *I have any coffee. I don't have some sugar.* Say: *Some and* any *are used with count nouns too. Some is used in affirmative statements. Any is used in questions and in negative statements.* Go over the examples in the chart.

2. Point out the Language Note. Review the rule. Stress that quantity words must be used with *homework, information,* and *advice* to talk about specific quantities of these things. Say and write on the board these examples: *I have to do three homework assignments tonight. Oh, that's an interesting piece of information! Can I give you a piece of advice?*

EXERCISE 1

ANSWERS: 1. any OR some; **2.** some; **3.** any; **4.** some; **5.** any; **6.** any OR some; **7.** some; **8.** some

5-10 mins

1. Have students read the direction line. Go over the example.

2. Have students complete Exercise 1 individually. Remind them to review grammar chart **6.8** on page 136 if necessary. Check the answers as a class.

Practice Idea: Writing

Have students write responses to the two questions in Exercise 1. Model this example for #1: *Do you have any homework today? Yes, I have a math assignment.*

EXERCISE 2

Answers will vary.

5-10 mins

1. Say: *You are going to give answers that are true for you.* Have students read the direction line. Ask: *When do we use* any? (in questions and in negatives) Go over the example in the book. Have a volunteer model the example.

2. Have students complete Exercise 2 individually. Remind them to review grammar chart **6.8** on page 136 if necessary. Have students compare answers with a partner. Have volunteers share their answers with the class.

Practice Idea: Speaking

Have students practice asking and answering the questions in pairs. Monitor pair work. Give help as needed.

6.9 Count and Noncount Nouns: *A Lot of* and *Much* vs. *Many* =★

5-10 mins

1. Have students look at grammar chart **6.9** on page 137. Go over the examples and explanations in the top half of the chart. Say: *A lot of* and *many can both be used with count nouns.*

2. Go over the examples and explanations in the bottom half of the chart. Then say: *A lot of* and *much are used with noncount nouns in questions and negatives.* Much *is not used in affirmative statements.*

EXERCISE 3 =★

ANSWERS: 1. a lot of, much; **2.** a lot of, many; **3.** Many; **4.** a lot of; **5.** a lot of; **6.** a lot of, much; **7.** Many OR A lot of

5-10 mins

1. Have students read the direction line. Go over the example.

2. Have students complete Exercise 3 individually. Remind them to review grammar chart **6.9** on page 137 if necessary. Check the answers as a class.

6.10 Count and Noncount Nouns: *A Few* vs. *A Little* =★

5-10 mins

Have students look at grammar chart **6.10** on page 138. Review the explanations. Say: *A few is used with count nouns.* A little *is used with noncount nouns.* Go over the examples.

EXERCISE 4 =★

ANSWERS: 1. a little; **2.** a few; **3.** a few; **4.** a little; **5.** a few

5-10 mins

1. Have students read the direction line. Go over the example in the book.

2. Have students complete Exercise 4 individually. Remind them to review grammar chart **6.10** on page 138 if necessary. Check the answers as a class.

EXERCISE 5

Answers will vary.

5-10 mins

1. Say: *In this exercise, you give information that is true about you.* Go over the example. Have a volunteer model the example.

2. Have students complete Exercise 5 individually. Remind them to review grammar chart **6.10** on page 138 if necessary. Then have students compare their answers in pairs. Have volunteers share their answers with the class.

Practice Idea: Speaking

Have students make questions about the statements (e.g., for *I have a few good friends: Do you have any friends?*). Then have students work in pairs and have partners ask and answer questions.

6.11 Count and Noncount Nouns: *How Much* vs. *How Many*

5-10 mins

Have students look at grammar chart **6.11** on page 139. Review the examples and explanations. Then ask: *What do we use with count nouns?* (how many) *What do we use with noncount nouns?* (how much) Ask: *Is this sentence correct: How many does this book cost?* (no) *Why?* (because you use *how much* to ask about cost)

EXERCISE 6
Answers will vary.

10-15 mins

1. Say: *In this exercise, you answer questions with information that is true about elementary schools in your country.* Have students read the direction line. Go over the example. Have a volunteer model the example.

2. Have students complete Exercise 6 individually. Remind them to review grammar chart **6.11** on page 139 if necessary. Then have students ask and answer questions in pairs. Monitor pair work. Give help as needed. Have volunteers share their answers with the class.

EXERCISE 7 ⚊★

ANSWERS: 1. many; **2.** much; **3.** much; **4.** many; **5.** many; **6.** much; **7.** much; **8.** many

1. Say: *In this exercise, you complete the sentences with information that is true about you.* Have students read the direction line. Go over the example. Have a volunteer model the example.

2. Have students complete Exercise 7 individually. Remind them to review grammar chart **6.11** on page 139 if necessary. Then have students compare their answers in pairs. Have volunteers share their answers with the class.

Practice Idea: Speaking

Have students practice asking and answering the questions in pairs. Monitor pair work. Give help as needed.

EXERCISE 8

CD 2
TR 15

ANSWERS: 1. a little; **2.** any OR some; **3.** a little; **4.** much; **5.** a lot of; **6.** many; **7.** much; **8.** much; **9.** a lot of; **10.** a lot of; **11.** many

10-15 mins

1. Say: *Maria is asking Victor some questions.* Have students read the direction line. Go over the example in the book.

2. Have students complete Exercise 8 individually. Remind them to review the grammar charts in the lesson if necessary. Then have students compare their answers in pairs. Play the audio and check the answers as a class.

Practice Idea: Speaking

Have students practice the conversation in pairs. Ask volunteers to role-play the conversations in front of the class.

Editing Advice

Have students close their books. Write the example sentences without editing marks or corrections on the board. For example:

1. *Schools must to serve a good lunch.*
2. *I like to eat a rice.*

Ask students to correct each sentence and provide a rule or explanation for each correction, e.g.: 1. Schools must serve a good lunch. (Don't use *to* after *must*.) 2. I like to eat rice. (Don't put *a* or *an* before a noncount noun.). This activity can be done individually, in pairs, or as a class. After students have corrected each sentence, tell them to turn to page 141. Say: *Now compare your work with the Editing Advice in the book.*

Editing Quiz

ANSWERS: 1. any; **2.** a glass of water; **3.** Ø; **4.** C; **5.** C; **6.** a lot of OR too much; **7.** a lot of; **8.** C; **9.** C; **10.** Ø; **11.** must; **12.** C; **13.** advice

10-15 mins

1. Tell students they are going to put the Editing Advice into practice. Have students read the direction line. Ask: *Do all the shaded words have mistakes?* (No) Go over the examples with the class. Then do #1 together.

2. Have students complete the rest of the quiz individually. Then have them compare their answers with a partner before checking answers as a class. Elicit the relevant grammar point for each correction.

3. For the items students had difficulty with, have them go back and find the relevant grammar chart and review it. Monitor and give help as necessary.

Expansion

These expansion activities provide opportunities for students to interact with one another and further develop their speaking and writing skills. Encourage students to use grammar from this unit whenever possible.

LEARNER'S LOG

10-15 mins

1. Have students close their books. Ask: *What did you learn about the following things in this unit: American lunch programs, healthy foods, and school supplies? What else do you want to know?* Brainstorm with students. Write ideas on the board. Discuss ways in which students can find out more about American elementary schools.

2. Have students open their books to complete the Learner's Log.

3. Have students compare logs in pairs.

WRITING ACTIVITIES

1. Have students turn to Exercise 6 on page 139. Say: *Use your partner's answers to the questions and write a paragraph about schools in his or her country.* Choose a country represented in the class and have students help you begin writing a paragraph on the board. Have students complete the activity individually. Collect for assessment.

2. Have students read the direction line. Go over the example. Do the first line of the paragraph together on the board. Have students complete the activity individually. Collect for assessment.

Practice Idea: Writing

Have students exchange papers with a partner. Ask students to help their partners edit their paragraph. Refer students to the Editing Advice on page 141.

OUTSIDE ACTIVITY

Tell students to ask an elementary-school child about his or her school. Tell them to find out what the child likes about the school. Have students get in pairs to write questions beforehand. After the interview, have them tell the class the name of the child's school and some interesting facts about this child's school.

INTERNET ACTIVITIES

1. Tell students to go to the government's Web site on school lunches (www.fns.usda.gov/cnd/lunch) and click on "Program Fact Sheet." Have them find a few interesting facts about the program. (Tell them they can also do a search with the name of their state and the words "school lunch program" for information in their state.) In class, have students get into groups to exchange facts.

2. Tell students to use a search engine and type in *fat counter* and find a list of foods showing fat and sodium (salt) content. Have them find out how much fat and how much salt are in *one* of the meals they have eaten that day. In class, have students get into groups and decide whose meal has the highest salt and fat counts.

Unit 7

Unit Overview

1. Say: *We're going to talk about shopping in this unit. I like to shop at small stores, but big stores are convenient. I can find everything I need in a big store.* Ask: *Where do you like to shop?*

2. Direct students' attention to the photos. Ask: *What kind of stores are these? Are they department stores? Supermarkets?* (pharmacy, home supply store/hardware store, clothes store/clothes section in a department store)

3. Ask: *Is it convenient to shop in these stores?* Have students share their personal experiences.

Presentation Ideas

The topic for this unit can be enhanced with the following items:

1. Circulars from home improvement stores and large discount and department stores

2. An envelope of coupons for local businesses sent out in the mail

Lesson 1 Overview

GRAMMAR

Say: *In Lesson 1, we are going to study time expressions with and without prepositions. We are also going to study prepositions of place and prepositions in common expressions.* Write the objectives and the following sentence on the board: *There is a class at 7:30 a.m. on Saturdays in this building at the university.* Underline time expressions once and place expressions twice. Have students name the prepositions. Elicit similar expressions from students. Prompt by asking: *Do you have another class? When is it? Where is it?*

CONTEXT

1. Say: *In this lesson, we're going to learn about buying necessary things.* Ask: *What are necessary things?* Elicit ideas from students and write them on the board

(For example, milk, bread, coffee, toothpaste, soap, aspirin, Band-Aids). Ask: *When do you buy these items? Where do you buy them?*

2. Direct students' attention to the picture of the convenience store on page 146. Ask: *Do you ever shop at convenience stores? When? What can you buy there?* (necessary things, basic items) *What is across from the convenience store?* (the pharmacy)

Twenty-Four/Seven READING

Have students look at the title of the reading and the picture on page 146. Say: *A lot of people have to shop after work. Some big stores are open all day and all night. Some small stores are also open 24/7.* Relate the topic to students' experiences. Make sure students understand the expression *24/7*. Tell them it means 24 hours a day, seven days a week. Ask: *Do you shop 24/7?* Say: *Skim through the reading. What two things does Sue want?* (coffee and aspirin) *Why does she want aspirin?* (She has a headache.) See if students can make more predictions about the reading.

BEFORE YOU READ

5-10 mins

1. Go over each question as a class. Have a volunteer read the questions or read them to the class yourself. Have students discuss the questions in pairs. If possible, put students together from different countries.

2. Ask a few volunteers to share their answers with the class.

Context Note

Convenience stores provide more services every year. Most now have ATMs and sell money orders. Many have car washes. Some even provide Internet services.

 Reading ☆

CD 2
TR 16

10-15 mins

1. Have students read the dialogue silently. Then play the audio and have students read along silently.

2. Check students' basic comprehension. Ask questions such as: *What does Rick want to*

watch on TV? (a news program) *What is Rick going to buy?* (coffee and aspirin) *What time does the pharmacy close?* (It doesn't close; it's open 24/7.)

Practice Ideas: Listening

1. To practice listening skills, have students listen to the audio before opening their books. Ask a few comprehension questions, such as: *How much does aspirin cost at the pharmacy this week?* (two bottles for $5.00) *What time is it?* (after 9:30 p.m.) Repeat the audio if necessary. Then have students open their books and read along as they listen to the audio.

2. Alternatively, have students begin by listening to the audio as they read along.

Practice Idea: Speaking

Have students practice the conversation in pairs. Ask volunteers to role-play the conversation in front of the class.

VOCABULARY IN CONTEXT

5-10 mins

1. Model the pronunciation of each new vocabulary item and have students repeat.

2. Make sure students understand the meaning of each vocabulary item. Review the examples in the book and create additional example sentences. Go over each new vocabulary item similarly, using visuals and realia when appropriate. For example, for *corner* draw a map of a local business on the corner of two well-known streets. Say: *[Business name] is on the corner of [street name] and [street name].* When possible, point to pictures in the book that illustrate the new vocabulary items, such as *convenience store, pharmacy,* and *corner* on page 146.

3. Have students underline an example of each vocabulary item in the reading.

Practice Idea: Speaking

To check comprehension, have volunteers in pairs or groups act out selected vocabulary, such as *headache* and *aspirin.*

Did You Know?

Point out the information to students. Tell students how much higher prices are at convenience stores. Say: *Prices at a convenience store are at least 10 percent more than prices at a supermarket. If an item costs $10 at the supermarket, it will cost $11 or more at a convenience store.* Ask: *Is it good to shop at convenience stores?* Have students discuss the advantages and disadvantages.

LISTENING ACTIVITY

CD 2
TR 17

ANSWERS: 1. True; **2.** True; **3.** False; **4.** False; **5.** True; **6.** False; **7.** False

5-10 mins

1. Say: *Listen to the sentences about Rick and Sue's conversation. Circle* true *or* false. Play the listening selection one time without pausing. Then play it through again, pausing and replaying as necessary.

2. Have students compare their answers, then play the audio again and check the answers as a class.

7.1 Time Expressions with Prepositions ≡★

1. Have students look at grammar chart **7.1** on page 149. Say: *Prepositions are small connecting words. We can use prepositions with time expressions.* Go over the examples. Give an additional example for each expression (e.g., *I exercise in the morning.*).

2. Point out the Language Note. Say: *A sentence can have more than one time expression.* Go over the examples. Ask volunteers to give additional examples.

Practice Idea: Writing

Have students work in pairs to write an example for each preposition of time (*in, at, after, before,* and *on*). Ask volunteers to share their examples.

EXERCISE 1

ANSWERS: **1.** on; **2.** in; **3.** on; **4.** in; **5.** at; **6.** at; **7.** after; **8.** in; **9.** before

5-10 mins

1. Have students read the direction line. Go over the example in the book.

2. Have students complete Exercise 1 individually. Remind them to review grammar chart **7.1** on page 149 if necessary. Check the answers as a class.

EXERCISE 2

Answers will vary.

5-10 mins

1. Say: *In this exercise, you'll ask and answer questions with a partner about when you do things.* Have students read the direction line. Go over the example. Model the example with a student.

2. Have students complete Exercise 2 in pairs. Remind them to review grammar chart **7.1** on page 149 if necessary. Monitor pair work. Give help as needed. Check the answers as a class.

Practice Idea: Speaking

Take a survey. Find out how the class answered some of the questions and write the results on the board (e.g., *In our class, [five] students wake up at 6:00 A.M.*).

7.2 Time Expressions without Prepositions

5-10 mins

1. Have students look at grammar chart **7.2** on page 150. Say: *Some time expressions don't have prepositions.* Go over the examples. Give an additional example for each expression (e.g., *The gas station on the corner is open 24 hours a day.*).

2. Write examples of incorrect sentences such as the following on the board: *The convenience store is open 9:30. I buy chocolate once day. The gas station is open 7/24.* Have students say why the sentences are incorrect.

Practice Idea: Writing

Have students work in pairs to write an example for each time expression. Ask volunteers to share their examples.

EXERCISE 3

Answers will vary.

5-10 mins

1. Say: *In this exercise, you'll write answers that are true for you.* Have students read the direction line. Go over the example. Model the example for yourself. Have a student model the example.

2. Have students complete Exercise 3 individually. Remind them to review grammar chart **7.2** on page 150 if necessary. Have students compare their answers with a partner. Have volunteers share their answers with the class.

EXERCISE 4

Answers will vary.

5-10 mins

1. Have students read the direction line. Say: *Answer about your own country.* Go over the example. Have a student model the example talking about their country.

2. Have students complete Exercise 4 individually. Remind them to review grammar chart **7.2** on page 150 if necessary. Then have students compare answers in pairs. Have volunteers share their answers with the class.

EXERCISE 5

ANSWERS: **Student responses will vary. Correct questions: 1.** How many times a day do you check your e-mail? **2.** How many hours a day do you talk on the phone? **3.** How many times a month do you go to the library? **4.** How many hours a night do you sleep? **5.** How many times a day do you cook? **6.** How many times a week do you shop for food?

5-10 mins

1. Say: *In this exercise, you'll ask and answer questions with a partner about how many times you do things.* Have students read the direction line. Go over the example. Model the example with a student volunteer.

2. Have students complete Exercise 5 in pairs. Remind them to review grammar chart **7.2** on page 150 if necessary. Monitor pair work. Give help as needed. Have volunteers share their questions and answers with the class.

7.3 Prepositions of Place

 1. Have students look at grammar chart **7.3** on page 151. Say: *Prepositions can be used with a place.* Go over the examples. Use the picture on page 146 to illustrate the prepositions.

2. Point out and explain the Language Note. Say: *The prepositions* in *and* at *do not mean the same thing. In means that you are inside the building/location. At is more general. You could be in the store, going into the store, or even in the parking lot of the store.*

 EXERCISE 6
CD 2
TR 18 **ANSWERS: 1.** at; **2.** in; **3.** in; **4.** to; **5.** at; **6.** near OR next to; **7.** on; **8.** next to OR near

 1. Have students read the direction line. Go over the example.
5-10 mins 2. Have students complete Exercise 6 individually. Remind them to review grammar chart **7.3** on page 151 if necessary. Then have students compare their answers in pairs. Play the audio and check the answers as a class.

7.4 Prepositions in Common Expressions

 Have students look at grammar chart **7.4** on page
5-10 mins 153. Say: *There are many common expressions with prepositions.* Go over the examples. Give additional examples to illustrate the expressions (e.g., *My daughter is on the phone 24 hours a day.*).

 EXERCISE 7
CD 2
TR 19 **ANSWERS: 1.** for; **2.** on; **3.** for; **4.** out of; **5.** at; **6.** on; **7.** next to; **8.** on

1. Have students read the direction line. Go over the example.
5-10 mins 2. Have students complete Exercise 7 individually. Remind them to review grammar chart **7.4** on page 153 if necessary. Then have students compare their answers in pairs. Play the audio and check the answers as a class.

EXERCISE **8**

CD 2
TR 20
ANSWERS: **1.** in; **2.** at; **3.** After; **4.** in; **5.** to; **6.** at;
7. after; **8.** on; **9.** at

5-10
mins

1. Have students read the direction line. Go over the example.

2. Have students complete Exercise 8 individually. Remind them to review grammar chart **7.4** on page 153 if necessary. Then have students compare their answers in pairs. Play the audio and check the answers as a class.

Practice Ideas: Speaking

1. Have students draw and label a map of locations mentioned in the conversation. Then have partners take turns telling where Sue is, where she has to go, and what she has to do (e.g., *She's at work now. She has to go to the gas station. She needs to buy gas.*).

2. Have students work in pairs to create a similar conversation with their own information.

Lesson 2 Overview

GRAMMAR

1. Say: *In Lesson 2 we are going to study* there is *and* there are *and quantity words.* Write the lesson's objectives on the board.

2. Activate students' prior knowledge. Elicit examples of quantity words (e.g., *some, enough, no, many*), and write them on the board. Then say and write: *There are no [flowers] in this room.* Underline *There are* and *no.* Ask volunteers to make more sentences using the quantity expressions on the board and *There is* and *There are.*

CONTEXT

1. Ask: *What stores do you like to shop at? Why?* Write students' ideas on the board. Say: *In this lesson we're going to talk about large stores and small stores.* Ask: *Do big stores have good service?* Have students share their ideas and personal experiences.

---

2. Direct students' attention to the pictures of Rick, Sue, and Peter on page 155. Ask: *What kind of stores are these?* (hardware stores, home supply stores) *Do these two stores have the same prices? Do they have the same level of service?*

Good Prices or Good Service

READING

Have students look at the title of the reading and the pictures on page 155. Ask: *What do you think Rick and Sue are talking about?* Have students quickly scan the reading. Ask: *What do they want to buy?* Have students use the title and pictures to make predictions about the reading.

BEFORE YOU READ

5-10
mins

1. Go over each question as a class. Have a volunteer read the questions or read them to the class yourself. Have students discuss the questions in pairs.

2. Ask a few volunteers to share their answers with the class.

Context Note

Not all people in the United States want a big superstore in their town. Some people say that big chain stores take businesses away from city centers, increase traffic, and provide only badly paid jobs to people living outside of town. Other people say that these stores offer more choices, have better prices, and provide more jobs than smaller businesses.

 Reading

CD 2
TR 21

10-15
mins

1. Have students read the conversations silently. Then play the audio and have students read along silently.

2. Check students' basic comprehension. Ask questions, such as: *What are Rick and Sue looking for?* (lightbulbs) *Are they happy with the service at the store?* (no) *Can Peter go downstairs?* (No. There's no elevator.) *Does Peter like the small store?* (yes)

Practice Ideas: Listening

1. To practice listening skills, have students listen to the audio before opening their books. Ask a few comprehension questions, such as: *Where are the lightbulbs in the big store?* (aisle 3) *Are the clerks helpful in the small store?* (yes) Repeat the audio if necessary. Then have students open their books and read along as they listen to the audio.

2. Alternatively, have students begin by listening to the audio as they read along.

Practice Idea: Speaking

Have students practice the conversations in groups. Ask volunteers to role-play all or part of the conversations in front of the class.

VOCABULARY IN CONTEXT

5-10 mins

1. Model the pronunciation of each new vocabulary item and have students repeat.

2. Make sure students understand the meaning of each vocabulary item. Review the examples in the book and create additional example sentences. For example, say: *enough. I don't have enough time to go to the gym today. I'll go tomorrow.* Go over each new vocabulary word similarly, using visuals and realia when appropriate. For example, for *elevator* draw a set of elevator doors on the board, with Up and Down buttons and a light over the doors. Say: *Stairs go up and down. Elevators go up and down.* When possible, point to pictures in the book that illustrate the new vocabulary items, such as *home supply store* and *clerk* on page 155 and *lightbulb* on page 156.

3. Have students underline an example of each vocabulary item in the reading. Let them know that *40% off* and *lamp* are not in the reading.

Practice Idea: Speaking

To check comprehension, have volunteers in pairs or groups act out selected vocabulary, such as *service* and *clerk*.

Did You Know?

Point out the information to students. Tell students that big home supply stores offer classes in painting, gardening, and installing various items the store sells. Tell students that people can save a lot of money by doing these jobs themselves.

 LISTENING ACTIVITY

CD 2
TR 22

ANSWERS: 1. False; **2.** False; **3.** False; **4.** True; **5.** False; **6.** True

5-10 mins

1. Say: *Listen to the sentences about the conversation. Circle* true *or* false. Play the listening selection one time without pausing. Then play it through again, pausing and replaying as necessary.

2. Have students compare their answers, then play the audio again and check the answers as a class.

7.5 *There Is* and *There Are*— Affirmative Statements ≡★

5-10 mins

1. Have students look at grammar chart **7.5** on page 158. Say: *To express the existence of something we use* there is *and* there are. *We use* there is *for singular subjects and* there are *for plural subjects.* Go over the examples. Give additional examples from the classroom (e.g., *There are four tables in the classroom.*).

2. Point out the Language Notes. Review the contraction rules. Have students close their books. Write on the board: *There're six oranges. There are six oranges. There's a dog. Theres' a dog.* Ask which sentences are correct and why.

Practice Idea: Speaking

Have students tell a partner what's in his or her apartment or house. Say and write the following examples on the board: *There are three bedrooms. There's a big kitchen.*

EXERCISE 1 ≡★

ANSWERS: **1.** There's; **2.** There are; **3.** There are; **4.** There are; **5.** There's; **6.** There's; **7.** There's

 5-10 mins

1. Have students read the direction line. Go over the example in the book. Remind students to use contractions when they can.

2. Have students complete Exercise 1 individually. Remind students to review grammar chart **7.5** on page 158 if necessary. Check the answers as a class.

EXERCISE 2

 CD 2 TR 23

ANSWERS: **1.** There are; **2.** There's; **3.** There's; **4.** There's; **5.** There's; **6.** There are; **7.** There are

10-15 mins

1. Have students look at the picture of Victor, Lisa, and Simon on page 159. Ask: *Where are Victor and Lisa? Where is Simon?* Then have students read the direction line. Go over the example in the book.

2. Have students complete Exercise 2 individually. Remind students to review grammar chart **7.5** on page 158 if necessary. Then have students compare their answers in pairs. Play the audio and check the answers as a class.

Practice Idea: Speaking

Have students describe who they see in the stores where they shop. Say and write on the board the following model sentences: *There are a lot of women in the shoe department. There's only one clerk in the jewelry department.*

7.6 *There Is* and *There Are*— Negative Statements ≡★

 10-15 mins

1. Have students look at grammar chart **7.6** on page 160. Say: *There isn't any* and *there is no are* used with noncount nouns. Go over the examples. Give additional examples from the classroom (e.g., *There isn't any paper on my desk. There is no coffee on my desk.*).

2. Say: *There aren't any* and *There is no* are used with plural nouns. Go over the examples. Give additional examples (e.g., *There aren't any dictionaries in this room. There are no computers.*).

3. Have students close their books. Write the following sentences on the board. Point out that the contraction of *There is no* is *There's no*. Have volunteers come to the board and fill in the blanks:

> *There's no [elevator].*
> *There are no [cheap TVs].*
> *There isn't a [good shoe department].*
> *There aren't any [nice clerks].*

Practice Idea: Speaking

Have students get into groups and describe to group members what's *not* in their neighborhood (e.g., There's no bank in my neighborhood.).

EXERCISE 3 ≡★

ANSWERS: **1.** There aren't any OR There are no; **2.** There aren't any OR There are no; **3.** There's no; **4.** There's no; **5.** There isn't any OR There's no

5-10 mins

1. Have students read the direction line. Go over the example in the book.

2. Have students complete Exercise 3 individually. Remind them to review grammar chart **7.6** on page 160 if necessary. Check the answers as a class.

7.7 Quantity Words ≡★

5-10 mins

Have students look at grammar chart **7.7** on page 161. Present the quantity words and examples. To check comprehension, ask volunteers to describe the contents of the room using the quantity words in the chart (e.g., There aren't any windows in this room.).

EXERCISE 4 ≡★
Answers will vary.

5-10 mins

1. Say: *In this exercise, you're going to make and share sentences about this class and this school.* Have students read the direction line. Go over

the examples in the book. Have a volunteer model the examples.

2. Have students complete Exercise 4 individually. Remind them to review grammar chart **7.7** on page 161 if necessary. Then have students compare their answers in pairs. Have volunteers share their answers with the class.

EXERCISE 5
Answers will vary.

 5-10 mins
1. Say: *In this exercise, you're going to tell about where you live.* Have students read the direction line. Go over the example in the book. Have a volunteer model the example.

2. Have students complete Exercise 5 individually. Remind them to review grammar chart **7.7** on page 161 if necessary. Give help as needed. Have volunteers share their answers with the class.

Practice Idea: Speaking

Have students share their answers with a partner. Encourage them to ask each other further questions about the places they live.

  10-15 mins

 EXERCISE 6
CD 2 TR 24
ANSWERS: 1. any; 2. some; 3. one; 4. any OR enough; 5. no; 6. any; 7. a lot of OR many

1. Have students read the direction line. Go over the example. You might have students scan the conversation for quantity and location phrases. Then review or pre-teach terms and phrases that might be difficult, such as *batteries*, *hall closet*, and *A battery is a battery*.

2. Have students complete Exercise 6 individually. Remind them to review grammar chart **7.7** on page 161 if necessary. Then have students compare their answers in pairs. Play the audio and check the answers as a class.

Practice Ideas: Speaking

1. Have students practice the conversation in pairs. Ask volunteers to role-play the conversation in front of the class.

2. Have students write a list of ten things in their refrigerator at home and then write a shopping list of five things they need. Put students into pairs. Say: *Ask your partner for something on your shopping list. Your partner will say if he or she has any.* Say and write the following model on the board:

   Student A: *I need milk.*

   Student B: *There isn't any milk in my refrigerator./There's no milk in my refrigerator.*

 EXERCISE 7
CD 2 TR 25
ANSWERS: 1. They're; 2. There's; 3. They're; 4. There isn't OR There's not; 5. It's; 6. isn't OR 's not; 7. isn't OR 's not; 8. They're

 10-15 mins
1. Have students look at the pictures of the tools on page 157. Have students name the tools. (hammer, screwdriver, pliers) Then have students read the direction line for this exercise. Do the example with the class.

2. Have students complete the rest of Exercise 7 individually. Remind them to review grammar chart **7.7** on page 161 if necessary. Then have students compare their answers in pairs. Play the audio and check the answers as a class.

Practice Idea: Speaking

Have students practice the conversation in pairs. Ask volunteers to role-play the conversation in front of the class.

Lesson 3 Overview

GRAMMAR

1. Say: *In Lesson 3, we are going to study how to make yes/no and information questions with* there is *and* there are. Write the lesson's objectives on the board. Ask students to use complete sentences to answer

the following questions: *Are there any students from Japan in the class? Is there anyone from Chile? How many students are there in this class?*

2. Activate students' prior knowledge. Ask: *What are some question words?* (what, who, how much, how many, etc.) Ask volunteers to make *yes/no* and information questions about the class with *there is* and *there are*.

CONTEXT

1. Say: *Stores usually offer many different things. They also offer many kinds of the same thing. When you shop, you have to choose. In this lesson, we're going to learn about smart shopping.* Relate the topic to students' experience. Ask: *When you decide what to buy, what do you think about?*

2. Direct students' attention to the photo. Ask: *What is in the woman's hand?* (shampoo) *Are all the different kinds of shampoo the same price?* (no)

Presentation Ideas

The topic for this lesson can be enhanced with the following items:

1. Circulars from different supermarkets, drugstores, and chain stores

2. Advertisements comparing two versions of one product or two brands of the same product

Choices READING

Have students look at the title of the reading and the photo on page 164. Ask: *What kinds of choices do we have to make when we are shopping?* Have students use the title, the photo, and the picture of the calculator on page 166 to make predictions about the reading. Prompt by asking: *What kinds of things will Halina and Peter compare at the supermarket?*

BEFORE YOU READ

5-10 mins

1. Go over each question as a class. Have a volunteer read the questions or read them to the class yourself.

2. Discuss the questions as a class. Have students share their ideas and personal experiences of comparing products and prices.

 Reading

CD 2
TR 26

10-15 mins

1. Have students read the dialogue silently. Then play the audio and have students read along silently.

2. Check students' basic comprehension. Ask questions such as: *Which shampoo do they buy?* (the cheap one) *Which bag of sugar do they buy?* (the five-pound bag) *Are they going to buy a calculator?* (no)

Practice Ideas: Listening

1. To practice listening skills, have students listen to the audio before opening their books. Ask a few comprehension questions, such as: *Where is the sugar?* (in aisle 6) *How many kinds of dog food are there?* (over 20) Repeat the audio if necessary. Then have students open their books and read along as they listen to the audio.

2. Alternatively, have students begin by listening to the audio as they read along.

Practice Idea: Speaking

Have students practice the conversation in pairs. Ask volunteers to role-play the conversation in front of the class.

VOCABULARY IN CONTEXT

5-10 mins

1. Model the pronunciation of each new vocabulary item and have students repeat.

2. Go over the meaning of each vocabulary item. Review the examples in the book and create additional example sentences. For example, say: *difference between.* Hold up two book bags from different students. Say: *What's the difference between these two bags?* Review each new vocabulary item similarly, using visuals and realia when appropriate. When possible, point to pictures that illustrate the new vocabulary items, such as *shampoo* on page 164 and *calculator* on page 166.

3. Have students underline an example of each vocabulary item in the reading.

Did You Know?

Point out the information to students. Explain to students that the U.S. uses the metric system for some things, such as measuring servings for food items.

LISTENING ACTIVITY

CD 2
TR 27

ANSWERS: 1. True; **2.** False; **3.** False; **4.** False; **5.** True; **6.** True

5-10 mins

1. Say: *Listen to the sentences about Peter and Halina's conversation. Circle* true *or* false. Play the listening selection one time without pausing. Then play it through again, pausing and replaying as necessary.

2. Have students compare their answers in pairs, then play the audio again and check the answers as a class.

7.8 *There Is* and *There Are— Yes/No Questions* ⩵★

5-10 mins

1. Have students cover up grammar chart **7.8** on page 166. Write the following sentence on the board: *There's a shampoo aisle.* Have students write a *yes/no* question for the statement. (Is there a shampoo aisle?) Then have students look at the chart. Say: *To make a question with* there is *and* there are, *reverse the word order.* Review each statement, question, and short answer.

2. Point out the Language Notes. Review the rules. Stress the use of *any.* Have students underline *any* in the chart examples and identify the noncount noun (*cat food*) and plural count noun (*bags of sugar*).

EXERCISE 1 ⩵★

ANSWERS: 1. there isn't; **2.** there are; **3.** there isn't; **4.** there are; **5.** there is; **6.** there aren't

5-10 mins

1. Have students read the direction line. Go over the example.

2. Have students complete Exercise 1 individually. Remind them to review grammar chart **7.8** on page 166 if necessary. Check the answers as a class.

Practice Idea: Speaking

Have students write questions about the classroom using *there is* and *there are.* Then have them ask and answer the questions with a partner. (e.g., Are there any chairs in this room? Yes, there are.)

EXERCISE 2 ⩵★

ANSWERS: 1. Are there; **2.** Is there; **3.** Is there; **4.** Are there; **5.** Is there; **6.** Are there

5-10 mins

1. Have students read the direction line. Go over the example in the book. Ask: *How do you know what to put in the blank?* (Look at the short answer.)

3. Have students complete Exercise 2 individually. Remind them to review grammar chart **7.8** on page 166 if necessary. Then have students compare their answers with a partner. Check answers as a class.

EXERCISE 3

ANSWERS: Student responses will vary. Correct questions: 1. Are there any Mexican students in this class? **2.** Are there any hard exercises in this lesson? **3.** Are there any new words in this lesson? **4.** Are there any pictures on this page? No, there aren't; **5.** Is there a verb chart in your dictionary? **6.** Is there a computer lab at this school? **7.** Are there any public telephones on this floor? **8.** Is there a gym at this school?

10-15 mins

1. Say: *You're going to ask and answer questions with a partner.* Have students read the direction line. Go over the example in the book. Then have two volunteers model the example.

2. Have students complete Exercise 3 in pairs. Remind them to review grammar chart **7.8** on page 166 if necessary. Monitor pair work. Give help as needed. Have volunteers ask and answer to check the answers as a class.

7.9 *There Is* and *There Are*— Information Questions

5-10 mins

1. Have students look at grammar chart **7.9** on page 168. Say: *How much, how many, and why are common question words with* is there/are there. *The question word goes before* is there *or* are there. Go over the examples in the chart. Note that the word *there* following *how much* or *how many* can often be omitted in everyday speech.

2. Ask: *What is the difference between yes/no questions and information questions?* (Yes/no questions can be answered by a simple *yes* or *no*. Information questions require a piece of information. Information questions have question words.) Review the examples in the chart. Point out the word order for both types of questions.

3. Note that in casual conversation, the short answers to *yes/no* questions are sometimes omitted. Give examples, e.g.:

   A: Is there any sauce?
   B: One can.

Practice Idea: Speaking

Have students go back to the reading on page 165. Tell students to circle the information questions. Have them underline the *yes/no* questions, and put a wavy line under the short answers (e.g., *Are there any other items on the shopping list? Just two.*). Have students practice the questions in pairs.

EXERCISE 4 =★

ANSWERS: 1. How many items are there on the list? **2.** How many ounces are there in two pounds? **3.** How many people are there in this line? **4.** Why are there many kinds of dog food? **5.** Why is there a pharmacy in the store? **6.** How much difference (in price) is there between these two shampoos? OR How much difference is there (in price) between these two shampoos?

5-10 mins

1. Have students read the direction line. Go over the example in the book.

2. Have students complete Exercise 4 individually. Remind them to review grammar chart **7.9** on page 168 if necessary. Check the answers as a class.

EXERCISE 5

ANSWERS: Answers will vary. Correct questions:
1. How many students are there in this class?
2. How many windows are there in this room?
3. How much paper is there on the floor? **4.** How many telephones are there in this room? **5.** How many men's washrooms are there on this floor?
6. How many floors are there in this building?
7. How many pages are there in this book? **8.** How much grammar information is there on this page?

5-10 mins

1. Say: *In this exercise, you'll ask and answer questions about this class or school with a partner.* Go over the example. Have volunteers model the example. Tell partners to take turns asking and answering questions.

2. Have students complete Exercise 5 in pairs. Remind them to review grammar chart **7.9** on page 168 if necessary. Monitor pair work. Give help as needed. Have volunteers ask and answer to check the answers as a class.

Practice Idea: Speaking

Have students ask and answer questions about their homes with a partner (e.g., How many bathrooms are there in your house?).

EXERCISE 6

ANSWERS: Answers will vary. Possible answers:
1. How many inches are there in a foot? There are 12 inches in a foot. **2.** How many ounces are there in a pound? There are 16 ounces in a pound. **3.** How many cups are there in a quart? There are 4 cups in a quart. **4.** How many quarts are there in a gallon? There are 4 quarts in a gallon. **5.** How many pints are there in a quart? There are 2 pints in a quart.

5-10 mins

1. Have students look at the pictures on page 169. Review the vocabulary for the units of measure: *feet, yard, inches, ounces, pounds, cup, pint, quart, gallon.* Then have students read the direction line. Go over the example.

2. Have students complete Exercise 6 individually. Remind them to review grammar chart **7.9** on page 168 if necessary. Check the answers as a class.

EXERCISE 7

CD 2
TR 28
ANSWERS: **1.** There are; **2.** There's; **3.** How many;
4. are there; **5.** Is there; **6.** there is; **7.** How many;
8. are there; **9.** Is there

10-15
mins

1. Point out the pictures of the CDs and the printer. Ask: *What are these?* (CDs and a printer) Have students read the direction line. Go over the example. Have a volunteer model the example.

2. Have students complete Exercise 7 individually. Remind them to review grammar chart **7.9** on page 168 if necessary. Then have students compare their answers in pairs. Play the audio and check the answers as a class.

Practice Ideas: Speaking

1. Have students practice the conversation in pairs. Ask volunteers to role-play the conversation in front of the class.

2. Have students work in pairs to create a similar conversation using their own information.

 EXERCISE 8

CD 2
TR 29
ANSWERS: **1.** Is there; **2.** there is; **3.** There are; **4.** There's; **5.** is there; **6.** There are

10-15
mins

1. Have students look at the pictures on page 171. Ask: *What can you see?* (a sweater, boots, gloves, the clothes section in a store/ jackets and tops, sweaters) *Are the clothes in the store at full price? What does* sale *mean?* (The prices are especially low.)

2. Have students read the direction line. Have a volunteer read the example. Ask: *Why is* There's *correct?* ("A sale" is singular.) Have students skim a few statements for the clue to choosing singular or plural. Remind them that *a lot of* means *many.*

3. Have students complete Exercise 8 individually. Remind them to review grammar charts **7.8** on page 166 and **7.9** on page 168 if necessary. Then have students compare their answers in pairs. Play the audio and check the answers as a class.

Practice Ideas: Speaking

1. Have students practice the conversation in pairs. Ask volunteers to role-play the conversations in front of the class.

2. Have students get into groups and talk about sales they know about, saying when the big sales occur and which items are marked down (e.g., *There's a big sale in January. All winter clothes are 50 percent off.*).

Editing Advice

10-15
mins
Have students close their books. Write the example sentences without editing marks or corrections on the board. For example:

1. *Sue likes to shop in the night. Your favorite program begins after 20 minutes.*
2. *Simon works five days in a week.*

Ask students to correct each sentence and provide a rule or explanation for each correction, e.g.: 1. Sue likes to shop at night. Your favorite program begins in 20 minutes. (Use the correct preposition) 2. Simon works five days a week. (Don't use prepositions with certain time expressions.) This activity can be done individually, in pairs, or as a class. After students have corrected each sentence, tell them to turn to page 172. Say: *Now compare your work with the Editing Advice in the book.*

Editing Quiz

ANSWERS: **1.** to; **2.** at; **3.** at; **4.** near OR next to; **5.** C; **6.** on OR for; **7.** C; **8.** C; **9.** Ø; **10.** There are; **11.** aren't any OR are no; **12.** C; **13.** in; **14.** C; **15.** C; **16.** next to; **17.** C; **18.** Ø; **19.** C; **20.** C; **21.** a; **22.** C

10-15
mins

1. Tell students they are going to put the Editing Advice into practice. Have students read the direction line. Ask: *Do all the shaded words have mistakes?* (no) Go over the examples with the class. Then do #1 together.

2. Have students complete the rest of the quiz individually. Then have them compare their answers with a partner before checking the answers as a class. Elicit the relevant grammar point for each correction.

3. For the items students had difficulties with, have them go back and find the relevant grammar chart and review it. Monitor and give help as necessary.

Expansion

These expansion activities provide opportunities for students to interact with one another and further develop their speaking and writing skills. Encourage students to use grammar from this unit whenever possible.

LEARNER'S LOG

10-15 mins

1. Have students close their books. Ask: *What did you learn about shopping, different types of stores, and getting good prices in the U.S.? What else do you want to know?* Write students' ideas on the board. Discuss ways in which students can find out more about shopping, stores, and prices.

2. Have students open their books to complete the Learner's Log. Remind them to write three questions about shopping in the U.S.

3. Have students compare logs in pairs.

WRITING ACTIVITY

10-15 mins

1. Have students read the direction line. Go over the example. Brainstorm ways to describe the pictures with the class and list the ideas on the board.

2. Have students complete the activity individually. Collect for assessment.

Practice Idea: Writing

Have students exchange papers with a partner. Ask students to help their partners edit their paragraph. Refer students to the Editing Advice on page 172.

OUTSIDE ACTIVITY

Tell students to check their local newspaper for ads for their favorite pharmacy or supermarket and find a product that's on sale. Have them write down the sale price. Tell them to find a product with a coupon and write down what the sale price is with the coupon. Then have them write about the ads in their notebook. In class, have students compare prices in groups, including sale prices and prices with coupons.

INTERNET ACTIVITIES

1. Tell students to use a search engine on the Internet and type in *metric conversion*, then choose a Web site to find out their weight and height in both metric and American measurements. If appropriate, in class, have them share their information.

2. In class, elicit from students the names of office supply stores they know and write them on the board. Tell students to find the Web site of a big office supply store and find the price of a package of printer paper. In class, have students compare prices in small groups.

Unit 8

Unit Overview

1. Begin by directing students' attention to the photos. Ask: *What do you see in the pictures?* (mailboxes, a bank drive-through window) *What is the man in his car doing?* (getting money from his account or putting money into his account)

2. Say: *We're going to talk about errands in Unit 8.* Errands *are short trips we take to get a task done.* Relate the topic to students' experience. Ask: *What errands do you do?*

Presentation Ideas

The topic for this unit can be enhanced with the following items:

1. Flyers from dry cleaners
2. Post office announcements of automated or other services giving rates for first-, second-, and third-class items
3. Magazine pictures of people doing errands
4. A postage scale

Lesson 1 Overview

GRAMMAR

1. Say and write the following sentences on the board:

    Now I'm writing on the board.

    Today, I'm teaching.

    This year, I'm teaching grammar.

    Write or point out the first lesson objective on the board: *The Present Continuous Tense—Affirmative Statements.* Say: *The present continuous tense tells what's happening in the present.* Point out the time phrases in the sentences on the board and say: *There are different kinds of present time.*

2. Elicit responses from students using different expressions of time. Prompt by asking: *What are you doing right now? What are you doing this year?*

CONTEXT

1. Begin by directing students' attention to the picture of the post office on page 176. Go over the names of the items in the post office, such as *package, letter,* and *envelope.* Say: *What will we talk about in Lesson 1?* (mail in the United States)

2. Relate the topic to students' experience. Ask: *Do you send mail? How often do you go to the post office? When you go, what are people doing there?* Write students' answers on the board (e.g., They are mailing packages. They're buying stamps.).

At the Post Office   READING

Have students look at the title of the reading and the picture on page 176. Ask: *What is happening at the post office?* Elicit some of the activities in the photo. Point to the clerk. Ask: *What is he doing?* (He is waiting on a customer; he is selling postal items.)

BEFORE YOU READ

1. Go over each question as a class. Have a volunteer read the questions or read them to the class yourself. Have students discuss the questions in pairs.

2. Ask a few volunteers to share their answers with the class.

5-10 mins

Context Note

The U.S. Post Office has been delivering mail for over 200 years. The U.S. Post Office , today called the U.S. Postal Service, began in 1775. Benjamin Franklin was the first postmaster general.

 Reading

CD 3 TR 01

1. Have students read the text silently. Then play the audio and have students read along silently.

10-15 mins

2. Check students' basic comprehension. Ask questions, such as: *Are people complaining about the slow service?* (no) *What is Marta doing?* (picking up a package) *Are people buying stamps?* (yes) *Are people buying phone cards?* (no)

Practice Idea: Listening

To practice listening skills, have students listen to the audio before opening their books. Ask a few comprehension questions, such as: *Is self-service fast?* (yes) *What day of the week is it?* (Friday) Repeat the audio if necessary. Then have students open their books and read along as they listen to the audio.

VOCABULARY IN CONTEXT

5-10 mins

1. Model the pronunciation of each new vocabulary item and have students repeat.

2. Make sure students understand the meaning of each new vocabulary item. Review the examples in the book and create additional example sentences. For example, *postage.* (Hold up an envelope with stamps on it.) Say: *The postage on this envelope is [amount].* For *automated postal center,* say: *A clerk doesn't help you. You can do everything by yourself. It's like an ATM.* Go over each new vocabulary item using visuals and realia when appropriate. When possible, point to pictures in the book that illustrate the new vocabulary items, such as *customer, scale,* and *counter* on page 176.

3. Have students underline an example of each vocabulary item in the reading.

Practice Idea: Speaking

To check comprehension, have volunteers in pairs or groups act out selected vocabulary from the reading, such as *customer, pick up,* and *wait in line.*

Did You Know?

Point out the information to students. Tell students that the first five-cent stamp pictured Benjamin Franklin. The first ten-cent stamp, also issued in 1847, pictured George Washington.

LISTENING ACTIVITY

CD 3
TR 02

ANSWERS: 1. False; **2.** False; **3.** True; **4.** True; **5.** True; **6.** True; **7.** False; **8.** False

5-10 mins

1. Say: *Listen to the sentences about the reading. Circle* true *or* false. Play the listening selection one time without pausing. Then play it through again, pausing and replaying as necessary.

2. Have students compare their answers, then play the audio again and check the answers as a class.

8.1 The Present Continuous Tense—Affirmative Statements

5-10 mins

1. Have students look at grammar chart **8.1** on page 179. Say: *We form the present continuous with* be *plus the verb with an* -ing *ending.* Go over the examples. Give an additional example for each expression.

2. Point out the Language Notes. Say: *Use contractions in the present continuous.* Remind students that they have already learned contractions with *be.* Explain that we don't use contractions with plural nouns.

3. Write the following sentences on the board:

   Bill is go to the store.

   The kids're playing.

   She studying now.

   Have the class decide which sentences have incorrect forms for the present continuous tense and explain how to correct them.

Practice Idea: Speaking

Have students work in pairs to create sentences about the class using *wear, hold, get,* and *use* (e.g., The teacher is wearing a sweater.).

EXERCISE 1

ANSWERS: Answers may vary. Possible answers:
1. 's standing; **2.** are waiting; **3.** 's giving;
4. 's buying; **5.** are helping; **6.** 's weighing;
7. are doing; **8.** are paying

5-10 mins

1. Have students read the direction line. Go over the example in the book. Be sure that the students understand that the sentences are based on the reading on page 177.

2. Have students complete Exercise 1 individually. Remind them to review grammar chart **8.1** on page 179 if necessary. Check the answers as a class.

8.2 Spelling of the *-ing* Form

5-10 mins

1. Have students cover up grammar chart **8.2** on page 180. Create an exercise on the board:

    go – going / eat – eating

    sit – sitting / plan – planning

    give – giving / write – writing

    show – showing / fix – fixing

    Ask: *What is the spelling rule for each set of verbs?*

2. Have students look at grammar chart **8.2** on page 180. Go over the verbs and the rules.

Practice Idea: Writing

Have students work in pairs. Ask the class to turn to the reading on page 177. Have students find all the verbs in the present continuous tense and match them to the relevant spelling rules in the chart. Go over the answers with the class.

EXERCISE 2

ANSWERS: 1. 's getting; **2.** 's waiting; **3.** 's taking;
4. are talking; **5.** 're looking at; **6.** are using; **7.** 's putting; **8.** 's weighing; **9.** 's planning; **10.** 's giving;
11. 's writing

5-10 mins

1. Have students read the direction line. Go over the example in the book. Remind students to use contractions correctly.

2. Have students complete Exercise 2 individually. Remind them to review grammar chart **8.2** on page 180 if necessary. Then have students compare their answers in pairs. Monitor pair work. Give help as needed. Check the answers as a class.

Practice Idea: Writing

Have students talk about the picture on page 176 in pairs (e.g., *The mail clerk is working. The customer is holding a package and letters.*). Ask students to write as many sentences about the photo as they can without looking at the reading. Then have volunteers share their sentences with the class.

8.3 Uses of the Present Continuous Tense

5-10 mins

1. Have students look at grammar chart **8.3** on page 181. Say: *We use the present continuous in three main ways.* Read the example sentences and explanations. Note that *stand, sleep, sit, wear, hold,* and *wait* are acts without movement and therefore "no action" verbs.

2. Point out the Language Note. Go over the time expressions. Elicit examples with the present continuous tense from the students (e.g., *I'm working all day.*).

EXERCISE 3

ANSWERS: Answers will vary. Possible answers:
1. A woman is holding a baby. The girl is holding the baby's hand. **2.** The clerk is giving stamps to the customer. The customer is buying the stamps.
3. People are waiting in line. A woman is writing.
4. A woman is mailing a letter. The man is waiting for her. **5.** A woman is buying mailing supplies.
6. The clerk's taking the man's letter. The man is using a credit card.

10-15 mins

1. Have students read the direction line. Go over the example. Say: *Your answers will vary.* Elicit sentences for picture 1 and write them on the board.

2. Have students complete Exercise 3 individually. Remind them to review grammar charts **8.2** on page 180 and **8.3** on page 181 if necessary. Check the answers as a class.

Practice Idea: Speaking

Have students play a game in groups. Write a list of verbs on the board. Ask students to take turns acting out one of the verbs in front of their groups. Group members guess the action. Say: *Use sentences, such as: She's walking.* OR *She's eating.*

8.4 The Present Continuous Tense—Negative Statements

5-10 mins

1. Have students look at grammar chart **8.4** on page 182. Ask: *How do we make the sentence negative?* (We write *not* after the verb *be* and before the main verb.) Go over the examples.

2. Point out the Language Note. Clarify the rule for making negative contractions with *be*. Make sure students understand that, while there are two negative contractions for other subject pronouns, there is only one negative contraction for *I am not.* (*I'm not*)

Practice Idea: Speaking

Have students go back to the reading on page 177. Say: *Rewrite some of the sentences to make them negative. Use contractions.* (e.g., People aren't doing errands.)

EXERCISE 4

ANSWERS: 1. He's not using his credit card. OR He isn't using his credit card. **2.** They aren't complaining about the service. OR They're not complaining about the service. **3.** They're not using self-service. OR They aren't using self-service. **4.** She's not mailing a package. OR She isn't mailing a package. **5.** She's not shopping with Peter. OR She isn't shopping with Peter.

5-10 mins

1. Have students read the direction line. Go over the examples.

2. Have students complete Exercise 4 individually. Remind them to review grammar chart **8.4** on page 182 if necessary. Check the answers as a class.

EXERCISE 5

ANSWERS: Answers will vary. Possible answers:
1. I'm (not) writing in a journal. **2.** The teacher's wearing sneakers. OR The teacher's not (OR The teacher isn't) wearing sneakers. **3.** We're using a dictionary. OR We're not (OR We aren't) using a dictionary. **4.** The teacher's looking at my ID. OR The teacher's not (OR The teacher isn't) looking at my ID. **5.** We're talking about the supermarket. OR We're not (OR We aren't) talking about the supermarket. **6.** The students are complaining about this exercise. OR The students aren't complaining about this exercise. **7.** I'm (not) trying to learn all the new words. **8.** The teacher's helping me now. OR The teacher's not (OR The teacher isn't) helping me now.

10-15 mins

1. Say: *You're going to write sentences about what is true in this class at this moment. The statements can be affirmative or negative. You must tell what is happening now.* Have students read the direction line. Go over the examples. Remind students to use contractions correctly.

2. Have students complete Exercise 5 individually. Remind them to review grammar chart **8.4** on page 182 if necessary. Check the answers as a class.

EXERCISE 6

ANSWERS: Answers will vary. Possible answers:
1. Dorota's son isn't living with her. He's living in Canada. **2.** Dorota's mailing a package. She isn't using the automated postal center. **3.** Dorota's son is expecting his winter clothes. She's sending them in the package. **4.** Dorota's complaining about the post office. She's not getting fast service. **5.** Marta's talking about online services. She's not using online services today. **6.** Peter's waiting outside in the car. He's waiting for Halina. **7.** Marta and Amy are leaving the post office. They're going to lunch now.

10-15 mins

1. Have students read the direction line. Then read the conversation as a class or have students read it silently. Go over the example. Remind students to use contractions.

2. Have students complete Exercise 8 individually. Remind them to review grammar charts **8.1** on page 179, **8.2** on page 180, and **8.4** on page 182 if necessary. Then have students compare their answers in pairs. Check the answers as a class.

EXERCISE 7

ANSWERS: 1. 'm staying, 'm not going, 'm doing; **2.** 's visiting; **3.** 's not (OR isn't) working; **4.** 'm planning; **5.** 's not (OR isn't) working; **6.** are waiting; **7.** 's using; **8.** isn't (OR 's not) printing

🕐 5-10 mins

1. Have students read the direction line. Go over the examples. Remind students to use contractions whenever possible.

2. Have students complete Exercise 7 individually. Remind them to review grammar charts **8.1** on page 179, **8.2** on page 180, and **8.4** on page 182 if necessary. Check the answers as a class.

Lesson 2 Overview

GRAMMAR

Write the following statement on the board: *He is going to the bank.* Ask: *Can you write a* yes/no *question for this statement?* (Is he going to the bank?) Then ask: *Can you write an information question for this statement?* (Where is he going?) Then ask: *Can you write a subject question for this statement?* (Who is going to the bank?) Write the lesson objectives on the board: *The Present Continuous Tense—Yes/No Questions, The Present Continuous Tense—Information Questions, and The Present Continuous Tense—Subject Questions.*

CONTEXT

1. Say: *Drive-throughs are very convenient. They are usually fast and easy for doing errands.* Ask: *What kinds of places use drive-throughs?* (fast-food restaurants, banks, pharmacies) *Do businesses in your countries use drive-throughs? Do you think they should or shouldn't?* Have students share their knowledge and experiences. Say: *Bank drive-throughs make banking easier for people. In this lesson, we will learn about easy banking.*

2. Direct students' attention to the picture on page 187. Ask: *Where are Marta and Amy?* (a bank drive-through) *What do you think they are doing?* (taking out money; depositing money) Go over some of the vocabulary in the picture.

The Drive-Through READING

Direct students' attention once more to the picture on page 187. Say: *In the reading on page 188, Marta and her daughter Amy are at the bank drive-through. In their car at the bank drive-through, Amy is asking her mother questions. Look at the picture. What do you think Amy is asking questions about?* (the other people, the cashier, the tube)

BEFORE YOU READ

🕐 5-10 mins

1. Go over each question as a class. Have a volunteer read the questions or read them to the class yourself. Have students answer the questions in pairs.

2. Ask a few volunteers to share their answers with the class.

 Reading

CD 3
TR 03

🕐 10-15 mins

1. Have students read the dialogue silently. Then play the audio and have students read along silently.

2. Check students' basic comprehension. Ask questions such as: *What does Marta want to get at the bank?* (quarters) *Why does she need quarters?* (for the laundromat/washing machine) *Who does Amy hear talking?* (the teller) *Why is the man holding a tube?* (to put his deposit in it)

Practice Idea: Speaking

Have students practice the conversation in pairs. Ask volunteers to role-play all or part of the conversation in front of the class.

VOCABULARY IN CONTEXT

5-10 mins

1. Model the pronunciation of each new vocabulary item and have students repeat.

2. Make sure students understand the meaning of each vocabulary item. Review the examples in the book and create additional example sentences. For example, say: *microphone. A microphone makes your voice louder.* Go over each new vocabulary word similarly, using visuals and realia when appropriate. For example, for *roll* show students rolls of items, such as coins or tape. For *turn* direct a volunteer to stand up and then turn left or right. When possible, point to pictures in the book that illustrate the new vocabulary items, such as *drive-through, tube, teller, microphone,* and *ahead of* on page 187.

3. Have students underline an example of each vocabulary item in the reading.

Practice Idea: Speaking

To check comprehension, have volunteers in pairs or groups act out selected vocabulary, such as *turn, teller, microphone,* and *ahead of.*

Did You Know?

Point out the information to students. Write *drive-thru* on the board. Ask: *Have you seen this word?* Explain that *drive-through* is often written as *drive-thru.*

CD 3
TR 04

LISTENING ACTIVITY

ANSWERS: 1. False; **2.** True; **3.** True; **4.** True; **5.** False; **6.** False; **7.** False; **8.** True

5-10 mins

1. Say: *Listen to the following questions about Marta and Amy's conversation. Circle* true *or* false. *Play the listening selection one time*

without pausing. Then play it through again, pausing and replaying as necessary.

2. Have students compare their answers, then play the audio again and check the answers as a class.

8.5 The Present Continuous Tense—*Yes/No* Questions

5-10 mins

1. Have students look at grammar chart **8.5** on page 189. Ask: *Where is the subject?* Then say: *To form* yes/no *questions, put the verb* be *before the subject.* Go over the examples.

2. Say: *The short answer contains just the subject and* be. *Do not include the verb in a short answer.* Go over the short answers.

Practice Idea: Speaking

Have students practice asking and answering the questions in the chart with a partner.

EXERCISE 1

ANSWERS: 1. Are Marta and Amy using the drive-through? Yes, they are. **2.** Is Marta cashing a check? No, she isn't. **3.** Are Marta and Amy waiting in the car? Yes, they are. **4.** Is Marta answering Amy's questions? Yes, she is. **5.** Is the teller helping Marta now? No, she isn't. **6.** Is the man holding the tube? Yes, he is. **7.** Is the man asking for a roll of quarters? No, he isn't. **8.** Are two customers getting service at the same time? Yes, they are.

10-15 mins

1. Have students read the direction line. Go over the example in the book. Be sure students understand that the questions and answers are based on the reading on page 188.

2. Have students complete Exercise 1 individually. Remind them to review grammar chart **8.5** on page 189 if necessary. Check the answers as a class.

EXERCISE

ANSWERS: Student responses will vary. Correct questions: 1. Are you asking for help? **2.** Is someone helping you now? **3.** Is your teacher complaining about your work now? **4.** Are you writing in your book now? **5.** Is your teacher standing in front of the class now? **6.** Are you learning a lot of new words today? **7.** Are you waiting for something now?

10-15 mins

1. Say: *In this exercise, you're going to ask your partner questions about what he or she is doing.* Then have students read the direction line. Go over the example in the book. Say: *There is only one correct answer for the questions, but different responses are possible.* Have two volunteers model #1. If they have difficulty, give an example answer (e.g., *Yes, I am. I'm raising my hand.*).

2. Have students complete the rest of Exercise 2 in pairs. Remind them to review grammar chart **8.5** on page 189 if necessary. Check the answers for the questions as a class. Monitor pair work. Give help as needed. Have a few volunteers share their responses to the questions with the class.

Practice Idea: Speaking

Have students write three new questions to ask their partner (e.g., *Are you watching TV now?*).

8.6 The Present Continuous Tense—Information Questions =★

5-10 mins

1. Have students close their books. Write the following on the board:

    helping / is / How many people / the teller

    Have students unscramble the words to make a question. (*How many people is the teller helping?*)

    Ask: *How do you begin an information question in the present continuous tense?* (with a question word)

2. Have students look at grammar chart **8.6** on page 191. Review the word order and the examples.

3. Say: *In a short answer, do not repeat the subject and verb of the question. Compare:* "We are waiting for service" *and* "Waiting for service." Review the short answers with the class. Then say or write on the board the following question and set of answers. Ask which answers are correct and why.

    What are you doing?

    Nothing.

    Yes, you do.

    Yes, I do.

    I'm not doing anything.

4. Point out the Language Notes. Elicit or give further examples as necessary.

Practice Idea: Writing

Have students write out the long answer for each question.

EXERCISE 3 =★

ANSWERS: 1. Who is the teller talking to? **2.** What is Marta waiting for (at the bank)? **3.** How many rolls of quarters is Marta expecting to get? **4.** Where is the customer putting a deposit? **5.** How is the teller talking to customers? **6.** How many customers is the teller helping at the moment? **7.** Who OR What are Marta and Amy talking about? **8.** Why is Marta using the drive-through? OR Why are people (OR customers) using the drive-through?

10-15 mins

1. Have students read the direction line. Go over the example in the book. Have a volunteer do #1.

2. Have students complete the rest of Exercise 3 individually. Remind them to review grammar chart **8.6** on page 191 if necessary. Check the answers as a class.

Practice Idea: Speaking

Have students practice asking and answering the questions with a partner.

EXERCISE 4

CD 3
TR 05 **ANSWERS: 1.** He's asking; **2.** What are you ordering; **3.** are waiting; **4.** Why are we going; **5.** 's putting OR is putting

10-15 mins

1. Point out the picture on page 193. Ask: *Where are Marta and Amy?* (at a restaurant drive-through) Have students read the direction line. Go over the example in the book.

2. Have students complete Exercise 4 individually. Then have them compare their answers with a partner. Play the audio and check the answers as a class.

8.7 The Present Continuous Tense—Subject Questions ≡★

5-10 mins

1. Have students look at grammar chart **8.7** on page 193. Say: *The question word is the subject in each of these examples.* Go over each example.

2. Check comprehension. Have students close their books. Say or write the following short answers on the board and have students make questions:

   Amy.

   Only three.

   Studying English.

3. Point out the Language Notes. Review the rules. Ask: *Why must you always use a plural verb after* how many? (because *many* is plural) Clarify the rule for *who*. Explain that *who* in the question can mean one or many. You might note that a long answer with a plural subject will need a plural verb. (e.g., *Who is talking? Amy and Marta are talking.*)

Practice Idea: Speaking

Have students practice the conversation in groups of three.

EXERCISE 5 ≡★

ANSWERS: 1. Who is using a microphone? **2.** How many customers are making a deposit? **3.** Which customers are getting help now? OR Who is getting help now? **4.** What is happening at the bank?

5. How many customers are using the drive-through? **6.** What's taking the man's deposit to the tellers?

10-15 mins

1. Say: *In this exercise, you're going to make questions. You will use a question word as the subject.* Have students read the direction line. Go over the example in the book.

2. Have students complete Exercise 5 individually. Remind them to review grammar chart **8.7** on page 193 if necessary. Check the answers as a class.

Editing Advice

5-10 mins

Have students close their books. Write the example sentences without editing marks or corrections on the board. For example:

1. *He working at that store.*
2. *Marta and Amy are wait at the drive-through.*

Ask students to correct each sentence and provide a rule or explanation for each correction., e.g.: 1. He's working at that store. (Always use a form of *be* with the present continuous tense.) 2. Marta and Amy are waiting at the drive-through. (Don't forget to use the *-ing* form with present continuous verbs.) This activity can be done individually, in pairs, or as a class. After students have corrected each sentence, tell them to turn to page 194. Say: *Now compare your work with the Editing Advice in the book.*

Editing Quiz

ANSWERS: 1. you use; **2.** are we going; **3.** C; **4.** She's talking; **5.** C; **6.** C; **7.** he's asking; **8.** giving; **9.** C; **10.** I'm eating

5-10 mins

1. Tell students they are going to put the Editing Advice into practice. Have students read the direction line. Ask: *Do all the shaded words have mistakes?* (No) Go over the examples with the class. Then do #1 together.

2. Have students complete the rest of the quiz individually. Then have them compare their answers with a partner before checking the answers as a class. Elicit the relevant grammar point for each correction.

3. For the items students had difficulties with, have them go back and find the relevant grammar chart and review it. Monitor and give help as necessary.

Expansion

These expansion activities provide opportunities for students to interact with one another and further develop their speaking and writing skills. Encourage students to use grammar from this unit whenever possible.

LEARNER'S LOG

5-10 mins

1. Have students close their books. Ask: *What did you learn about post offices, banks, and drive-throughs in the U.S.? What else do you want to know?* Write students' ideas on the board. Discuss ways in which students can find out more about U.S. postal services, banks, and drive-through windows.

2. Have students open their books to complete the Learner's Log. Remind students to write three questions about post offices, banks, or drive-throughs in the U.S.

3. Have students compare logs in pairs.

WRITING ACTIVITIES

10-15 mins

1. Have students read the direction line. Go over the example. Elicit a few more ideas about the picture.

2. Have students complete the activity individually. Collect for assessment.

Practice Idea: Writing

Have students exchange papers with a partner. Ask students to help their partners edit their paragraph. Refer students to the Editing Advice on page 194.

OUTSIDE ACTIVITIES

1. Tell students to go to a post office in their city and bring a package to weigh. Have them ask how much it costs to send the package to their home country. (They don't have to send it.) If the post office has an automated postal center, tell students to use it to weigh the package and find the price. Have students share their experiences at the post office in groups.

2. Tell half the class to look for mailing supplies at the post office and to find out how much a small box or a large mailing envelope costs. Tell the other half to do the same at office supply stores. Have students compare prices in groups.

3. Tell students to go to a fast-food restaurant in their neighborhood and find out if it has a drive-through. Have them write some sentences about what is happening at the restaurant or drive-through. In class, ask volunteers to share their sentences with the class.

INTERNET ACTIVITIES

1. Tell students to go to the Web site of a bank in their area and find out how to open an online account.

2. Tell students to go to the U.S. Postal Service Web site (www.usps.gov) and find out how to buy stamps and how to send a package to their country.

Have students discuss their online research in groups. Then have volunteers tell the class how to open an online account, buy stamps online, or send a package home.

Unit 9

Unit Overview

1. Ask: *What's this unit about?* (making changes) *What big changes do people make?* Elicit examples and write them on the board (e.g., going to college, moving to a new place, getting married, having a baby, changing jobs).

2. Direct students' attention to the photos. Ask: *What's happening in these two pictures?* (A family is moving to a new house. A couple is looking at a new baby.)

3. Relate the topic to students' experience. Ask: *How many times have you moved? Do you have any children?* Ask students to share their experiences.

Presentation Ideas

The topic for this unit can be enhanced with the following items:

1. Mail-order catalogs or store catalogs with baby equipment and baby accessories
2. Change-of-address forms from the post office

Lesson 1 Overview

GRAMMAR

Point out or write on the board the lesson's objectives. (*affirmative statements with* be going to, *negative statements with* be going to, *uses of the future tense with* be going to, and *time expressions with* be going to) Say: *We use the future tense to talk about future events and to predict what will happen.* Write *to predict = to make a guess about something in the future* on the board. Say and write on the board these example sentences: *They're going to have a baby. I think they're going to have a boy.* Ask: *Which sentence is a prediction?* Ask volunteers to give additional examples, and write them on the board. Prompt by asking questions about topics such as moving, going to college, or other life changes.

CONTEXT

1. Ask: *What's this lesson about?* (baby needs) *How is your life going to change when you have a baby? What new things are you going to need?* Have students share their knowledge and experiences.

2. Direct students' attention to the picture of the resale shop for baby clothes and furniture on page 198. Ask: *What's in this store?* (clothes and furniture for babies) Review some of the new words in the illustration.

Getting Ready for a New Baby
READING

Have students look at the title of the reading and the picture on page 198. Say: *Shafia is going to have a baby. What do you think she, Halina, and Dorota are talking about?* Have students use the title and picture to make predictions about the reading.

BEFORE YOU READ

5-10 mins

1. Go over each question as a class. Have a volunteer read the questions or read them to the class yourself. Have students discuss the questions in pairs.

2. Ask a few volunteers to share their answers with the class.

Context Note

Baby showers are small parties for new mothers usually given by a friend or relative one or two months before the baby is born. Guests bring gifts, such as baby clothing, blankets, and diapers, often chosen from the new mother's gift registry list at a department store. In the past, only women attended showers, but today men sometimes come too.

 Reading ═★

CD 3
TR 06

10-15 mins

1. Have students read the dialogue silently. Then play the audio and have students read along silently.

2. Check students' basic comprehension. Ask questions such as: *When is the baby going to*

arrive? (in two months, in August) *What is Halina going to give Shafia?* (a crib) *Why isn't Shafia going to buy a lot of things?* (She's going to get a lot of gifts because she and Ali have a lot of relatives.)

Practice Ideas: Listening

1. To practice listening skills, have students listen to the audio before opening their books. Ask a few comprehension questions, such as: *How long is Shafia's mother going to stay with them?* (one month) *Is this her first grandchild?* (yes) Repeat the audio if necessary. Then have students open their books and read along as they listen to the audio.

2. Alternatively, have students begin by listening to the audio as they read along.

Practice Idea: Speaking

Have students practice the conversation in groups of three. Ask volunteers to role-play all or part of the conversation in front of the class.

VOCABULARY IN CONTEXT

5-10 mins

1. Model the pronunciation of each new vocabulary item and have students repeat.

2. Make sure students understand the meaning of each vocabulary item. Review the examples in the book and create additional example sentences. Go over each new vocabulary item similarly, using visuals and realia when appropriate. When possible, point to pictures in the book that illustrate the new vocabulary items, such as *crib*, *high chair*, *stroller*, and *resale shop* on page 198.

3. Have students underline an example of each vocabulary item in the reading.

Practice Idea: Speaking

To check comprehension, have volunteers in pairs or groups act out selected vocabulary, such as *crib*, *stroller*, and *excited.*

Did You Know?

Point out the information to students. Ask students if they know the average age of first-time mothers in their country. Ask if they think the age is going up, going down, or staying the same.

 LISTENING ACTIVITY

CD 3
TR 07   **ANSWERS: 1.** False; **2.** True; **3.** True; **4.** False; **5.** True; **6.** False; **7.** True; **8.** True

5-10 mins

1. Say: *Listen to the sentences about the reading. Circle* true *or* false. Play the listening selection one time without pausing. Then play it through again, pausing and replaying as necessary.

2. Have students compare their answers, then play the audio again and check the answers as a class.

9.1 The Future Tense— Affirmative Statements ⭐

5-10 mins

1. Have students look at grammar chart **9.1** on page 201. Review word order for affirmative statements. Say: *Put* be going to *before the verb.* Point out that the verb after *be going to* is in the base form. Go over the examples. Write the following on the board, and have students unscramble the parts and make a correct statement:

    a stroller/is/She/buy/going to

2. Point out the Language Note. Model the relaxed pronunciation of *going to.*

Have students work in pairs to practice saying the sentences in the chart with relaxed pronunciation. Tell students that the relaxed pronunciation is only used when *going to* is followed by a verb, not by a noun. Write the following sentences on the board:

I'm going to tell my mother.

They're going to the store.

She's going to have a baby.

We're going to the hospital.

Have students practice saying the sentences, using the relaxed pronunciation of *going to* where possible.

EXERCISE 1 ≡★

ANSWERS: 1. are going to see; **2.** 's going to help; **3.** 's going to arrive; **4.** are going to bring; **5.** are going to take; **6.** 's going to need; **7.** are going to be; **8.** 's going to be; **9.** 's going to visit; **10.** are going to enjoy

🕐 5-10 mins

1. Have students read the direction line. Go over the example in the book. Remind students to use contractions when possible.

2. Have students complete Exercise 1 individually. Remind them to review grammar chart **9.1** on page 201 if necessary. Check the answers as a class.

9.2 The Future Tense— Negative Statements ≡★

🕐 5-10 mins

1. Have students look at grammar chart **9.2** on page 202. Say: *To make negative statements, write* not *after the verb* be.

2. Say: *We use contractions with negative forms of* be. Go over the examples. Ask: *What are the two ways to make contractions with negative forms of* be? (subject + be, be + not). Review the examples in the book. Then write additional examples on the board (e.g., *My friend's not going to go to school tomorrow. My friend isn't going to go to school tomorrow.*).

Have students identify the type of contraction in each example. Remind students not to use contractions with plural nouns and *are*.

Have students change the sentences in Exercise 1 to negative statements. Ask students to use both forms of contractions where possible. (e.g., for #2: *Shafia's mother's not going to help her with the baby./ Shafia's mother isn't going to help her with the baby.*)

EXERCISE 2 ≡★

ANSWERS: 1. aren't going to get; **2.** isn't going to stay OR 's not going to stay; **3.** isn't going to need OR 's not going to need; **4.** aren't going to shop; **5.** isn't going to be OR 's not going to be; **6.** aren't going to give; **7.** isn't going to be OR 's not going to be; **8.** aren't going to buy; **9.** isn't going to take OR 's not going to take

🕐 5-10 mins

1. Have students read the direction line. Review the example in the book.

2. Have students complete Exercise 2 individually. Remind them to review grammar chart **9.2** on page 202 if necessary. Then have students compare their answers in pairs. Check the answers as a class.

9.3 The Future Tense— Uses ≡★

🕐 5-10 mins

1. Have students look at grammar chart **9.3** on page 203. Say the title of the chart. Then say and write on the board:

Two Uses:

1. *future plans*

2. *predictions*

Review the examples in the chart. Give students the following situations and have them make three predictions with *be going to* for each situation:

She is late today.

He's at the bank now.

2. Point out the Language Note. Say: *Going to go is often shortened to just going*. Go over the example and provide additional examples (e.g., *I'm going to go to Boston next week. I'm going to Boston next week.*). Ask volunteers for additional examples.

> ### Practice Idea: Speaking
>
> Have students work in pairs to talk about future plans. Say and write the following model sentence on the board: *I'm going to a baby shower next week.*

EXERCISE 3

ANSWERS: 1. isn't going to buy OR 's not going to buy; **2.** 's going to be; **3.** 's going to give; **4.** 's going to need; **5.** aren't going (to go); **6.** isn't going to arrive OR 's not going to arrive; **7.** 's going to be; **8.** are going to get; **9.** are going to be; **10.** 's going to help; **11.** 's not going to spend OR isn't going to spend

10-15 mins

1. Have students read the direction line. Go over the examples. Remind students to use contractions whenever possible.

2. Have students complete Exercise 3 individually. Remind them to review grammar chart **9.3** on page 203 if necessary. Check the answers as a class.

9.4 Time Expressions

5-10 mins

1. Have students look at grammar chart **9.4** on page 204. Say: *Time expressions can go at the beginning or end of the sentence.* Point out the prepositions in the time expressions. (*in, on, for, at*) Go over the examples and explanations.

2. Say the following rules. Ask the class to name the appropriate time expressions:

   with a date (on)

   with names of months (in)

   with a specific amount of time (for)

   for the day after today (tomorrow)

with names of days (on/this)

with a specific time in the future (at)

3. Write the answers on the board. Add *soon* and *for a while*. Ask volunteers to make sentences with the expressions.

> ### Practice Idea: Writing
>
> Have students write five sentences that are true for them using the time expressions in the chart.

EXERCISE 4

ANSWERS: 1. on; **2.** for; **3.** at; **4.** in; **5.** for; **6.** on; **7.** in

5-10 mins

1. Have students read the direction line. Review the example.

2. Have students complete Exercise 4 individually. Remind them to review grammar chart **9.4** on page 204 if necessary. Check the answers as a class.

EXERCISE 5

Answers will vary.

10-15 mins

1. Have students read the direction line. Say: *Now you're going to make predictions about your future.* Go over the example. Model #1 yourself. Then have a student model #1.

2. Have students complete Exercise 5 individually. Remind them to review grammar chart **9.4** on page 204 if necessary. Then have students compare their answers in pairs. Monitor pair work. Give help as needed. Have volunteers share their answers with the class.

> ### Practice Ideas: Speaking
>
> 1. Have students make predictions about a friend or family member's life in ten years.
>
> 2. Survey the class. What are students' predictions for their future? Write the results on the board.

EXERCISE 6

ANSWERS: Answers will vary. Possible answers:
1. Ali's going to be out of town on Friday, June 26. He isn't going to be out of town this week. **2.** Shafia's going to take an exercise class in two weeks. Shafia's going to take an exercise class on Wednesday, June 17. **3.** Dorota's going to come to Shafia's house in three weeks. She's not going to visit her this weekend. **4.** Shafia's going to see the doctor on June 9 at 3 P.M. She isn't going to see the doctor every Tuesday. **5.** Ali's going to get ready for his trip at the end of this month. He isn't going to get ready for his trip this weekend. **6.** Shafia, Halina, and Dorota are going (to go) to the resale shop this Thursday at 1 P.M. They're not going (to go) to the resale shop next Thursday. **7.** Shafia and Ali are going to have dinner with Halina and Peter on Friday the 19th at 7 P.M. They're not going to have dinner with them this week. **8.** Shafia and Ali are going to visit Ali's parents next Friday. They're not going to visit Ali's parents this Friday. **9.** Shafia's going to have free time on Wednesday and Friday this week. She's not going to have much free time the last week in June.

10-15 mins

1. Have students read the direction line. Go over the example and point out the information on the calendar page. Do #1 as a class, write it on the board.

2. Have students complete the rest of Exercise 6 individually. Remind them to review grammar chart **9.4** on page 204 if necessary. Then have students compare their answers in pairs. Monitor pair work. Give help as needed. Check the answers as a class.

EXERCISE 7

CD 3
TR 08

ANSWERS: Conversation A: **1.** aren't going to leave OR 're not going to leave; **2.** 's going to move; **3.** 's going to help; **4.** 're going to paint; **5.** 's not going to be OR isn't going to be. Conversation B: **1.** aren't going to choose; **2.** 're going to ask; **3.** 's not going to have OR isn't going to have; **4.** 're going to give; **5.** 're going to wait

10-15 mins

1. Tell students they are going to complete two conversations. Point out the picture of Halina and Shafia. Ask: *What do you think they're talking about?* (the baby's room)

Have students read the direction line. Have a volunteer complete #1 in Conversation A.

2. Have students complete both conversations in Exercise 7 individually. Remind them to review grammar chart **9.1** on page 201 and **9.2** on page 202 if necessary. Then have students compare their answers in pairs. Play the audio and check the answers as a class.

Practice Ideas: Speaking

1. Have students rewrite the first dialogue as a conversation about a different situation, such as making room for a guest, a boarder, or a new pet.

2. Have students practice the conversations in pairs. Ask volunteers to role-play the conversations in front of the class.

Lesson 2 Overview

GRAMMAR

1. Say: *In Lesson 1, we studied the future tense and time expressions with* be going to. Write the objectives for Lesson 2 on the board: Yes/No *Questions with* Be Going To, *Information Questions with* Be Going To, *Questions with* How Long *and* Be Going To, *and Subject Questions with* Be Going To.

2. Write this statement on the board: *Hui is going to be a doctor.* As a class, make each type of question for the statement. (e.g., Is he going to be a doctor? Why is he going to be a doctor? How long is he going to be in medical school? Who is going to be a doctor?)

CONTEXT

1. Take a quick survey of the class. Ask: *How many times do people usually move in their lifetime? I have moved* [number of times] *in the last ten years. It's a lot of work to move!*

2. Direct students' attention to the picture of Simon and Victor on page 209. Go over new vocabulary in the picture. Ask: *What are Victor and Simon doing?* (Victor is moving. Simon is helping him.) Point to the change-of-address card. Ask: *What do you write on this card?* (your old address and your new address)

Moving to a New Apartment
READING

Have students look at the title of the reading and the pictures on page 209. Ask: *What is the form for?* (to change your mailing address) *What are Victor and Simon doing?* (moving boxes into a truck) Have students use the title and pictures to make predictions about the reading.

BEFORE YOU READ

5-10 mins

1. Go over each question as a class. Have a volunteer read the questions or read them to the class yourself. Have students answer the questions in pairs.

2. Ask a few volunteers to share their answers with the class.

Context Note

Many Americans use professional movers who supply boxes, pack the contents of the house or apartment, and transport the belongings to the new address. Others rent trucks and pack their own belongings.

  Reading

CD 3
TR 09

10-15 mins

1. Have students look at the title of the reading and the picture on page 209. Say: *Victor is moving. He asks Simon lots of questions. What does he want to know? Skim the reading and find out.* (Is Simon going to be available to help? What should he do about his mail? What's going to happen with his phone? What should he do with the things he doesn't want?)

2. Have students read the dialogue silently. Then play the audio and have students read along silently.

3. Check students' basic comprehension. Ask questions, such as: *Who is moving?* (Victor) *When is he going to move?* (in two weeks) *Who is going to help him?* (Simon) *Where is Victor's new apartment going to be?* (in the same neighborhood) *Is he going to have the same phone number?* (yes, probably) *Does Victor have boxes?* (Yes, but he doesn't have enough.) *Where is he going to get more boxes?* (at some stores in the neighborhood)

Practice Ideas: Listening

1. To practice listening skills, have students listen to the audio before opening their books. Ask a few comprehension questions, such as: *What can Victor do with his old things?* (give them to charity) Repeat the audio if necessary. Then have students open their books and read along as they listen to the audio.

2. Alternatively, have students begin by listening to the audio as they read along.

Practice Idea: Speaking

Have students practice the conversation in groups. Ask volunteers to role-play all or part of the conversation in front of the class.

VOCABULARY IN CONTEXT

5-10 mins

1. Model the pronunciation of each new vocabulary item and have students repeat.

2. Make sure students understand the meaning of each vocabulary item. Review the examples in the book and create additional example sentences. For example, say: *move. We're going to move to a new classroom next semester.* Review each new vocabulary item similarly, using visuals and realia when appropriate. When possible, point to pictures in the book that illustrate the new vocabulary items, such as *truck* on page 209.

3. Have students underline an example of each vocabulary item in the reading.

Practice Idea: Speaking

To check comprehension, have volunteers in pairs or groups act out selected vocabulary, such as *move, mover, hire,* and *pack.*

Did You Know?

Point out the information to students. Tell students some reasons why Americans might be moving less often:

More people commute.

More people buy houses.

More husbands and wives have careers that make moving difficult.

  ## LISTENING ACTIVITY

CD 3
TR 10

ANSWERS: 1. False; **2.** True; **3.** True; **4.** False; **5.** True; **6.** False

1. Say: *Listen to the sentences about Victor and Simon's conversation. Circle* true *or* false. Play the listening selection one time without pausing. Then play it through again, pausing and replaying as necessary.

2. Have students compare their answers, then play the audio again and check the answers as a class.

9.5 The Future Tense— *Yes/No* Questions

1. Have students look at grammar chart **9.5** on page 211. Say: *To form* yes/no *questions with* be going to, *put the subject after* be *and before* going to. *The verb in the base form follows* going to. Go over the examples.

2. Say: *The short answer contains just the subject and* be. *Do not include the verb in the short answer.* Review the short answers.

3. Point out the Language Note. Write additional affirmative statements on the board and have students make questions (e.g., *He is going to pack his things. Is he going to pack his things in boxes?*).

> ### Practice Idea: Speaking
> Have students practice the questions and short answers in the chart with a partner.

EXERCISE 1

ANSWERS: 1. Is Victor going to hire a mover? No, he's not. OR No, he isn't. **2.** Is he going to buy some boxes? No, he isn't. OR No, he's not. **3.** Is his new apartment going to be in the same neighborhood? Yes, it is. **4.** Is he going to change his phone number? No, he isn't. OR No, he's not. **5.** Is it going to take a long time to get new phone service? No, it isn't. OR No, it's not. **6.** Is the post office going to send Victor's mail to his new address? Yes, it is. **7.** Is there going to be a fee to change phone service? Yes, there is. **8.** Is Victor going to move all his things to his new apartment? No, he isn't. OR No, he's not.

1. Have students read the direction line. Go over the example in the book.

2. Have students complete Exercise 1 individually. Remind students to review grammar chart **9.5** on page 211 if necessary. Check the answers as a class.

EXERCISE 2

ANSWERS: 1. Are you going to change your phone number too? **2.** Is he going to pay more than $50? **3.** Are they going to move to a house? **4.** Is Marta going to help too? **5.** Is Victor going to give some things to charity? **6.** Is he going to rent a new apartment in a different city? **7.** Is he going to get a change-of-address card (OR it) online?

1. Have students read the direction line. Go over the example in the book. Have two volunteers model #1.

2. Have students complete the rest of Exercise 2 individually. Remind students to review grammar chart **9.5** on page 211 if necessary. Then have students compare their answers. Check the answers as a class.

> ### Practice Idea: Speaking
> Have students practice the short dialogues in pairs.

9.6 The Future Tense—Information Questions

10-15 mins

1. Have students look at grammar chart **9.6** on page 213. Say: *Information questions begin with a question word followed by* be *plus the subject plus* going to *plus the verb in the base form.* Go over the examples.

2. Say: *The short answer does not include the subject or the verb. Compare:* They're going to get boxes next week./Next week. Go over the other short answers in the chart.

3. Have students close their books. Write the following phrases on the board:

   When he move to California

   Why Mi Son buy a new car

   How many there be

   Ask volunteers to come to the board and write complete questions using *be going to* and the phrases.

4. Point out the Language Notes. Go over the examples.

Practice Idea: Writing

Have students write out the long answer for each question.

EXERCISE 3

ANSWERS: 1. When are you going to rent a truck? **2.** Why is Victor (OR he) going to change his phone service? **3.** What kind of problems are there going to be? **4.** How are Victor's (OR his) friends (OR they) going to help him? **5.** How many boxes am I going to need? **6.** How much is the truck (OR it) going to cost? **7.** Which items are you going to give (to charity)? **8.** Where are we (OR you) going to get some boxes (OR them)?

10-15 mins

1. Have students read the direction line. Go over the example in the book. Have a volunteer do #1.

2. Have students complete the rest of Exercise 3 individually. Remind them to review grammar chart **9.6** on page 213 if necessary. Check the answers as a class.

Practice Idea: Speaking

Have students practice asking and answering the questions from Exercise 3 with a partner.

EXERCISE 4

ANSWERS: 1. What are Victor and Lisa going to rent? **2.** How much is the fee going to be for the new phone service? **3.** Why are they going to move? **4.** When is Simon going to help Victor? **5.** Where is Victor going to get boxes? **6.** What kind of apartment are Victor and Lisa going to rent? **7.** How many boxes are Victor and Lisa going to pack? **8.** What is Victor going to do with his old items? **9.** When is the phone company going to change your service? **10.** Why are you going to have the same phone number?

10-15 mins

1. Have students read the direction line. Go over the example in the book. Have a volunteer do #1.

2. Have students complete the rest of Exercise 4 individually. Remind them to review grammar chart **9.6** on page 213 if necessary. Then have students compare their answers with a partner. Check the answers as a class.

Practice Ideas: Speaking

1. Have students practice asking and answering the questions with another partner.

2. Have students take turns making up short answers and questions. Ask a student to make up an answer and have the class make up the question for the answer.

9.7 The Future Tense—Questions with *How Long*

5-10 mins

Have students look at grammar chart **9.7** on page 216. Say: *We use* how long *to ask about specific amounts of time. When we answer with a specific time, we use* until *and* for. Until *means up to or before a particular time.* Review the examples and the explanations. Have students give additional example questions and answers. Prompt by writing on the board topics, such as *be in the U.S., study at this school* and *be at work today*. Ask two volunteers to make questions and answers.

EXERCISE 5

ANSWERS: Student responses will vary. Correct questions: 1. How long is our class going to work on this exercise? **2.** How long are we going to use this book? **3.** How long are you going to stay at school today? **4.** How long is this school going to be open today? **5.** How long are you going to be a student? **6.** How long are you going to stay in the U.S.?

10-15 mins

1. Have students read the direction line. Say: *Now you're going to ask and answer questions with a partner about how long you're going to do something.* Go over the example in the book. Have volunteers model the example.

2. Have students first write only the questions to Exercise 5 individually. Then have them ask their partner the questions and write down the answers. Remind them to review grammar chart **9.7** on page 216 if necessary. Monitor pair work. Give help as needed. Have volunteers share questions and answers.

Practice Idea: Writing

Have students write three more questions to ask their partner.

9.8 The Future Tense— Subject Questions ≡★

5-10 mins

1. Have students look at grammar chart **9.8** on page 217. Ask: *What is the subject of these questions?* (a question word) Say: *To form the question, write the question word or phrase plus the verb* be *plus* going to *plus the verb in the base form.* Write on the board:

   question word(s) + be + going to + *verb (base form)* + *complement*

   Review the examples and the short answers.

2. Have students write a question using the formula on the board. Then have several students share their questions with the class.

EXERCISE 6

ANSWERS: 1. What is (OR What's) going to change? **2.** How many people are going to move this year? **3.** Which services are going to be expensive? **4.** Who is (OR Who's) going to give you (OR me) some boxes? **5.** What is (OR What's) going to happen on Thursday? **6.** Which mover is going to help you? **7.** How many apartments are going to be available?

5-10 mins

1. Have students read the direction line. Go over the example.

2. Have students complete Exercise 6 individually. Remind them to review grammar chart **9.8** on page 217 if necessary. Check the answers with the class.

Practice Idea: Speaking

Have students practice saying the statements and asking the questions in pairs.

◀)) **EXERCISE 7**
CD 3
TR 11

ANSWERS: 1. What kind of truck are you going to need; **2.** how many rooms are you going to move; **3.** Is it going to have room for my sofa; **4.** When are you going to move; **5.** Is it going to be; **6.** Are there going to be; **7.** Is one day going to be; **8.** How are you going to pay

10-15 mins

1. Tell students they are going to complete Victor's conversation. Have students read the direction line. Ask: *Who is Victor speaking to?* (a clerk at the truck rental company) *What are they talking about?* (Victor wants to rent a truck.) Go over the example. If necessary, clarify to students that they are going to make questions with the words in parentheses.

2. Have students complete Exercise 7 individually. Remind them to review the grammar charts in Lesson 2 if necessary. Then have students compare their answers with a partner. Play the audio and check the answers as a class.

Practice Idea: Speaking

Have students practice the conversation in pairs. Have volunteers role-play the conversation in front of the class.

EXERCISE 8

ANSWERS: 1. I'm going to get; **2.** aren't going to move; **3.** Are you going to be; **4.** are going to help; **5.** We're going to meet; **6.** I'm going to invite

1. Direct student's attention to the photo on page 219. Ask: *What do you see? What's happening?* (Someone is moving.) Have students read the direction line. Have a volunteer complete #1.

2. Have students complete the rest of Exercise 8 individually. Remind them to review the grammar charts in Unit 9 if necessary. Then have students compare their answers in pairs. Check the answers as a class.

Practice Idea: Speaking

Have students practice the conversation in pairs. Have volunteers role-play the conversation in front of the class.

Editing Advice

Have students close their books. Write the example sentences without editing marks or corrections on the board. For example:

1. *We going to shop at a resale shop.*
2. *Where they are going to work?*

Ask students to correct each sentence and provide a rule or explanation for each correction, e.g.: 1. We're going to shop at a resale shop. (Use a form of *be* with *going to*.) 2. Where are they going to work? (Use the correct word order in questions.) This activity can be done individually, in pairs, or as a class. After students have corrected each sentence, tell them to turn to page 220. Say: *Now compare your work with the Editing Advice in the book.*

Editing Quiz

ANSWERS: 1. are you going to have; **2.** is it going to be; **3.** The party's going to be; **4.** C; **5.** Who's going to be; **6.** C; **7.** C; **8.** we're going; **9.** is the party going to start; **10.** At; **11.** C

1. Tell students they are going to put the Editing Advice into practice. Have students read the direction line. Ask: *Do all the shaded words have mistakes?* (no) Go over the examples with the class. Then do #1 together.

2. Have students complete the rest of the quiz individually. Then have them compare their answers with a partner before checking the answers as a class. Elicit the relevant grammar point for each correction.

3. For the items students had difficulties with, have them go back and find the relevant grammar chart and review it. Monitor and give help as necessary.

Expansion

These expansion activities provide opportunities for students to interact with one another and further develop their speaking and writing skills. Encourage students to use grammar from this unit whenever possible.

LEARNER'S LOG

1. Have students close their books. Ask: *What did you learn about resale shops, getting ready for a baby, moving, and renting a truck? What else do you want to know?* Write students' ideas on the board. Discuss ways in which students can find out more about these topics.

2. Have students open their books to complete the Learner's Log. Remind students to write two questions they still have about each of the four topics.

3. Have students compare logs in pairs.

WRITING ACTIVITY

Have students look at the picture and elicit what is happening and what is going to happen. Write some of the verbs and vocabulary on the board. Then have students read the direction line and the three example sentences. Have students help you write a fourth sentence. Have students complete the activity individually. Collect for assessment.

Practice Idea: Writing

Have students exchange papers with a partner. Ask students to help their partners edit their paragraph. Refer students to the Editing Advice on page 220.

OUTSIDE ACTIVITIES

1. Tell students to call a truck rental company in their city and find out how much it costs to rent a 15-foot truck for the following Saturday.

2. Tell students to find a resale or thrift shop in their neighborhood, visit the shop, and tell the class about their experience.

Have students report their information to the class. Ask volunteers to explain how to rent a truck and how to get the best buy at a resale store.

INTERNET ACTIVITIES

1. Tell students to use a search engine on the Internet and type in *moving tips* to find some advice about moving. Have them write three sentences to share with the class. Have students discuss the moving tips they found online in groups. Then ask groups to share with the class some of the best tips.

2. Tell students to use a search engine on the Internet and type in *baby names* or *names*. Have them find an interesting name (or their own name) and read about its origin. Have them answer these questions: What does it mean? Where does it come from? Have them tell the class about the name. Discuss names with the class. Ask volunteers to discuss the names they liked or didn't like and why.

Unit 10

Unit Overview

1. Say: *In Unit 9, we talked about making big changes. Now, we're going to talk about making big choices.* Activate students' knowledge. Ask: *What big choices do people make?*

2. Direct students' attention to the photos. Ask: *What are the choices in these photos?* (choosing a car, choosing what color to paint a house/room)

Presentation Ideas

The topic for this unit can be enhanced with the following items:

1. College catalogs

2. Car magazines or other magazines with car ratings

Lesson 1 Overview

GRAMMAR

Ask: *What is comparing?* (telling how things are alike and different) Say: *In Lesson 1, we are going to study forms of adjectives called* comparatives, *such as* nicer, older, better, *and* smaller. *How are these adjectives the same?* (They end in -er.) Point to two books and say: *This book is <u>bigger</u> than that book.* Write the sentence on the board. Elicit more comparative sentences from volunteers. Say: *We are also going to study comparisons with nouns using* more, less, fewer, *and* than, *as well as the comparative form after verbs.*

CONTEXT

1. Ask: *What is higher education?* (education after high school; universities and colleges) Direct students' attention to the picture of Shafia at the computer. Ask: *What is Shafia looking at?* (information about different colleges) *Why is Shafia looking at college brochures?* (She's comparing colleges. She's going to choose a college.)

2. Ask: *When you choose a college, what do you need to know about the college?* Have students share their knowledge and experiences.

Community Colleges and Universities READING

Have students skim the reading and look at the picture on page 224. Ask: *What is the reading about?* (community colleges and universities) *What are community colleges being compared to?* (four-year colleges) Have students use the title and picture to make predictions about the reading.

BEFORE YOU READ

5-10 mins

1. Go over each question as a class. Have a volunteer read the questions or read them to the class yourself. Have students discuss the questions in pairs.

2. Ask a few volunteers to share their answers with the class.

Reading =★

CD 3 TR 12

1. Have students read the text silently. Then play the audio and have students read along silently.

10-15 mins

2. Check students' basic comprehension. Ask questions such as: *Are community colleges four-year colleges?* (No. They're two-year colleges.) *On average, how much does it cost to go to a community college?* (over $2,000 a year) *Do community colleges have large or small classes?* (small) *Why are community college students busier?* (Students usually have a full- or part-time job and a family.)

Practice Ideas: Listening

1. To practice listening skills, have students listen to the audio before opening their books. Ask a few comprehension questions, such as: *Which has more night and weekend classes—a community college or a four-year college?* (a community college) Repeat the audio if necessary. Then have students open their books and read along as they listen to the audio.

2. Alternatively, have students begin by listening to the audio as they read along.

VOCABULARY IN CONTEXT

5-10 mins

1. Model the pronunciation of each new vocabulary item and have students repeat.

2. Make sure students understand the meaning of each vocabulary item. Review the examples in the book and create additional example sentences. For example, say: *bachelor's degree. I have a bachelor's degree in Teaching English as a Second Language. I studied at [college name] for four years.* Go over each new vocabulary item similarly, using visuals and realia when appropriate. For example, for *tuition* print on the board: *Courses: $500.00 per semester hour.* Elicit from students the tuition for your school. For *campus* show students a map of the campus at your institution. When possible, point to pictures in the book that illustrate the new vocabulary, such as *certificate* on page 225.

3. Have students underline an example of each vocabulary item in the reading.

LISTENING ACTIVITY

CD 3
TR 13

ANSWERS: 1. True; **2.** False; **3.** True; **4.** True; **5.** False; **6.** True

5-10 mins

1. Say: *Listen to the sentences about the reading on community colleges. Circle* true *or* false. Play the listening selection one time without pausing. Then play it through again, pausing and replaying as necessary.

2. Have students compare their answers in pairs, then play the audio again and check the answers as a class.

10.1 Comparative Forms of Adjectives ≡★

10-15 mins

1. Have students look at grammar chart **10.1** on page 226. Say: *We compare two things or two people. We usually compare using one of two forms.* Activate students' knowledge. Ask: *What are the two forms?* (add *-er* or add *more*)

2. Go over the adjectives, comparative forms, examples and explanations in the chart. Answer any questions students may have.

3. Write these sentences on the board. Elicit from students the correct explanation from the chart for each sentence:

   I'm busier than Joe.

   Sheila is more beautiful than Maria.

   My house is newer than your house.

   My English is better than my French.

   My mother is more cautious than my father.

4. Point out the Language Notes. For #1, ask: *What two things are being compared?* (the college and the university). For #2, explain that *much* means *a lot.* For #3, write this sentence on the board: *She is richer than I am, but I am happier _____.* Ask the class to fill in the blank with both possibilities. (than she is/than her) Then have them tell you which is more formal (than she is)

10.2 Spelling of the *-er* Form ≡★

5-10 mins

1. Have students cover up grammar chart **10.2** on page 227. Write the following adjectives on the board:

   1. *old/older; cheap/cheaper*
   2. *big/bigger; hot/hotter*
   3. *nice/nicer; late/later*
   4. *busy/busier; easy/easier*

2. Say: *Here are the spelling rules for comparatives.* Then read out the spelling rules in random order and ask students to match the adjectives to the rules.

3. Have students look at grammar chart **10.2** on page 227. Go over the adjectives and the explanations.

Practice Idea: Speaking

Have students go back to the reading on page 225. Have students find the comparative adjectives and say what pattern each comparative form follows.

EXERCISE 1

ANSWERS: 1. more convenient; 2. bigger; 3. finer;
4. lazier; 5. harder; 6. funnier; 7. more expensive;
8. friendlier OR more friendly; 9. more interesting;
10. quieter OR more quiet; 11. hotter; 12. better;
13. kinder; 14. madder; 15. later; 16. worse;
17. cheaper; 18. simpler OR more simple;
19. longer; 20. more beautiful

 5-10 mins

1. Have students read the direction line. Go over the examples in the Student Book.
2. Have students complete Exercise 1 individually. Remind them to review grammar charts **10.1** on page 226 and **10.2** on page 227 if necessary. Check the answers as a class.

EXERCISE 2

ANSWERS: 1. more expensive than; 2. smaller than; 3. busier than; 4. more convenient than OR better than; 5. bigger than; 6. older than; 7. better

10-15 mins

1. Tell students they are going to compare a community college and a university. Have students read through the information on the colleges in the chart. You might pre-teach terms that may be unfamiliar to students, such as *child-care center* and *credit hour*. Then have students read the direction line. Go over the example in the Student Book.
2. Have students complete Exercise 2 individually. Remind them to review grammar charts **10.1** on page 226 and **10.2** on page 227 if necessary. Then have students compare their answers in pairs. Check the answers as a class.

Practice Idea: Speaking

Have students give explanations for each comparison (e.g., Wilson College is more convenient because they have night and weekend classes.).

EXERCISE 3

CD 3 TR 14

ANSWERS: Conversation 1: 1. closer; 2. older; 3. younger than. Conversation 2: 1. more convenient; 2. busier than. Conversation 3: 1. more expensive than; 2. better than; 3. cheaper;

4. slower; 5. more convenient. Conversation 4: 1. harder than; 2. worse than; 3. more interesting than

10-15 mins

1. Tell students they are going to complete short conversations that compare two schools. Have students read the direction line. Go over the example in the Student Book.
2. Have students complete Exercise 3 individually. Remind them to review grammar charts **10.1** on page 226 and **10.2** on page 227 if necessary. Then have students compare their answers in pairs. Check the answers as a class.

Practice Idea: Speaking

Have students practice the conversations in pairs. Ask volunteers to role-play the conversation in front of the class.

Practice Idea: Speaking

In pairs, have students write similar short dialogues, comparing two schools they know, including courses of study, teachers, types of students, and location. Have volunteers role-play their dialogue for the class.

EXERCISE 4
Answers will vary.

5-10 mins

1. Say: *Now you're going to compare you and another person.* Have students read the direction line. Go over the example in the Student Book. Have a volunteer model the example. Go over the adjectives in the exercise, having students explain their meanings.
2. Have students complete Exercise 4 individually. Remind them to review grammar charts **10.1** on page 226 and **10.2** on page 227 if necessary. Then have students compare their answers in pairs. Check the answers as a class.

10.3 Comparisons with Nouns and Verbs

 5-10 mins

1. Have students look at grammar chart **10.3** on page 231. Go over the examples and explanations.

2. For comparisons with nouns, explain that *more* can be used before both plural count and noncount nouns. Point out that *less* is only used with noncount nouns and *fewer* with plural count nouns. Write a mixed list of plural count and noncount nouns on the board, e.g., *people, water, books, trains, rice, cars.* Then ask students whether *less* or *fewer* is correct with each noun. For comparisons with verbs, stress the location of the comparative form after verbs. Note that these comparatives are adverbs.

EXERCISE 5
Answers will vary.

10-15 mins

1. Say: *Now you're going to compare you and your partner.* Have students read the direction line. Go over the example in the Student Book. Have volunteers model the example.

2. Have students complete Exercise 5 in pairs. Remind them to review grammar chart **10.3** on page 231 if necessary. Monitor pair work. Give help as needed.

EXERCISE 6
ANSWERS: 1. less; **2.** more night classes than; **3.** fewer books; **4.** more campuses than; **5.** fewer students; **6.** more students; **7.** fewer married students than

10-15 mins

1. Have students look at the pictures and read through the information on the colleges in the chart. Then have students read the direction line. Go over the example in the Student Book.

2. Have students complete Exercise 6 individually. Remind them to review grammar chart **10.3** on page 231 if necessary. Then have students compare their answers in pairs. Monitor pair work. Give help as needed.

EXERCISE 7
ANSWERS: Answers will vary. Possible answers: 1. more; **2.** less; **3.** harder than OR more difficult than; **4.** more; **5.** bigger than; **6.** older than

10-15 mins

1. Have students read the direction line. Go over the example in the Student Book. Say: *In this exercise, you can fill in the blanks with* more, less, *and comparative forms of adjectives. Include* than *when necessary.*

2. Have students complete Exercise 7 individually. Remind them to review grammar chart **10.3** on page 231 if necessary. Check the answers as a class.

Lesson 2 Overview

GRAMMAR

Say: *In Lesson 1, we learned how to compare two things. Now we're going to learn to compare three or more things. We are going to study the superlative forms of adjectives, the spelling of the -est form, and superlatives with nouns and verbs.* Write on the board:

Superlatives

Then write the following statement on the board:

Mt. Everest is the <u>highest</u> mountain in the world.

Elicit more examples from volunteers.

CONTEXT

1. Ask: *What are we going to learn about in this lesson?* (buying a car) Say: *It's easy to buy the cheapest car, but it's important to buy a good car. There are many things to think about: mileage, economy, safety.* Ask: *How do you choose a car? What do you think about?* Have students share their ideas.

2. Direct students' attention to the picture of Simon and Victor on page 234. Ask: *What kind of Web site are Victor and Simon looking at?* (They're looking at a Web site about cars.)

Choosing a Used Car READING

Direct students' attention to the title of the reading on page 234. Ask the following questions and have students scan the reading for the answers: *Who is buying a used car?* (Victor) *What does the price of a used car depend on?* (the condition of the car, mileage, and extras) Ask: *What do you think Victor will ask Simon? What will Simon say?* Have students make predictions about the reading.

BEFORE YOU READ

5-10 mins

1. Go over each question as a class. Have a volunteer read the questions or read them to the class yourself. Have students answer the questions in pairs.

2. Ask a few volunteers to share their answers with the class.

Context Note

Consumer Reports magazine compares many used and new cars in a special list every year. The magazine compares price, mileage, performance, and much more.

 Reading ━★

CD 3
TR 15

10-15 mins

1. Have students read the dialogue silently. Then play the audio and have students read along silently.

2. Check students' basic comprehension. Ask questions such as: *What costs $6,000?* (the car Victor wants to buy) *What is the "blue book"?* (a book that gives information about cars) *What kind of information does the blue book have?* (prices and other information on new and used cars) *Why does Simon tell Victor to take the car to a mechanic?* (so the mechanic can find out if it's in good condition) *What else does Simon think Victor should consider before buying the car?* (fuel economy)

Practice Idea: Listening

To practice listening skills, have students listen to the audio before opening their books. Ask a few comprehension questions, such as: *How many miles per gallon does Victor's coworker's car get?* (19 miles per gallon) Repeat the audio if necessary. Then have students open their books and read along as they listen to the audio.

Practice Idea: Speaking

Have students practice the conversation in pairs. Ask volunteers to role-play all or part of the conversation in front of the class.

VOCABULARY IN CONTEXT

5-10 mins

1. Model the pronunciation of each new vocabulary item and have students repeat.

2. Make sure students understand the meaning of each vocabulary item. Review the examples in the book and create additional example sentences. For example, say: *coworker. [Name of another English teacher] is my coworker. [He/She] teaches here too.* Go over each new vocabulary item similarly, using visuals and realia when appropriate. For example,

for *consider* mime the action by tilting your head to one side and looking thoughtful. For *make a decision* act out making a decision. Put books on your desk, and act out choosing one. For *repair* give examples of things that need repairing (e.g., *The car won't start; the window is broken.*).

3. Have students underline an example of each vocabulary item in the reading.

Practice Idea: Speaking

To check comprehension, have volunteers in pairs or groups act out selected vocabulary, such as *consider*, *mechanic*, and *decision*.

Did You Know?

Point out the information to students. Explain to students that the price the car dealership advertises is called the *asking price* or the *sticker price*.

LISTENING ACTIVITY

CD 3
TR 16

ANSWERS: 1. True; **2.** True; **3.** False; **4.** False; **5.** False; **6.** True; **7.** True

1. Have students look at the photo on page 236. Ask: *What do they sell here?* (cars) Say: *Listen to the sentences about the conversation. Circle* true *or* false. Play the listening selection one time without pausing. Then play it through again, pausing and replaying as necessary.

2. Have students compare their answers in pairs, then play the audio again and check the answers as a class.

10.4 Superlative Forms of Adjectives ≡★

10-15 mins

1. Have students look at grammar chart **10.4** on page 237. Say: *Superlatives name the number-one item in a group. We usually make superlatives in two ways.* Activate students' knowledge. Ask: *What are the two ways?* (Add *-est* or *the most.*) Review the forms, examples, and explanations in the chart.

---

2. Write these sentences on the board. Elicit from students the correct explanation for each sentence from the chart:

   I think Will Ferrell is the funniest comedian.

   To me, math is the most interesting subject.

   Jennie is the smartest student in the class.

   This is the worst storm in 20 years.

   He is the most careful worker in the company.

3. Go over the Language Notes. Review the rules and example sentences. For Note 1, explain that a prepositional phrase after a superlative often identifies the group. Give an additional example: *My mother is the best mother <u>in the world</u>.* Ask: *What is the group?* (all the mothers in the world) For Note 2, explain that *one of the* is used to describe one of the items in a group of items that are all described by the following superlative. Give additional examples (e.g., *This show is one of the worst shows on TV. That is one of the best songs ever written.*).

Practice Idea: Writing

Have students use the pictures on page 237 to write sentences comparing the three cars.

Practice Idea: Speaking

Have students go back to the reading on page 235. Ask them to circle all the superlatives and discuss which explanation in chart **10.4** on page 237 each form follows. Then ask several students to share their conclusions with the class.

10.5 Spelling of the *-est* Form ≡★

5-10 mins

1. Have students look at grammar chart **10.5** on page 238. Review the examples of simple and superlative adjectives and the explanations.

2. Check comprehension by asking students the superlative form of familiar and unfamiliar adjectives. Tell students they do not need to know what the words mean. Say the words as you write them on the board:

fast (fastest)

dry (driest)

handy (handiest)

sad (saddest)

young (youngest)

early (earliest)

weird (weirdest)

strange (strangest)

Elicit the answers from the class and write them on the board. Ask volunteers to identify the spelling rule for each word.

EXERCISE 1

ANSWERS: 1. the most convenient; **2.** the biggest; **3.** the finest; **4.** the laziest; **5.** the funniest; **6.** the most expensive; **7.** the friendliest OR the most friendly; **8.** the quietest OR the most quiet; **9.** the hottest; **10.** the best; **11.** the kindest; **12.** the maddest; **13.** the latest; **14.** the most helpful; **15.** the busiest; **16.** the commonest OR the most common

5-10 mins

1. Have students read the direction line. Have a volunteer do #1.

2. Have students complete the rest of Exercise 1 individually. Remind them to review grammar charts **10.4** on page 237 and **10.5** on page 238 if necessary. Check the answers as a class.

EXERCISE 2

ANSWERS: 1. the biggest; **2.** the oldest; **3.** the newest; **4.** the most expensive; **5.** the cheapest; **6.** the best; **7.** the worst

10-15 mins

1. Have students read the direction line. Have a volunteer create a superlative statement about the cars in the chart.

2. Have students complete Exercise 2 individually. Remind them to review grammar charts **10.4** on page 237 and **10.5** on page 238 if necessary. Then have students compare their answers in pairs. Check the answers as a class.

EXERCISE 3

ANSWERS: Part A: 1. the best; **2.** the closest; **3.** the most convenient; **4.** the best; **5.** the hardest; **6.** the best. **Part B: 1.** the earliest; **2.** the hardest; **3.** the best OR the fastest; **4.** the most expensive; **5.** the most economical; **6.** the slowest

10-15 mins

1. Have students read the direction line. Go over the example in the Student Book.

2. Have students complete Exercise 3 individually. Remind them to review grammar charts **10.4** on page 237 and **10.5** on page 238 if necessary. Then have students compare their answers in pairs. Check the possible answers as a class.

EXERCISE 4
Answers will vary.

10-15 mins

1. Say: *You're going to talk about your family members. Who's the most intelligent? Who's the most beautiful?* Have students read the direction line. Go over the example in the book. Have a volunteer model the example.

2. Have students complete the rest of Exercise 4 individually. Remind them to review grammar charts **10.4** on page 237 and **10.5** on page 238 if necessary. Then have students

compare their answers with a partner. Monitor pair work. Give help as needed. Have volunteers share their answers with the class.

10.6 Superlatives with Nouns and Verbs

 5-10 mins

1. Have students look at grammar chart **10.6** on page 241. Activate students' prior knowledge. Ask: *How do we use* more, less, *and* fewer *in comparative statements?* (They go before a noun; *less* is used with noncount nouns, *fewer* is used with count nouns.) Ask: *What are the superlatives we use with nouns and verbs? (the most, the least, the fewest)* Review the examples and explanations. Point out that the superlative form can also be used after verbs.

2. Have students give additional examples. Prompt by asking questions such as: *Who eats the most candy in your family? Who watches the least TV?*

Practice Idea: Writing

Have students create three more superlative statements about family members (e.g., *My sister [name] is the most athletic.*).

 EXERCISE 5
CD 3 TR 17

ANSWERS: 1. The cheapest; **2.** the most expensive; **3.** the most repairs; **4.** the most economical; **5.** the best OR the most; **6.** the most extras; **7.** best

 10-15 mins

1. Have students read the direction line. Go over the example in the Student Book.

2. Have students complete Exercise 5 individually. Remind them to review grammar chart **10.6** on page 241 if necessary. Then have students compare their answers with a partner. Play the audio and check the possible answers as a class.

Practice Idea: Speaking

Have students practice the conversation in pairs. Then have volunteers role-play the conversation in front of the class.

 EXERCISE 6

Answers will vary.

 10-15 mins

1. Say: *Now you're going to make superlative statements about the students in the class.* Have students read the direction line.

2. Have students complete Exercise 6 in groups of three if possible. Remind them to review grammar chart **10.6** on page 241 if necessary. Have each group share some of their answers with the class.

EXERCISE 7

ANSWERS: 1. more expensive than; **2.** the most expensive; **3.** more information than; **4.** the most economical; **5.** better than; **6.** cheaper than; **7.** the prettiest; the best; the fewest; **8.** more beautiful than; **9.** more convenient than

10-15 mins

1. Have students read the direction line. Say: *Remember, you're going to be completing sentences with both comparatives and superlatives.* Have a volunteer do #1.

2. Have students complete the rest of Exercise 7 individually. Remind them to review the grammar charts in this unit if necessary. Then check the answers as a class.

Editing Advice

10-15 mins

Have students close their books. Write the example sentences without editing marks or corrections on the board. For example:

1. *My new car is more better than my old car.*
2. *I want to buy the most cheapest car.*

Ask students to correct each sentence and provide a rule or explanation for each correction., e.g.: 1. My new car is better than my old car. (Don't use *-er* and *more* together.) 2. I want to by the cheapest car. (Don't use *-est* and *most* together.) This activity can be done individually, in pairs, or as a class. After students have corrected each sentence, tell them to turn to page 243. Say: *Now compare your work with the Editing Advice in the book.*

Editing Quiz

10-15 mins

1. Tell students they are going to put the Editing Advice into practice. Have students read the direction line. Ask: *Do all the shaded words have mistakes?* (no) Go over the examples with the class. Then do #1 together.

2. Have students complete the rest of the quiz individually. Then have them compare their answers with a partner before checking the answers as a class. Elicit the relevant grammar point for each correction.

3. For the items students had difficulties with, have them go back and find the relevant grammar chart and review it. Monitor and give help as necessary.

Expansion

These expansion activities provide opportunities for students to interact with one another and further develop their speaking and writing skills. Encourage students to use grammar from this unit whenever possible.

LEARNER'S LOG

10-15 mins

1. Have students close their books. Ask: *What did you learn about community colleges and four-year universities? What did you find out about comparing used cars? What else do you want to know?* Write students' ideas on the board. Discuss ways in which students can find out more about these topics.

2. Have students open their books to complete the Learner's Log. Remind students to write three questions about colleges or comparing used cars.

3. Have students compare logs in pairs.

WRITING ACTIVITIES

10-15 mins

1. Have students read the direction line and the example sentence. Have students make brief notes on three classes they are taking.

Then have students complete the activity individually. Collect for assessment.

2. Have students look at the pictures. Then elicit differences from students between the two classes. Write their ideas on the board. Then have students read the direction line and the example sentence. Have students help you write another on the board. Have students complete the activity individually. Collect for assessment.

Practice Idea: Writing

Have students exchange papers with a partner. Ask students to help their partners edit their paragraph. Refer students to the Editing Advice on page 243.

OUTSIDE ACTIVITY

Tell students to compare their family car to another car in their neighborhood, or compare the cars of two friends. Tell them to compare age, condition, price, comfort, and how much they like each car. In class, have students share their comparisons in groups.

INTERNET ACTIVITIES

1. Tell students to use a search engine on the Internet and type in *blue book* and *used car prices*. Have them find the prices of three used cars. In class, have students discuss the used cars they found online in groups: the names of the cars, the condition, and the prices. Then have groups share their information with the class.

2. Tell students to use a search engine on the Internet and type in *compare fuel economy* and find two cars they like. Have them tell the class about them. Compare students' information as a class. Make a chart on the board and write in car names and miles per gallon.

Unit 11

Unit Overview

1. Begin by directing students' attention to the photos. Ask: *What's happening in the photos?* (Someone's writing/filling out a job application. The man is interviewing the woman. He's smiling.)

2. Ask: *What are we going to talk about in this unit?* (getting a job) *How do you get a job? What do you do?* Have students share their knowledge and experiences.

Presentation Ideas

The topic for this unit can be enhanced with the following items:

1. Job application forms
2. Lists of typical interview questions

Lesson 1 Overview

GRAMMAR

1. Say: *In Lesson 1, we're going to learn the past tense of* be. Ask: *What kind of statements are we going to study?* (affirmative and negative) *What kind of expressions?* (time expressions in the past) *What kind of questions?* (yes/no, information, and subject) Write the lesson objectives on the board.

2. Write the following examples on the board:

    Why were you late?

    They weren't ready.

    last week

    Were you in class yesterday?

    She was late.

    Which bus were you on?

    Have students match each example with a grammar objective on page 248.

CONTEXT

Say: *In this lesson, we're going to talk about applying for jobs. I worked [in a bank] many years ago. The interview wasn't easy.*

Say: *Think about your job interviews. Were they easy? What were the questions?* Have students share their experiences.

Applying for a Job in a Store
READING

Have students look at the title of the reading and the photo on page 248 to make predictions about the reading. Say: *Halina is talking to Dorota on the phone. What are they talking about? Why was Halina at the store?* (They're talking about applying for a job at the store. Halina was at the store to apply for a job.)

BEFORE YOU READ

1. Go over each question as a class. Have a volunteer read the questions or read them to the class yourself. Have students discuss the questions in pairs.

    5-10 mins

2. Ask a few volunteers to share their answers with the class.

Context Note

Jobs in Retail   There are many different kinds of careers involved in selling goods to the public:

finance

human resources

information systems

inventory control

management

marketing

merchandising and buying

 Reading

CD 3
TR 18

1. Have students read the dialogue silently. Then play the audio and have students read along silently.

10-15 mins

2. Check students' basic comprehension. Ask questions such as: *What store was Halina at?* (Baker's Department Store) *Why were the people there not happy?* (There was a long line to apply for jobs.) *Why did Halina write Dorota's name on the application?* (Dorota was one

of her references.) *What were the application questions about?* (job history and education)

Practice Ideas: Listening

1. To practice listening skills, have students listen to the audio before opening their books. Ask a few comprehension questions, such as: *Were there interviews today?* (no) Repeat the audio if necessary. Then have students open their books and read along as they listen to the audio.

2. Alternatively, have students begin by listening to the audio as they read along.

Practice Idea: Speaking

Have students practice the conversation in pairs. Ask volunteers to role-play the conversation in front of the class.

VOCABULARY IN CONTEXT

5-10 mins

1. Model the pronunciation of each new vocabulary item and have students repeat.

2. Review each vocabulary item. Make sure students understand the examples in the book and create additional example sentences. For example, say: *apply for. My daughter is going to apply for a job as a waitress in a restaurant.* Go over each new vocabulary item similarly, using visuals and realia when appropriate. When possible, point to pictures in the book that illustrate the new vocabulary, such as *interview* on page 247.

3. Have students underline an example of each vocabulary item in the reading.

Practice Idea: Speaking

To check comprehension, have volunteers in pairs or groups act out selected vocabulary, such as *interview, employer,* and *employee.*

Did You Know?

Point out the information to students. Tell the class about different kinds of job interviews:

selection interview: the employer knows you're qualified but wants to find out if you would work well in the company

group interview: the employer interviews you and other candidates at once to separate leaders from followers

panel interview: several interviewers interview you at one time

 LISTENING ACTIVITY

CD 3
TR 19

ANSWERS: 1. False; **2.** True; **3.** False; **4.** False; **5.** True; **6.** False; **7.** True

1. Say: *Listen to the sentences about Dorota and Halina's conversation. Circle* true *or* false. Play the listening selection one time without pausing. Then play it through again, pausing and replaying as necessary.

2. Have students compare their answers, then play the audio again and check the answers as a class.

11.1 The Past Tense of *Be*—Affirmative Statements ≡★

5-10 mins

Have students look at grammar chart **11.1** on page 251. Go over the examples. Ask: *What form of* be *in the past do we use with* he *or* she? (was) Ask: *What form of* be *in the past do we use with* you, we *or* they? (were)

EXERCISE 1 ≡★

ANSWERS: 1. was; **2.** were; **3.** was; **4.** were; **5.** were; **6.** was; **7.** were; **8.** was

5-10 mins

1. Have students read the direction line. Go over the example in the book. Remind students that the answers are based on the conversation on page 249.

2. Have students complete Exercise 1 individually. Remind them to review grammar chart **11.1** on page 251 if necessary. Check the answers as a class.

11.2 The Past Tense of *Be*—Negative Statements

5-10 mins

1. Have students look at grammar chart **11.2** on page 252. Remind students that adding *not* to the verb negates the verb.

2. Point out the Language Notes. Ask: *What words are contracted in the examples?* (*be* + not)

Practice Idea: Speaking

Have students return to the reading on page 249. In pairs, ask students to review each use of *was* and *were* and underline the subject.

EXERCISE 2 ≡★

ANSWERS: 1. weren't; **2.** was; **3.** wasn't, was; **4.** weren't; **5.** were; **6.** wasn't; **7.** were; **8.** weren't; **9.** was

5-10 mins

1. Have students read the direction line. Go over the example in the book. Remind students that the answers are based on the conversation on page 249.

2. Have students complete Exercise 2 individually. Remind them to review grammar chart **11.2** on page 252 if necessary. Check the answers as a class.

11.3 Time Expressions in the Past ≡★

5-10 mins

Have students look at grammar chart **11.3** on page 253. Say: Ago, yesterday, *and* last *are expressions we use with the past.* Go over the examples and the explanations. Give additional examples (e.g., *It's October. My mother was in the hospital a month ago, in September. We didn't have class yesterday. I wasn't at work last month. I was on vacation.*).

Practice Idea: Writing

Have students write three additional sentences using the time expressions in the chart.

EXERCISE 3 ≡★
Answers will vary.

5-10 mins

1. Say: *You're going to make the following statements true for you.* Have students read the direction line. Go over the example in the book. Ask a volunteer to model the example.

2. Have students complete Exercise 3 individually. Remind them to review grammar charts **11.1** on page 251, **11.2** on page 252, and **11.3** on page 253 if necessary. Then have students compare their answers in pairs. Monitor pair work. Give help as needed. Have volunteers share their sentences with the class.

11.4 The Past Tense of *Be*—*Yes/No* Questions ≡★

5-10 mins

1. Have students look at grammar chart **11.4** on page 254. Say: *When making a* yes/no *question with the past tense of* be, *write* was *or* were *before the subject.* Go over the questions.

2. Say: *Short answers contain the subject and* was *or* were. *They don't contain the complement.* Go over the questions and short answers. Check students' comprehension. Point to various example answers and ask students to name the implied complement (e.g., For the first example, ask: *You were* what? *On time today.*).

Practice Idea: Speaking

Have students practice answering the questions in the chart with long answers.

EXERCISE 4

ANSWERS: 1. Were many people (OR they) at Baker's to apply for jobs? Yes, they were. **2.** Were there (any) questions about her family? No, there weren't. **3.** Was the job application (OR it) easy to fill out? Yes, it was. **4.** Was Halina (OR she) surprised by some of the questions? Yes, she was. **5.** Were many people (OR they) in line for interviews? No, they weren't. **6.** Was Halina (OR she) with Dorota this morning? No, she wasn't.

5-10 mins

1. Say: *In this exercise, you're going to write* yes/no *questions and short answers.* Have students read the direction line. Go over the example in the book. Remind students that the answers are based on the conversation on page 249.

2. Have students complete Exercise 4 individually. Remind them to review grammar chart **11.4** on page 254 if necessary. Check the answers as a class.

11.5 The Past Tense of *Be*— Information Questions ≡★

5-10 mins

1. Have students look at grammar chart **11.5** on page 255. Say: *When making an information question with the past tense of* be, *write the question word plus* was *or* were *before the subject.* Go over the examples in the chart.

2. Say: *Short answers only contain the information requested. They don't contain the subject or* be. Review the questions and short answers. Note the example: *It was great!* Remind students that some short answers can be in complete sentences if they give a very general piece of information as an answer. If necessary, have students review similar grammar rules for question words in chart **4.9** on pages 88–89.

EXERCISE 5 ≡★

ANSWERS: 1. Why was your employer (OR he OR she) surprised? **2.** How were the questions (OR they)? **3.** Where were they? **4.** When were you there (OR at Baker's)? **5.** How long were you there?

10-15 mins

1. Have students read the direction line. Go over the example in the book.

2. Have students complete Exercise 5 individually. Remind them to review grammar chart **11.5** on page 255 if necessary. Have students compare their answers with a partner. Check the answers as a class.

> ### Practice Idea: Speaking
>
> Have students practice the short conversations in pairs. Ask volunteers to role-play the conversation in front of the class.

11.6 The Past Tense of *Be*— Subject Questions ≡★

5-10 mins

1. Have students look at grammar chart **11.6** on page 256. Remind students that in subject questions, the subject is a question word or phrase. Review the examples and short answers. Say: *Short answers do not state the complement. They go back to the subject.*

2. Write the following short answers on the board:

   The student by the window.

   Three or four.

   Ask students to write questions that could be answered by these short answers. Ask several students to share their questions with the class.

EXERCISE 6 ≡★

ANSWERS: 1. questions were on the application? **2.** was surprised? **3.** positions were available (in that company last month)? **4.** was wrong (with my application)? **5.** questions were funny?

5-10 mins

1. Say: *In this exercise, you're going to complete questions about statements.* Have students read the direction line. Go over the example in the book. Note the answer. Ask: *Who does* Who *mean?* (some employees) *What does* there *mean?* (at the office) Have volunteers model the example.

2. Have students complete Exercise 6 individually. Remind them to review grammar chart **11.6** on page 256 if necessary. Have volunteers share and discuss their answers with the class.

EXERCISE 7

CD 3
TR 20

ANSWERS: 1. What was; **2.** Were there; **3.** Was; **4.** were; **5.** wasn't; **6.** Were there; **7.** There were; **8.** weren't; **9.** was

10-15 mins

1. Have students read the direction line. Review the example in the book. Remind students that some of the expressions will be used more than once. Remind students that the first word in a sentence must be capitalized.

2. Have students complete Exercise 7 individually. Remind them to review the grammar charts in this lesson if necessary. Then have students compare their answers in pairs. Play the audio and check the answers as a class.

Lesson 2 Overview

GRAMMAR

1. Write the following statement on the board: *The teacher <u>asked</u> a lot of questions.* Say: *In the last lesson, you learned how to form the past tense of* be *and how to make questions with the past tense of* be. *Now you're going to learn how to form the simple past tense of regular and irregular verbs.*

2. Elicit prior knowledge. Ask: *What regular verbs do you know? What irregular verbs do you know?* Write a few regular verbs on the board (e.g., *talk, live, ask*). Ask volunteers to give the past tense form and make a sentence with the verb.

CONTEXT

1. Say: *In the last lesson, you learned about job applications. In this lesson, you're going to learn about job interviews.* Have students share their opinions. Ask: *When you apply for a job, what questions do employers ask you? What do they want to know?*

2. Direct students' attention to the picture of Halina in a job interview on page 258. Ask: *What is going on in this picture?* (Halina is speaking with two people about her last job. She is in a job interview.) Point to the woman. Ask: *What is she thinking about?*

Applying for a Job in an Office
READING

Have students use the title and picture to make predictions about the reading. Ask: *Where is Halina applying for a job?* (in an office) Say: *Halina is telling Dorota about the job interview. What is Halina going to say about the interview? Did she think it went well?* (No. She made a lot of mistakes.)

BEFORE YOU READ

5-10 mins

1. Go over each question as a class. Have a volunteer read the questions or read them to the class yourself. Have students answer the questions in pairs.

2. Ask a few volunteers to share their answers with the class.

Reading ≡★

CD 3
TR 21

10-15
mins

1. Have students read the dialogue silently. Then play the audio and have students read along silently.

2. Check students' basic comprehension. Ask questions such as: *Did Halina get to the interview on time?* (No. She was 15 minutes late.) *How long was the interview?* (one hour) *Why didn't she like the interview?* (They asked her a lot of questions and she was nervous.) *What did she say about her last job?* (She had to work too hard and they didn't pay her enough money.) *What did she say about the company she was interviewing with?* (The company isn't too far away and it's easy to get there.)

Practice Ideas: Listening

1. To practice listening skills, have students listen to the audio before opening their books. Ask a few comprehension questions, such as: *Should you complain about your past jobs in an interview?* (no) Repeat the audio if necessary. Then have students open their books and read along as they listen to the audio.

2. Alternatively, have students begin by listening to the audio as they read along.

Practice Idea: Speaking

Have students practice the conversation in pairs. Ask volunteers to role-play all or part of the conversation in front of the class.

VOCABULARY IN CONTEXT

1. Model the pronunciation of each new vocabulary item and have students repeat.

2. Make sure students understand the meaning of each vocabulary item. Review the examples in the book and create additional example sentences. For example, say: *instead. I don't want to drive to work. I want to walk instead.* Review each new vocabulary item similarly, using visuals and realia when appropriate.

3. Have students underline an example of each vocabulary item in the reading.

Practice Idea: Speaking

To check comprehension, have volunteers in pairs or groups act out selected vocabulary, such as *résumé*, *positive*, and *instead*.

Did You Know?

Point out the information to students. Tell students about personnel or temping agencies. Explain that some agencies charge fees. If you accept a job and then quit before a specific time period (e.g., six months), you may have to pay the agency.

 LISTENING ACTIVITY

CD 3
TR 22

ANSWERS: 1. False; **2.** False; **3.** True; **4.** True; **5.** False; **6.** True; **7.** True

5-10
mins

1. Say: *Listen to the questions about Halina and Dorota's conversation. Circle* true *or* false. Play the listening selection one time without pausing. Then play it through again, pausing and replaying as necessary.

2. Have students compare their answers, then play the audio again and check the answers as a class.

11.7 The Simple Past Tense of Regular Verbs— Affirmative Statements ≡★

5-10
mins

1. Have students look at grammar chart **11.7** on page 261. Ask: *How do you form the past tense of regular verbs?* (add *-ed* to the base form)

2. Review the Language Note and the Pronunciation Note. Write on the board:

   -ed = /d/, /t/, /ld/.

   Read the rule and then read out the example sentences for each sound. Have students look at the verbs in the chart. Pronounce each verb and ask students to name the sound. (/d/: *complained, filled out;* /t/ *parked, asked;* /ld/: *needed, wanted*)

EXERCISE 1

ANSWERS: 1. filled out; **2.** called; **3.** interviewed; **4.** asked; **5.** complained; **6.** talked; **7.** needed (to have); **8.** used

⏱ 5-10 mins

1. Have students read the direction line. Go over the example in the book.

2. Have students complete Exercise 1 individually. Remind them to review grammar chart **11.7** on page 261 if necessary. Check the answers with the class.

11.8 Spelling of the *-ed* Form

⏱ 5-10 mins

1. Have students look at grammar chart **11.8** on page 262. Review the examples and explanations.

2. Write additional examples on the board. Ask students what the spelling rule is (e.g., *carry/carried, pray/prayed, drop/dropped, fire/fired, talk/talked*).

EXERCISE 2

ANSWERS: 1. applied; **2.** studied; **3.** stopped; **4.** planned; **5.** stayed; **6.** hired

⏱ 5-10 mins

1. Have students read the direction line. Go over the example.

2. Have students complete Exercise 2 individually. Remind them to review grammar chart **11.8** on page 262 if necessary. Check the answers as a class.

11.9 The Simple Past Tense of Irregular Verbs— Affirmative Statements

⏱ 5-10 mins

1. Have students look at grammar chart **11.9** on page 262. Say: *You have to memorize the past tense forms of irregular verbs.* Go over the verbs in the chart.

2. Review the Language Notes and have students find the list of irregular verbs in Appendix D.

3. Have students close their books. Check comprehension by asking students to give the past tense form of some of the verbs in the chart. Write the verbs on the board (e.g., *take, make, give, do, say, know*). Ask various students to say and spell the past tense form. Ask volunteers to make sentences.

EXERCISE 3

ANSWERS: 1. had; **2.** sent; **3.** went; **4.** took; **5.** got; **6.** told; **7.** gave

⏱ 5-10 mins

1. Have students read the direction line. Go over the example.

2. Have students complete Exercise 3 individually. Remind them to review grammar chart **11.9** on page 262 if necessary. Check the answers as a class.

11.10 The Simple Past Tense— Negative Statements =★

5-10 mins

1. Have students look at grammar chart **11.10** on page 263. Say: *We use* didn't *plus the base form for the negative of regular and irregular verbs in the past.* Write on the board:

   didn't + the base form of verb

   Go over the examples in the chart. Stress that *didn't + the base form* is used for all verbs in the past, both regular and irregular.

2. Review the Language Note. Give additional examples for *went* (e.g., *Jay went yesterday. He didn't go last week.*). Write the past tense form of a few irregular verbs on the board (e.g., *knew, gave, told*) and ask volunteers to give an affirmative and negative sentence for each one.

Practice Idea: Writing

Have students go back to Exercise 3 on page 263. Say: *Make the sentences in this exercise negative.*

EXERCISE 4 =★

ANSWERS: 1. she didn't park close to the office building. **2.** she didn't have an interview for a job at Baker's. **3.** she didn't go with Halina (OR her) to her job interview. **4.** they didn't work on the weekends. **5.** she didn't use Simon as a reference.

5-10 mins

1. Have students read the direction line. Review the example in the book.

2. Have students complete Exercise 4 individually. Remind them to review grammar chart **11.10** on page 263 if necessary. Check the answers as a class.

EXERCISE 5

ANSWERS: 1. didn't get; **2.** made; **3.** didn't have; **4.** didn't expect; **5.** sent, didn't see; **6.** told

10-15 mins

1. Have students read the direction line. Go over the examples in the book. Remind students to use *didn't + the base form* for both regular and irregular verbs in negative statements.

Have students skim the conversations first. Explain any unfamiliar terms (e.g., *out of town on business* = in another city for business).

2. Have students complete Exercise 5 individually. Remind them to review grammar charts **11.9** on page 262 and **11.10** on page 263 if necessary. Then have students compare their answers with a partner. Monitor pair work. Give help as needed. Check the answers as a class.

Practice Idea: Speaking

Have students practice the short conversations in pairs. Ask volunteers to role-play the dialogues in front of the class. Have the class listen for and, when needed, correct pronunciation of past tense regular verbs in the affirmative.

EXERCISE 6

ANSWERS: Answers will vary. They will begin with: 1. I applied OR I didn't apply; **2.** I used OR I didn't use; **3.** I went OR I didn't go; **4.** I took OR I didn't take; **5.** I studied OR I didn't study; **6.** I got OR I didn't get; **7.** I took OR I didn't take; **8.** I saw OR I didn't see; **9.** I needed OR I didn't need; **10.** I made OR I didn't make

10-15 mins

1. Say: *You're going to make these statements true for you by using the affirmative or the negative.* Have students read the direction line. Go over the example in the book. Have a volunteer model #1.

2. Have students complete Exercise 6 individually. Remind them to review grammar charts **11.9** on page 262 and **11.10** on page 263 if necessary. Then have students compare their answers in pairs. Monitor pair work. Give help as needed. Have volunteers share their answers with the class.

Practice Idea: Speaking

Do a quick survey of students' answers. Record the results on the board.

EXERCISE 7

ANSWERS: 1. had; **2.** didn't make; **3.** learned; **4.** told; **5.** didn't complain; **6.** didn't ask; **7.** didn't know

 10-15 mins

1. Say: *Halina is talking to Dorota about another job interview.* Have students read the direction line. Be sure that students understand this is Halina's second interview. Have a volunteer complete the first sentence.

2. Have students complete the rest of Exercise 7 individually. Remind them to review the grammar charts in this lesson if necessary. Then have students compare their answers in pairs. Play the audio and check the answers as a class.

Practice Ideas: Speaking

1. Have students practice the conversation in pairs. Then have volunteers role-play the conversation in front of the class.

2. Have students work in pairs to create their own conversation about a successful or unsuccessful job interview.

Lesson 3 Overview

GRAMMAR

1. Briefly review the objectives of Lessons 1 and 2. Give examples of present and past tense forms of some verbs taught in the lessons (e.g., *be, go, talk, do, say, work*) and of affirmative and negative sentences in the past (e.g., *I went to class. I didn't go to class.*). Say: *In Lesson 3, we're going to study more irregular verbs and more questions in the past tense.* Write the lesson objectives on the board.

2. Activate students' knowledge. Ask students to make questions in the past tense based on statements. Prompt with statements such as: *Jenny was a waitress many years ago; Tim worked there for only one day.* Elicit and list question words on the board if necessary.

CONTEXT

1. Say: *We're going to learn about choosing a career. Nowadays, many people choose to work in medicine.* Point out the fastest-growing jobs listed in the following Context Note. Ask: *Why do people choose these jobs?* Have students share their ideas.

2. Direct students' attention to the pictures of the professionals. Ask: *What careers or professions do you see here?* Then ask: *How long does it take to prepare for these jobs?*

Jobs of the Future   READING

Have students look at the title of the reading and the pictures on page 267. Ask: *What do you think are jobs of the future?* Have them read the direction line. Tell students to make predictions about the reading. Ask: *What is the reading about? What questions will Marta and Simon ask Matt?*

BEFORE YOU READ

 5-10 mins

1. Go over each question as a class. Have a volunteer read the questions or read them to the class yourself. Have students discuss the questions in pairs.

2. Ask a few volunteers to share their answers with the class.

Context Note

According to the U.S. Department of Labor, these are some of the fastest-growing jobs in the U.S.:

Medical assistants

Network systems and data communications analysts

Physician assistants

Social and human service assistants

Home health aides

Medical records and health information technicians

Computer software engineers, applications

Computer software engineers, systems software

Physical therapist (PT) assistants

Reading

CD 3
TR 24

10-15 mins

1. Have students read the dialogue silently. Then play the audio and have students read along silently.

2. Check students' basic comprehension. Ask questions, such as: *Is Matt a physical therapist?* (No. He's a PT assistant.) *What does he like about the career?* (He likes the physical activity and he likes to help people.) *What other kind of job did he have?* (He was a fitness instructor at an athletic club.)

Practice Idea: Listening

1. To practice listening skills, have students listen to the audio before opening their books. Ask a few comprehension questions, such as: *Who was in the hospital?* (Marta's father) Repeat the audio if necessary. Then have students open their books and read along as they listen to the audio.

2. Alternatively, have students begin by listening to the audio as they read along.

Practice Idea: Speaking

Have students practice the conversation in groups of three. Ask volunteers to role-play the conversation in front of the class.

VOCABULARY IN CONTEXT

5-10 mins

1. Model the pronunciation of each new vocabulary item and have students repeat.

2. Make sure students understand the meaning of each vocabulary item. Review the examples in the book and create additional example sentences. For example, say: *career. I started my teaching career 15 years ago after graduating from college.* Ask: *What's the difference between a career and a job? A career is a profession that you have training for. A job is an activity you do to earn money.* For *patient,* say: *When you receive medical care, you are a patient.* Go over each

new vocabulary item similarly, using visuals and realia when appropriate. When possible, point to pictures in the book that illustrate the new vocabulary, such as *patient* on page 267.

3. Have students underline an example of each vocabulary item in the reading.

Practice Idea: Speaking

To check comprehension, have volunteers in pairs or groups act out selected vocabulary, such as *patient, physical therapist,* and *fitness instructor.*

Did You Know?

Point out the information to students. Elicit other jobs in health care (e.g., social service assistants, physician assistants, and so on).

LISTENING ACTIVITY

CD 3
TR 25

ANSWERS: 1. True; **2.** False; **3.** True; **4.** True; **5.** False; **6.** True; **7.** False

5-10 mins

1. Say: *Listen to the sentences about Simon and Marta's conversation with Matt. Circle* true *or* false. Play the listening selection one time without pausing. Then play it through again, pausing and replaying as necessary.

2. Have students compare their answers, then play the audio again and check the answers as a class.

11.11 The Simple Past Tense— *Yes/No* Questions

5-10 mins

1. Have students look at grammar chart **11.11** on page 270. Say: *To make yes/no questions in the past, we use* did *plus the base form of the verb.* Remind students that the pattern is the same for regular and irregular verbs. Go over the example questions and short answers.

2. Read and review the Language Notes. Model the pronunciation of *did you* and *did he* in Note 1. For Note 2, elicit additional examples of affirmative and question forms for verbs in the chart, such as *choose, visit,* and *know.*

Practice Idea: Speaking

Have students work individually to write three *yes/no* questions in the simple past tense to ask their partner. Tell students to use verbs from the grammar chart. Then put students in pairs to ask and answer their questions. Have volunteers ask and answer their questions for the class.

Practice Idea: Speaking

Have students work individually to write three questions in the simple past tense to ask their partner. Tell students to use the verbs from the grammar chart. Then put students in pairs to ask and answer their questions. Have volunteers ask and answer their questions for the class.

EXERCISE 1

ANSWERS: 1. Did Matt get a bachelor's degree? No, he didn't. **2.** Did Matt's employer offer on-the-job training? Yes, he (OR she) did. **3.** Did Simon and Marta ask about Matt's family? No, they didn't. **4.** Did Simon hear about health careers on TV? No, he didn't. **5.** Did Matt help Simon's father in the hospital? No, he didn't. **6.** Did Simon and Marta ask Matt a lot of questions? Yes, they did.

5-10 mins

1. Have students read the direction line. Go over the example in the book. Remind them that the questions are based on the conversation on page 268.

2. Have students complete Exercise 1 individually. Remind them to review grammar chart **11.11** on page 270 if necessary. Check the answers as a class.

11.12 More Irregular Verbs in the Simple Past Tense

5-10 mins

1. Have students close their books. Write the following verbs from the chart on the board: *eat, choose, read, write, spend, keep, leave, hear.* Have students say and spell the past tense forms.

2. Have students open their books and look at grammar chart **11.12** on page 271. Have them check to see how many forms they got correct. Then review all of the verbs in the chart and the Pronunciation Note. Ask volunteers to write short sentences using a past tense form and share the sentence with the class.

EXERCISE 2

ANSWERS: 1. met; **2.** came OR went; **3.** chose; **4.** thought; **5.** read; **6.** took; **7.** got OR took; **8.** gave; **9.** took OR had OR got; **10.** took; **11.** kept, left; **12.** told; **13.** met OR saw; **14.** knew; **15.** ate OR had

5-10 mins

1. Have students read the direction line. Ask a volunteer to do #1. Tell students the sentences are based on the conversation on page 268.

2. Have students complete the rest of Exercise 2 individually. Remind them to review grammar chart **11.12** on page 271 if necessary. Check the answers as a class.

11.13 The Simple Past Tense— Information Questions

5-10 mins

1. Have students close their books. Write on the board:

   ? word + did + subject + base form of verb + complement

   Then write the following scrambled sentences:

   did / at her last job / Susie / ? / work / How long

   ? / What kind of job / Mr. Woods / find / did

   Ask: *What is the order of an information question in the past with* did? Have the class work together to put the questions and punctuation in order. Rewrite the questions correctly on the board. (*How long did Susie work at her last job? What kind of job did Mr. Woods find?*)

2. Have students look at grammar chart **11.13** on page 272. Review the example questions and short answers.

3. Direct students' attention to the Language Note. Have volunteers notice and explain to the class the differences between the affirmative statements and information questions.

EXERCISE 3

ANSWERS: 1. Where did you take classes? **2.** What did Simon read about? **3.** How many PT assistants did Matt meet (in that hospital)? **4.** Who did the PT assistants (OR they) help? **5.** How long did Marta's father stay in the hospital? **6.** What kind of part-time job did Matt get? **7.** How long did Matt (OR he) keep that job?

5-10 mins

1. Have students read the direction line. Go over the example.

2. Have students complete Exercise 3 individually. Remind them to review grammar chart **11.13** on page 272 if necessary. Check the answers with the class.

Practice Idea: Speaking

Have students practice the short conversations in pairs.

11.14 The Simple Past Tense— Subject Questions

5-10 mins

1. Have students look at grammar chart **11.14** on page 273. Say: *Subject questions begin with the question word followed by the verb in the past tense.* Go over the examples.

2. Review the short answers. Remind students that short answers for subject questions in the simple past tense usually contain just the subject and *did* or another verb in the simple past tense.

EXERCISE 4

ANSWERS: 1. What happened at the health club yesterday? **2.** Who told you about that job? **3.** How many people applied for the job as a fitness instructor? **4.** Which patient spent two weeks at the hospital? **5.** Which student chose a job in health services? **6.** Who wrote about jobs of the future? **7.** What kinds of patients needed help with their injuries? **8.** How many physical therapists went to community colleges?

5-10 mins

1. Have students read the direction line. Go over the example. Tell students that they will make questions. They will not answer the questions.

2. Have students complete Exercise 4 individually. Remind them to review grammar chart **11.14** on page 273 if necessary. Check the answers as a class.

11.15 More Irregular Verbs in the Simple Past Tense

5-10 mins

Have students look at grammar chart **11.15** on page 274. Point out that some verbs use the base form as the simple past tense. Go over the verbs and ask volunteers to write sentences in the simple past tense on the board using the verbs.

Practice Idea: Speaking

Have students work individually to write three questions to ask their partner using verbs from grammar chart **11.15** on page 274. Then put students in pairs to ask and answer their questions. Have volunteers ask and answer their questions for the class.

EXERCISE 5

ANSWERS: 1. How did she hurt her arm? She fell and broke it. **2.** Which arm did she break? She broke her right arm. **3.** Who drove her to the hospital? Her husband drove her. **4.** How long did the woman stay in the hospital? She stayed only a few hours. **5.** What kind of help did she get later? She got help from a good physical therapist. **6.** Who helped her in her house? She paid for a service. **7.** How much did this service cost? It cost $15.00 an hour. **8.** Where did she find this service? She found it online. **9.** How much work time did she lose? She lost only a week.

10-15 mins

1. Have students read the direction line. Go over the example. Remind students to use the words in parentheses to answer the questions.

2. Have students complete Exercise 5 individually. Remind them to review grammar charts **11.14** on page 273 and **11.15** on page 274 if necessary. Then have students compare their answers in pairs. Monitor pair work. Give help as needed. Check the answers as a class.

Practice Idea: Speaking

Have students work individually to write three to five questions to ask their partner. Tell students that the questions should be in the simple past tense and use verbs from grammar chart **11.15.** Then put students in pairs to ask and answer their questions. Ask volunteers to share their questions and answers with the class.

Editing Advice

10-15 mins

Have students close their books. Write the example sentences without editing marks or corrections on the board. For example:

1. *He wanted to spent some time at the health club.*
2. *Where did they went after work?*

Ask students to correct each sentence and provide a rule or explanation for each correction, e.g.: 1. He wanted to spend some time at the health club. (Don't use the simple past tense after *to* (the infinitive).) 2. Where did they go after work? (Use the base form after *did* and *didn't*.) This activity can be done individually, in pairs, or as a class. After students have corrected each sentence, tell them to turn to page 275. Say: *Now compare your work with the Editing Advice in the book.*

Editing Quiz

ANSWERS: 1. What happened; **2.** did you hurt; **3.** fell; **4.** C; **5.** didn't see; **6.** Did you call; **7.** wanted to call; **8.** C; **9.** helped; **10.** helped; **11.** stopped; **12.** did the woman do; **13.** Did she take; **14.** called; **15.** C; **16.** came; **17.** took; **18.** C; **19.** C; **20.** thank; **21.** C

10-15 mins

1. Tell students they are going to put the Editing Advice into practice. Have students read the direction line. Ask: *Do all the shaded words have mistakes?* (no) Go over the examples with the class. Then do #1 together.
2. Have students complete the rest of the quiz individually. Then have them compare their answers with a partner before checking the

answers as a class. Elicit the relevant grammar point for each correction. For example, for the first example, ask: *What's the rule?* (Use *did* plus the base form for *yes/no* questions in the past.)

3. For the items students had difficulties with, have them go back and find the relevant grammar chart and review it. Monitor and give help as necessary.

Expansion

These expansion activities provide opportunities for students to interact with one another and further develop their speaking and writing skills. Encourage students to use grammar from this unit whenever possible.

LEARNER'S LOG

10-15 mins

1. Have students close their books. Ask: *What did you learn about applying for a job, interviews, and jobs of the future? What else do you want to know?* Write students' ideas on the board. Discuss ways in which students can find out more about these topics.
2. Have students open their books to complete the Learner's Log. Remind students to write three to five sentences about each topic and to write two questions they still have about each of the topics.
3. Have students compare logs in pairs.

WRITING ACTIVITY

10-15 mins

Have students read the direction line and the example. Then have students help you write the next line of the conversation on the board. Have students complete the activity individually. Collect for assessment.

Practice Idea: Writing

Have students exchange papers with a partner. Ask students to help their partners edit their paragraph. Refer students to the Editing Advice on page 275.

OUTSIDE ACTIVITIES

1. Tell students to find a health or exercise club in their city or town and call or visit it to ask how much it costs to be a member. Tell them to ask about the activities at the club. In class, have students tell the class about the club and then exchange information about health clubs in groups. Find out which ones are the most economical.

2. Tell students to go to a store near them and ask for a job application and fill it out for practice. Have students bring their job applications to class and compare and correct applications with classmates in pairs or groups.

INTERNET ACTIVITY

Tell students to use a search engine on the Internet and type in *Occupational Outlook Handbook* and look for an interesting job or a job of the future. Tell them to find it in the handbook and find the answers to these questions about the job.

• What education is necessary?

• What is the average pay for this job?

• Are jobs like this growing faster than average?

In class, have students discuss the jobs they researched in groups and decide which seem the best. Have groups share their ideas with the class.

Unit 12

Unit Overview

1. Have students look at the pictures. Ask: *What do you think this unit is going to be about?* (helping people; giving back to the community) Say: *Look at the pictures again. How do people give back to the community?* (They do things for people who need help.)

2. Ask: *Should everyone give back? Who should we help?* Have students share their ideas and experience.

Presentation Ideas

The topic for this unit can be enhanced with the following items:

1. Announcements of local volunteer opportunities in flyers and brochures, and Web site addresses of volunteer organizations

2. Information about volunteer organizations and the groups they help

Lesson 1 Overview

GRAMMAR

Say: *In Lesson 1, we're going to review verb tenses. What else are we going to review?* (infinitives, modal verbs, and time expressions) Point out or write the lesson objectives on the board. Activate students' knowledge. Ask for examples of infinitives and time expressions. Write the examples on the board.

CONTEXT

1. Say: *We're going to read about helping people. What's a volunteer?* (a person who helps people in need but doesn't get paid for his/her work) Ask: *Are you a volunteer? Do you like to help people? Who do you help? What do you do?* Have students share their experiences.

2. Direct students' attention to the picture. Activate students' prior knowledge. Ask: *How did Simon and*

Dorota help newcomers to the United States? (e.g., showed them how to use the laundromat, find a new apartment, move, fill out applications, get a job, get a Social Security Card, take a driver's test, buy an infant car seat)

Helping Others   READING

Have students look at the title of the reading and the picture on page 280. Say: *Quickly skim the reading. What do Halina and Victor say they want to do now?* (help Dorota and Simon with other newcomers) Have students use the title and pictures to make predictions about the reading.

BEFORE YOU READ

5-10 mins

1. Go over each question as a class. Have a volunteer read the questions or read them to the class yourself. Have students discuss the questions in pairs.

2. Ask a few volunteers to share their answers with the class.

Context Note

Most volunteering in the U.S. is done for religious organizations or educational/youth service organizations. People also volunteer for social or community organizations and for hospital/health organizations.

 ### Reading

CD 3
TR 26

1. Have students read the dialogue silently. Then play the audio and have students read along silently.

10-15 mins

2. Check students' basic comprehension. Ask questions such as: *Who do Victor and Lisa thank?* (Simon) *What did Simon do?* (helped them move, gave advice about used cars) *Did Victor buy a car?* (no) *Who thanked Dorota?* (Halina) *What did Dorota do?* (taught her about places in the city, helped with getting a Social Security card, gave advice about job

interviews) *How can Halina help Dorota?* (She can be a volunteer.) *Are Victor and Lisa going to volunteer?* (Victor is; Lisa doesn't say.)

Practice Ideas: Listening

1. To practice listening skills, have students listen to the audio before opening their books. Ask a few comprehension questions, such as: *Does Halina like her new job?* (yes) Repeat the audio if necessary. Then have students open their books and read along as they listen to the audio.

2. Alternatively, have students begin by listening to the audio as they read along.

Practice Idea: Speaking

Have students practice the conversation in groups of five. Ask volunteers to role-play the conversation in front of the class.

VOCABULARY IN CONTEXT

5-10 mins

1. Model the pronunciation of each new vocabulary item and have students repeat.

2. Make sure students understand the meaning of each vocabulary item. Review the examples in the book and create additional example sentences. For example, say: *really. I really wanted to play tennis today, but it's raining.* For *count on*, write on the board: *Count on me = I will do it. / I will be there.* Go over each new vocabulary item similarly, using visuals and realia when appropriate. When possible, point to pictures in the book that illustrate the new vocabulary.

3. Have students underline an example of each vocabulary item in the reading.

Practice Idea: Speaking

To check comprehension, have volunteers in pairs or groups act out selected vocabulary, such as *volunteer* and *newcomer*.

Did You Know?

Point out the information to students. Tell students that *mentoring* is a popular type of volunteer work in the U.S. Adults work with young people in need. They help out with homework, give advice, offer emotional support, and much more.

CD 3
TR 27

LISTENING ACTIVITY

ANSWERS: **1.** True; **2.** False; **3.** True; **4.** False; **5.** False; **6.** False; **7.** False; **8.** False

1. Say: *Listen to the sentences about the conversation. Circle* true *or* false. Play the listening selection one time without pausing. Then play it through again, pausing and replaying as necessary.

2. Have students compare their answers in pairs, then play the audio again and check the answers as a class.

12.1 Review of Verb Tenses— Affirmative and Negative ═★

10-15 mins

1. Have students look at grammar chart **12.1** on pages 283–284. Review the information about each tense.

2. Have students close their books. Write sentences on the board and ask students to tell you what tense each verb is.

Practice Idea: Speaking

List one or more pieces of information from the EXPLANATION column of grammar chart **12.1** on pages 283–284 on the board for each tense. Have students say or write an example sentence. You might write this example on the board:

Simple Present: Age.

Brett is six years old.

Make a list of many verbs on the board, mixing all of the tenses in the chart. Put students in pairs or groups. Have them sort out the verbs by tense and then share their answers with the class.

EXERCISE 1

ANSWERS: 1. are sitting; **2.** found; **3.** likes; **4.** are enjoying; **5.** gave; **6.** is going to buy OR 's going to buy; **7.** were; **8.** has; **9.** helped; **10.** is going to help OR 's going to help; **11.** is going to be OR 's going to be

5-10 mins

1. Have students read the direction line. Go over the example in the book. Remind students to use the ideas from the conversation on page 281 for the answers.

2. Have students complete Exercise 1 individually. Remind them to review grammar chart **12.1** on pages 283–284 if necessary. Check the answers as a class.

EXERCISE 2

ANSWERS: 1. They aren't (OR They're not) talking about their problems now. **2.** He didn't want to stay in his old apartment. **3.** It wasn't big enough for his family. **4.** He doesn't feel strange anymore. **5.** He didn't give him advice about jobs. **6.** They didn't have much free time then. **7.** They don't need a new car. **8.** She isn't going to look for another job soon.

5-10 mins

1. Have students read the direction line. Go over the example in the book.

2. Have students complete Exercise 2 individually. Remind them to review grammar chart **12.1** on pages 283–284 if necessary. Check the answers with the class.

12.2 Review of Infinitives

5-10 mins
Have students look at grammar chart **12.2** on page 285. Say: *The infinitive form is* to *plus the base form of a verb.* Review the explanations. Ask: *Can you remember the verbs we use with the infinitive?* (*want, need, like, expect,* and *try*) Give an example sentence (e.g., *I want to go to the movies on Saturday.*). Write the example on the board. Remind students that expressions with *it* are often followed by an infinitive.

EXERCISE 3

ANSWERS: Answers will vary. Possible answers:
1. to buy a used car. **2.** to get a Social Security card. **3.** to volunteer. **4.** to be a newcomer. **5.** to help other people. **6.** to have another meeting. **7.** to help newcomers.

5-10 mins

1. Have students read the direction line. Go over the example in the book. Remind students to use the ideas from the conversation on page 281 for the answers. Say: *Your answers will vary.*

2. Have students complete Exercise 3 individually. Remind them to review grammar charts **4.7** on page 77 and **12.2** on page 285 if necessary. Check the answers as a class.

12.3 Review of Modal Verbs—Affirmative and Negative

⏱ **5–10 mins**

1. Have students look at grammar chart **12.3** on page 286. Review the examples and explanations.

2. Have students close their books. Give students additional examples and ask students to explain what the sentences mean. For example, write on the board: *I can build a house.* Ask: *What does this mean?* (I have the ability to build a house. OR It's OK to build a house; I have permission.)

Practice Ideas: Writing

1. Have students change the affirmative sentences to negative, and vice versa, for each example sentence in the chart.

2. Have students write an affirmative and negative sentence for each modal verb phrase in the chart.

EXERCISE 4
Answers will vary.

⏱ **5–10 mins**

1. Say: *In this exercise, you're going to make the sentences true for you by using affirmative or negative modals.* Have students read the direction line. Go over the examples in the book. Have volunteers model the examples.

2. Have students complete Exercise 4 individually. Remind them to review grammar chart **12.3** on page 286 or grammar charts **5.1–5.3** in Unit 5 and **6.1–6.3** in Unit 6. Go over the answers with the class.

EXERCISE 5

CD 3 TR 28

ANSWERS: Part 1: **1.** don't get; **2.** don't know; **3.** aren't; **4.** can help; **5.** are going to meet; **6.** has to drive; **7.** practiced; **8.** 'm going to be; **9.** want to help; **10.** don't have; **11.** bought; **12.** doesn't need to use. Part 2: **1.** 're going to prepare; **2.** 're looking

for; **3.** to find; **4.** want to help; **5.** can cook; **6.** 'm going to tell; **7.** prepares; **8.** came; **9.** weren't; **10.** didn't have; **11.** volunteered to help; **12.** got; **13.** had

⏱ **10–15 mins**

1. Have students read the direction line. Have a volunteer do #1.

2. Have students complete the rest of Exercise 5 individually. Remind them to review grammar chart **12.1** on pages 283–284 if necessary. Then have students compare their answers in pairs. Play the audio and check the answers as a class.

Practice Idea: Speaking

Have students practice the conversation in groups. Ask volunteers to role-play the conversations in front of the class.

12.4 Review of Time Expressions

⏱ **5–10 mins**

Have students look at grammar chart **12.4** on page 288. Activate students' knowledge. Ask students to separate the expressions by their use. Begin by having students give examples of expressions that mean habit or custom. (*always, never, from now on, often, usually, hardly ever, sometimes, rarely, every week*) Repeat the procedure for expressions used to show something happening now (*right now, at the moment*), future plans or predictions (*in a few weeks, next week, soon, tomorrow, right away*), past events (*yesterday, last year, two weeks ago*), and events thought of as present, past, or future (*this week: I go this week; I went this week; I'm going to go this week*).

Practice Idea: Writing

Have students work in pairs to write two or three sentences for each of these four categories of time expressions: habit or custom, things happening now, future plans or predictions, and past events. Make sure students know to include a time expression in each sentence.

EXERCISE 6

ANSWERS: **1.** helps/often; **2.** have/hardly ever; **3.** gives OR tries to get OR finds/usually; **4.** teaches OR tells/always; **5.** moved/Last year; **6.** gave OR found/In just a month; **7.** tried to get OR found/later; **8.** are enjoying/now; **9.** is going to invite OR 's going to invite/later this year; **10.** came/Last year; **11.** was/a week later; **12.** are helping/now; **13.** is teaching OR 's teaching/now

10-15 mins

1. Have students read the direction line. Then go over the example.

2. Have students complete Exercise 6 individually. Remind them to review the grammar charts on time expressions, including **4.4** on page 69, **8.3** on page 181, **9.4** on page 204, **11.3** on page 253, and **12.4** on page 288 if necessary. Check the answers as a class.

EXERCISE 7

ANSWERS: Answers will vary. Possible answers: Dorota and the volunteers prepared food for the Thanksgiving dinner. She got a lot of volunteers to help her. Volunteers are bringing out food on trays. A volunteer is going to cut the turkey. Everyone is having a good time. They're going to eat a lot of food. After that, Dorota and the volunteers are going to clean up.

10-15 mins

1. Have students look at the picture of the Thanksgiving dinner. Ask: *What's happening in this picture?* (People are eating Thanksgiving dinner.) Ask: *Are these Americans or are they newcomers?* (newcomers) Then have students read the direction line. Go over the examples.

2. Have students complete Exercise 7 individually. Then have students compare paragraphs in pairs. Ask volunteers to read some of their sentences.

3. If necessary, review grammar chart **12.1** on pages 283–284.

Practice Idea: Speaking

Have students get into groups to talk about how they're going to spend their next Thanksgiving or other important holiday. Say and write on the board: *Tell your group where you are going to be, who you are going to be with, what you're going to do, and what you're going to eat.*

Lesson 2 Overview

GRAMMAR

1. Write the following questions on the board:
   Do you do any volunteer activities?
   What do you do?

2. Ask: *What's the difference between these two questions?* (The first is a *yes/no* question. The second is an information question.) Have students provide more examples of each type of question.

CONTEXT

1. Talk with students about any volunteer activities you do (e.g., *I volunteer my time at the public library teaching ESL.*). Encourage students to ask *yes/no* and information questions about your work (e.g., *How many hours a month do you work in the library?*).

2. Direct students' attention to the photo on page 291. Ask: *What are these people doing?* (They're unloading food and supplies from an airplane.)

Charity Work READING

Have students look at the title of the reading and the photos on page 291. Then ask students to scan the reading. *What did the volunteers do last year?* (They brought a sick little boy from South America to the U.S. He needed an operation.)

BEFORE YOU READ

5-10 mins

1. Go over each question as a class. Have a volunteer read the questions or read them to the class yourself. Have students answer the questions in pairs.

2. Ask a few volunteers to share their answers with the class. Ask if anyone in the class volunteers.

Context Note

Reasons why people volunteer:

It's an important thing to do.

Other people respect you.

It helps you become a better person.

You can help many people.

You can help create change.

You can make friends.

  ### Reading

CD 3
TR 29

10-15
mins

1. Have students read the dialogue silently. Then play the audio and have students read along silently.

2. Check students' basic comprehension. Ask questions, such as: *What do the three women do?* (They are volunteers.) *What does Rhonda's volunteer group do?* (They have a program to help poor children in other countries.) *Where are they going this month?* (to South America) *What are they going to bring?* (medical supplies, wheelchairs, and eyeglasses) *What did Rhonda's group do last year?* (They brought a sick little boy from South America to the U.S. for an operation.) *What are they going to do next?* (bring gifts to the kids of one village at a special holiday party)

Practice Ideas: Listening

1. To practice listening skills, have students listen to the audio before opening their books. Ask a few comprehension questions, such as: *Was the little boy healthy after his operation?* (yes) *How long did he stay in the U.S.?* (two months) Repeat the audio if necessary. Then have students open their books and read along as they listen to the audio.

2. Alternatively, have students begin by listening to the audio as they read along.

 ### Practice Idea: Speaking

Have students practice the conversation in pairs. Ask volunteers to role-play all or part of the conversation in front of the class.

VOCABULARY IN CONTEXT

5-10
mins

1. Model the pronunciation of each new vocabulary item and have students repeat.

2. Make sure students understand the meaning of each vocabulary item. Review the examples in the book and create additional example sentences. For example, say: *fly. I don't like to fly in airplanes. I prefer to drive.* Go over each new vocabulary item similarly, using visuals and realia when appropriate. For example, for *airline* write the names of various countries' airlines on the board, such as *British Airways, Air France, Japan Airlines*, and *Korean Airlines*. Ask students the names of their countries' airlines and write them on the board. When possible, point to pictures in the book that illustrate the new vocabulary, such as *wheelchair* and *toys* on page 293.

3. Have students underline an example of each vocabulary item in the reading.

Did You Know?

Point out the information to students. Say: *More women than men in the U.S. volunteer regardless of age, economic status, or educational level.*

 ## LISTENING ACTIVITY

CD 3
TR 30

ANSWERS: 1. False; **2.** True; **3.** True; **4.** False; **5.** True; **6.** False; **7.** False; **8.** True

5-10
mins

1. Say: *Listen to the sentences about the conversation. Circle* true *or* false. Play the listening selection one time without pausing. Then play it through again, pausing and replaying as necessary.

2. Have students compare their answers, then play the audio again and check the answers as a class.

12.5 Review of *Yes/No* Questions

 10-15 mins

1. Have students look at grammar chart **12.5** on pages 294–295. Review the questions and short answers.

2. Point out the Language Note. Say: Must *isn't usually used in questions.*

Practice Idea: Writing

Play a game. Prepare a list of 20 to 30 verbs that students have learned. Divide the class into two to four teams. Write a verb and a verb tense on the board (e.g., *talk/present continuous*). Someone from each team must go to the front of the board to write a *yes/no* question using the verb in the given tense. The next team member has to write a logical (but not necessarily true) answer.

Practice Idea: Speaking

Have students work in pairs to write *yes/no* questions for another pair. Then have pairs ask and answer questions. Tell students to use the simple present, the present continuous, the future with *be going to*, the simple past, and modals.

EXERCISE 1

ANSWERS: 1. Is Rhonda (OR she) talking about her job with the airline? No, she isn't. **2.** Does Rhonda (OR she) bring wheelchairs to poor children? Yes, she does. **3.** Did the little boy (OR he) need an operation last year? Yes, he did. **4.** Was the sick boy from the U.S.? No, he wasn't. **5.** Did Rhonda (OR she) bring the boy back to his parents? Yes, she did. **6.** Are they (OR the volunteers) going to have a party in the U.S.? No, they aren't. **7.** Are there any volunteers at Marta's house today? Yes, there are. **8.** Should they (OR people) save their toys too? Yes, they should. **9.** Can they (OR people) ask Rhonda (OR her) about other projects? Yes, they can.

 10-15 mins

1. Have students read the direction line. Remind students to use the same tense that's in the

affirmative statement. Go over the example in the book. Point out that the exercise is based on the conversation on page 292.

2. Have students complete Exercise 1 individually. Remind them to review grammar chart **12.5** on pages 294–295 if necessary. Check the answers as a class.

12.6 Review of Information Questions

 10-15 mins

1. Have students look at grammar chart **12.6** on pages 296–297. Say: *Let's look at how to form information questions.* Review how to form questions and short answers for each tense and go over all examples.

2. For the simple present tense, write the following on the board to begin the review:

   question word + *be*

   question word + *be* + *there*

   question word + verb

   question word + *do* + complement + verb

   Say: *These are the four ways to make questions in the present tense.* Remind students not to use *do* or *does* in subject questions. Have students cover their books. Give a formula and ask volunteers to make a question using that formula.

3. For the present continuous tense, ask: *How do you form a verb in this tense?* (*be* + verb -*ing*) Ask: *Can you use* do *with the* -ing *verb?* (no)

4. Have students compare information questions about the complement and information questions about the subject in the chart. (Both begin with question words, but in subject questions there is no noun or pronoun for the subject. The question word or phrase is the subject.) Go over examples in the present continuous tense to illustrate.

5. Direct students' attention to the future tense in the bottom part of the chart on page 296. Ask: *What form of the verb do we use after* be going to *in questions?* (the base form)

6. For questions in the simple past tense, remind students that *did* is used with both regular and irregular verbs, but not with *be*.

Unit 12 **135**

7. For modal verbs, say: *Questions with* can *and* should *are formed the same way. To form questions with* have to, *use* does *OR* do *followed by the subject plus* have to. *All information questions begin with a question word.* Point out the Language Note. Say: Must *isn't usually used in questions.*

Practice Idea: Speaking

Have students turn to the reading on page 147 in Unit 7. Say: *Write information questions about the reading.* Then have students take turns asking and answering questions about the reading. (e.g., *What is Rick going to buy? Coffee and aspirin.*)

EXERCISE

ANSWERS: **1.** What kind of volunteer work does Rhonda (OR she) do? She helps poor children in other countries. **2.** Why did Rhonda (OR she) go to South America last year? She brought a little sick boy here to the U.S. for an operation. **3.** Who pays for the flights to South America? The airline pays for the flights. **4.** When are the volunteers (OR they) going to have a party for children? They're going to have a party for children on a holiday. **5.** Why did the sick boy (OR he) have to come to the U.S.? He needed an operation. **6.** How can people (OR they) help with the holiday project? They can give clothing and toys. **7.** What (kinds of things) should we collect? We should collect supplies. **8.** What is Rhonda (OR she) explaining to the new volunteers? She's explaining the volunteer program.

1. Have students read the direction line. Say: *Use the ideas from the reading on page 292 to complete this exercise.* Go over the examples. Say: *You're going to write a question and an answer.*

2. Have students complete Exercise 2 individually. Remind them to review grammar chart **12.6** on pages 296–297 if necessary. Then have students take turns asking and answering the questions in pairs. Monitor pair work. Give help as needed. Have volunteers share their questions and answers with the class.

EXERCISE 3

ANSWERS: **Answers will vary. Possible answers:**
1. Who are the children waiting for? For Santa.
2. Are all the children going to talk to Santa? Yes, they are. **3.** Did some children get gifts from Santa? Yes, they did. **4.** Did one boy get a new ball? Yes, he did. **5.** What kind of ball did a boy get? He got a basketball. **6.** Are the children going to open their presents now? Yes, they are.

1. Say: *In this exercise, you're going write questions about the picture.* Have students read the direction line. Go over the examples.

2. Have students complete Exercise 3 individually. Remind them to review grammar charts **12.5** on pages 294–295 and **12.6** on pages 296–297 if necessary. Then have students ask and answer questions about the picture with a partner. Monitor pair work. Give help as needed. Have volunteers share their questions and answers with the class.

Practice Idea: Speaking

Have students choose a different illustration in the book and make six questions about the picture. Then have students ask and answer questions about the picture with a partner.

EXERCISE 4

ANSWERS: **1.** children are there; **2.** does each volunteer have to work; **3.** happened; **4.** did you do; **5.** did you learn; **6.** are the volunteers planning; **7.** are the children learning to do; **8.** is the sale going to be; **9.** is the center going to do

1. Say: *Val is being interviewed about her volunteer activities. The answer will help you write the question.* Have students read the direction line. Go over the example.

2. Have students complete Exercise 4 individually. Remind them to review grammar charts **12.5** on pages 294–295 and **12.6** on pages 296–297 if necessary. Then have students compare their answers in pairs. Play the audio and check the answers as a class.

Practice Idea: Speaking

Have students practice the conversation as a class. Ask one student to play Val. The rest of the students can take turns asking the questions.

EXERCISE 5

CD 3
TR 31

ANSWERS: 1. are you going to help; **2.** does this woman do; **3.** Does she have to take; **4.** Can she swim; **5.** did she start; **6.** did you find; **7.** wants to help

1. Say: *Now Elsa is being interviewed about her volunteer activities.* Have students read the direction line. Go over the example.

2. Have students complete Exercise 5 individually. Remind them to review grammar charts **12.5** on pages 294–295 and **12.6** on pages 296–297 if necessary. Then have students compare their answers in pairs. Play the audio and check the answers as a class.

Practice Idea: Speaking

Have students practice the conversation as a class. Ask one student to play Elsa. The rest of the students can take turns asking the questions.

Editing Advice

10-15 mins

Have students close their books. Write the example sentences without editing marks or corrections on the board. For example:

> *Peter didn't went to the meeting last Saturday.*
>
> *He had to worked last Saturday.*
>
> *Volunteers should to go to the meetings.*

Ask students to correct each sentence and provide a rule or explanation for each correction, e.g.: *Peter didn't go to the meeting last Saturday.* (Use the base form after *didn't*.) *He had to work last Saturday.* (Use the base form after *have to*.) *Volunteers should go to the meetings.* (Use the base form after modals.) This activity can be done individually, in pairs, or as a

Editing Quiz

ANSWERS: 1. came; **2.** helped; **3.** had to write; **4.** didn't know; **5.** did you hear; **6.** found; **7.** C; **8.** does this site work; **9.** gives; **10.** to use; **11.** don't have to look; **12.** is it; **13.** it isn't; **14.** I have; **15.** C; **16.** should put; **17.** C; **18.** are going to; **19.** There was; **20.** C; **21.** we're going to have; **22.** are you going to stay; **23.** C

1. Tell students they are going to put the Editing Advice into practice. Have students read the direction line. Ask: *Do all the shaded words have mistakes?* (no) Go over the examples with the class. Then do #1 together.

2. Have students complete the rest of the quiz individually. Then have them compare their answers with a partner before checking the answers as a class. Elicit the relevant grammar point for each correction. For example, for the first example, ask: *What's the rule?* (In questions in the simple present, use *do/does* and the base form of the verb.)

3. For the items students had difficulties with, have them go back and find the relevant grammar chart and review it. Monitor and give help as necessary.

Expansion

These expansion activities provide opportunities for students to interact with one another and further develop their speaking and writing skills. Encourage students to use grammar from this unit whenever possible.

LEARNER'S LOG

10-15 mins

1. Have students close their books. Ask: *What did you learn about Val's, Elsa's, and Rhonda's volunteer jobs? What else do you want to know?*

2. Have students open their books to complete the Learner's Log. Remind students to write three questions about volunteering in the U.S.

3. Have students compare logs in pairs.

WRITING ACTIVITIES

10-15
mins

1. Have students read the direction line. Make sure they understand that they should only answer one of the questions. Go over the example with students. Have students complete the activity individually. Collect for assessment.

2. Have students look at the picture and say what they can see. Write the vocabulary and verbs on the board. Have students read the direction line and the example. Then have students help you write another sentence about the picture on the board. Have students complete the activity individually. Collect for assessment.

Practice Idea: Writing

Have students exchange papers with a partner. Ask students to help their partners edit their paragraph. Refer students to the Editing Advice on page 302.

OUTSIDE ACTIVITY

Tell students to ask some Americans about their volunteer work. Tell them to find out what they do and how often. Elicit questions they can ask (e.g. *Do you volunteer? Where do you volunteer? What do you do? How often do you volunteer? Why do you volunteer?*). In class, have students get into groups to share the information about the volunteers they spoke with. Ask: *What were their reasons for volunteering? Were they the same or different?*

INTERNET ACTIVITIES

1. Tell students to use a search engine on the Internet and type in *volunteer opportunities* and the name of their city. Have them find some organizations that offer volunteer opportunities. Have students discuss in groups the volunteer opportunities they found in their area.

2. Tell students to go to the Web site www.serve.gov. This site offers volunteer jobs all over the country. Tell them to find an interesting volunteer opportunity in their city. Have them discuss in groups what they found. Then ask groups to share with the class the opportunities they found most interesting. Ask students if they're going to volunteer.